AN INTRODUCTION
TO ENGINEERED
SOFTWARE

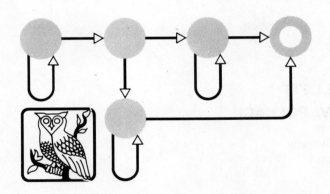

HRW SERIES IN COMPUTER SCIENCE

Seymour V. Pollack, Series Editor

Seymour V. Pollack and Theodor Sterling
     Guide To PL/1 and Structured Programming, Third Edition

Will Gillett and Seymour V. Pollack
     An Introduction to Engineered Software

James Bradley
     File and Data Base Techniques

AN INTRODUCTION TO ENGINEERED SOFTWARE

WILL D. GILLETT
SEYMOUR V. POLLACK

Washington University
St. Louis, Missouri

Holt, Rinehart and Winston

New York   Chicago   San Francisco   Philadelphia
Montreal   Toronto   London   Sydney   Tokyo
Mexico City   Rio de Janeiro   Madrid

Printed in the United States of America

2 3 4 144 9 8 7 6 5 4 3 2 1

Library of Congress Cataloging in Publication Data

Gillett, Will D.

  Software engineering.
  Includes index.
  1. Electronic digital computers—Programming.
I. Pollack, Seymour V. II. Title.
QA76.6.G554   001.64′2   81-13253
ISBN 0-03-056902-8   AACR2

CBS College Publishing
Holt, Rinehart and Winston
The Dryden Press
Saunders College Publishing

Contents

Preface

The continuing revolution in computer science and technology is not restricted to hardware. It also has manifested itself as a changing perception of the software development process. We are well past the point where it can be considered reasonable to treat software development as being predominantly an art. While not a science, this process has progressed from its ad hoc origins to a point where many of its activities can be systematized. Moreover, the scope and complexity of today's software requirements make it generally impractical to undertake large software development projects without considerable systematization.

Over the past several years, the approaches to the orderly production of computer programs have begun to coalesce into a collection of principles, techniques, and tools known as *software engineering*. The term is not applied frivolously. In large measure, the concepts stem from traditional engineering practices that have been applied effectively over a wide range of products. The central idea can be stated simply: Programs, too, are products, amenable to the same approaches that guide the development of other, more physical products. Starting as a tentative opinion, this attitude has gained credence very rapidly, supported by a growing body of successful experience in business, industrial, and government settings. As a result, the software effort in an increasing number of organizations is conducted in accordance with an orderly progression in which there is an explicit design phase, motivated by carefully defined requirements and objectives. The outcome of that activity, documented by a set of ''blueprints,'' as it were, guides the actual formulation and testing of the software. In this context, the ''programming'' activity (i.e., the preparation of executable code) becomes a task whose purpose it is to implement algorithmic processes that have already been defined, reviewed, and accepted. In other words, the *fabrication* of a software product has formally been separated from its *design*.

The evolution of software engineering has seen these notions fortified with an increasing array of specialized aids that continue to reduce the chaos associated with software production. Prominent in this regard are powerful techniques such as functional decomposition, structured programming, stepwise refinement, and systematic testing. Each of these contributes to the overall software production process by making some aspect of it more orderly. The ability to *apply* these techniques effectively is enhanced by the use of convenient tools such as structure diagrams, pseudocode, stubs, and drivers. It is this combination of concepts, techniques, and tools that concerns us here.

This book presents a disciplined approach to the production of effective, reliable software. It focuses on the processes involved in:

Preparing a cohesive product design;

Systematically breaking it down into a reasonable assemblage of components;

Perfecting each component in isolation;

Integrating the completed component into the overall product;

Documenting the activities as they progress.

After an initial chapter that provides background and motivation for systematic software production, there is a detailed exploration of the software design activity. This takes two forms: Chapter 2 discusses and illustrates the design process and its associated techniques. This material then is reinforced by applying it (in Chapter 3) to the design of a realistic, nontrivial software product. Chapter 3 also includes a very extensive set of project specifications varying in scope and difficulty and covering a wide range of applications. Most are taken from actual practice, so that the student establishes and maintains contact with reality. These projects are sustained in subsequent chapters, along with more sharply focused problems and exercises designed to emphasize particular techniques or concepts.

Chapter 4 carries the process forward by examining the philosophy, techniques, and tools for structured programming. These are applied subsequently (Chapter 5) to the product designed in Chapter 3.

The final three chapters offer a detailed presentation of the software implementation and testing processes. The highly effective techniques of stepwise refinement and systematic testing, supported by such tools as stubs, drivers, and planned instrumentation, are applied to a variety of realistic examples. As a result, their efficacy is established and reinforced immediately.

One of the most dramatic assets of systematic software development lies in the simplicity of its techniques and tools. Consequently, its acquisition and use emphatically should not be deferred. No good purpose is served in learning chaotic practices, only to have to unlearn them later. Accordingly, this book is designed to be used in a one- or two-semester course (its length depending on the number and scope of assigned projects) in which students' prerequisites can be limited to familiarity with a high-level programming language. In fact, the text also has been used successfully in situations in which the students were acquainted with a language's fundamental features; additional experience and expertise were acquired along the way.

It would be counterproductive to view this material as being the exclusive bailiwick of computer science. Sound methods leading to clear, reliable software are needed in any situation in which computer programs are to be written. Accordingly, the text is designed to provide appropriate background and skills for any student intending to engage in nontrivial involvement with computers.

The authors wish to acknowledge, with thanks, the help of Messrs. Robert Benson and Tom Bugnitz in providing the facilities for preparing the manuscript, Dr. Jerome R. Cox in providing the opportunity to use the material in several classes, and Myrna Harbison in preparing manuscript copies for class use. Special thanks are due to Cathy Gurganus for her help during the production process.

Will D. Gillett
Seymour V. Pollack

AN INTRODUCTION TO ENGINEERED SOFTWARE

Programs as Products   1

The rapid growth of computer usage rivals and may even exceed that of artifacts such as the telephone, automobile, or television. Two distinct sources of this sustained growth are evident: First, there is the introduction of computer science and technology to areas in which they played no role heretofore. Part of this process involves identifying new areas whose feasibility would have been beyond contemplation without computers because of their complexity or the massive amount of data to be processed. Second, an already existing application within an area is expanded in response to newly perceived opportunities. Thus an arbitrary group of computer deliveries is likely to be split between organizations expanding or replacing their configurations and those taking a first step.

This second type of growth is of particular interest because the new computer applications that stimulate it often are substantially more ambitious and complex than their predecessors. Consequently, their implementation generally requires more extensive programs with increasingly intricate procedural logic. Based on successes achieved with earlier applications, the tendency was to apply ad hoc programming methods to these more demanding applications. It has become painfully clear that the ad hoc approach to the specification, development, and perfection of programs, characteristic of practices followed during the first two decades of the computer age, could not be extended indefinitely.

For many organizations, the gap between what reasonably could be programmed and what was required grew so large that it constituted a ''software crisis.'' While recognition was slow in coming at first, it is now beyond dispute that these larger, more challenging computerization problems cannot be solved effectively by bombarding them with additional people or machines. It is abundantly clear now that economical and reliable implementations of arbitrarily large software products are not out of reach and are often attainable at costs (in time and effort) surprisingly below those previously associated with much more modest undertakings. The key lies in perceiving a program as a product designed (*designed* is an important word here) to exhibit certain operational properties that fill needs which are well thought out and carefully defined.

In the following sections we shall explore the nature of this software crisis to develop some insights regarding its origins and characteristics. With this perspective it will be easier to characterize structured methodologies as effective responses to this crisis. Moreover, it will allow a natural generalization so that this approach can be seen as a universal methodology for producing an arbitrarily wide spectrum of software products, including those that may seem simple enough to be handled in an ad hoc way.

1.1 MAJOR PROBLEMS WITH SOFTWARE

One interesting side effect of the widespread use of computers is the emergence of the computer as a popular national scapegoat. When a newspaper needs an inch or so at the bottom of a column or a television newscast needs 15 seconds and the producer does not believe that the anchorperson can smile and/or collate papers for that long, it always is possible to find (or construct) a story in which "the computer" has done something amusing or outrageous. So here is poor Mrs. Fenwick who answers a knock at her door to find her front yard filled with 417 cubic feet of fresh organic fertilizer. The impassive driver, having established that delivery was made to the address indicated on the shipping order, wants only a signature. When the distraught Mrs. Fenwick finally gets hold of someone in the accounting department, all that person can do is assure her that she really did order the merchandise delivered; the computer says so. Elsewhere, a computer "ran amok," printing 3729 paychecks made out to the same person (who does not even work for the company).

Of course, the overwhelming majority of the boners, bloopers, and bad news eventually can be traced back to errors or oversights in programs, but that does not make good copy. For us, however, the direction of blame (if *blame* is the right word) is rather important because it underscores a disturbing but nonetheless unmistakable fact: many of the computer programs released for routine use as being "checked out" and "operational" contain serious flaws. Sometimes these are logical errors in a program stemming from the fact that the program does not do exactly what the programmer intended it to do. In other instances the program is an accurate implementation of the programmer's intent, but that intent turns out to be an inaccurate or incomplete reflection of the *problem's* requirements. The frequency with which this type of situation occurs makes it important to understand its characteristics so they can be reflected against the principles, attitudes, and techniques that offer relief.

1.1.1 Characteristics of the Software Crisis

The present level of concern about the software crisis does not mean that there was a better time, a "golden age" for programming, programmers, and programs. We have always had problems with software, but most of these eventually were removed or reduced to minor irritants. Moreover, the costs involved in producing such software rarely were monitored carefully because the equipment costs were overwhelming by comparison. Now the situation has changed dramatically. The tremendous increase in the amount of "computing power" that can be bought for a given amount of money has not been paralleled by anything even remotely similar in the way of software productivity. In many instances the software trend is going in the opposite direction. Consequently, the fraction of a system's cost attributable to software has been rising steadily. For example, the U.S. Department of Defense figured that its software costs in the early 1960s were about 20 percent of its total computer system costs. In the 1980s the fraction is expected to exceed 90 percent. Findings in a variety of industries and businesses indicate that this is not peculiar to the Defense Department.

Such statistics have prompted more detailed investigations in an effort to identify the primary problems. These inquiries, which still continue, have identified a number of major difficulties that characterize this crisis.

1. Much of the software cost (often exceeding 50 percent) is incurred during production use—after the software has been released as "developed" and "operable." In other words, software maintenance is a significant portion of the total development process.

2. The ability to determine the resources (for instance, time, cost, personnel) required to complete a given software project that is not particularly well defined to begin with, has not kept pace with software demands. As a result, the gap between what is promised and what is delivered is increasing. Time and cost overruns are so common that a software project completed to specifications within a prescribed period of time is often singled out for high praise and special study.

3. The scope and implications of a project are often unclear until well into the project's life cycle. Only after the expenditure of considerable resources does it become evident that some of the aspirations may be unexpectedly ambitious or downright unrealistic. Ad hoc regrouping and redefinition late in the development cycle make it difficult to avoid leaving a mess.

4. It is normal for many (probably most) computer applications to change and evolve; yet much of today's software is difficult to modify. Surprisingly modest alterations may require abandoning large pieces of operational software rather than attempting to build on what is there already.

The presence or absence of these symptoms is not governed by the size of the enterprise, the nature and diversity of its information processing applications, or the length of its involvement with computers. The causes of these difficulties transcend such factors. Examination of these relatively well-understood causes can provide valuable insights in developing techniques for improvement.

A major reason for the magnitude of the current software crisis is the failure of previous methodologies to analyze software costs over the *entire* life cycle of any given system. This life cycle extends from the design phase through initial implementation and testing, and includes modification and maintenance. Previous methodologies have failed to recognize the magnitude of the effort required to maintain and modify existing software. Software systems are "living," "growing" entities that require significant care and attention in order to reach maturity. For various reasons, it may be either impossible or unadvantageous to incorporate all the aspects of a complicated software system in its initial implementation. Any methodology used in developing significant software products *must* address these observations by producing code that can be understood (by someone other than the original programmer), verified, and modified. Code without these properties is *doomed* to be discarded whenever even minor modifications must be made.

1.1.2 Traditional Approaches and Current Requirements

The history of computer applications is about as chaotic as any history can be. During the first decade of the computer age many of the most productive sources for this new technology were organized around university laboratories equipped with one-of-a-kind computers. The speed and capacity of these machines were very modest by today's standards, so that storage and machine time were extremely precious commodities. Each installation was likely to have its own collection of independent programs, its own techniques for implementation, and its own conventions for operating the facility and documenting the programs. Much of the educational effort centered around these laboratories and was characterized by a master-apprentice approach.

This general type of atmosphere was instrumental in establishing several important attitudes with regard to computer applications.

1. Program preparation was thought to be the primary (if not dominant) factor in the development of a computer application. It was expected that most of the effort involved in such an endeavor would be devoted to writing, testing, and perfecting the program. (Many still cling to this belief.)

2. Programming and coding—the production of useful instruction sequences—was perceived as a highly serendipitous, almost artistic activity subject to tremendous variation among individuals. The "right" programmer was seen as a crucial factor in the success or failure of an application.

3. Programs that used storage sparingly (even ingeniously) and executed rapidly, were considered to be ideal. Effort directed toward reducing program size and execution time was effort well spent.

These tendencies evolved quickly into operational facts, so that the perception of a programmer was not drastically different from, for example, a ceramist: There are good ceramists and mediocre ones. All use basically the same resources, but each has a particular way with clay.

Consequently, the computerization process was perceived to pivot conceptually around programming. As soon as the requirements for an application were known (or somebody thought he or she understood them), it was taken as a signal to jump in with both feet and start writing code. Supervisory personnel were conditioned to react accordingly. Once the program was actually being written, we were Getting Somewhere.

1.1.2.1 Solving the Wrong Problem

The urge to begin writing the program as early as possible in an application's development often indicates the likelihood that the underlying requirements are not yet completely understood. When the person writing the program was also the person interested in using it, this deficiency tended to be resolved as the program evolved. However, when these were different individuals, the anomaly between what was required and what was being programmed sometimes did not become evident until the program was working (or, actually, not working)! Once it became clear that the program was supplying "correct" answers to the wrong questions, some reprogramming and retesting had to be done, and the extent of such repairs sometimes approached the original effort. In some cases there was a more insidious consequence: In their eagerness to salvage as much as possible of the "good" code (after all, the program was working), people would compromise their requirements (if the results were not completely outlandish) so that, in effect, the questions now matched the answers.

1.1.2.2 A Trade Full of Tricks

Emphasis on program size and speed, even when not necessitated by equipment or scheduling restrictions, often became objectives in their own right. As a result, programmers concocted a bewildering assortment of highly individualized techniques, shortcuts, and secret passages that produced time and space economies highly specific to the particular machine, program, or both. For example, someone needing the constant 12 might use an operation code of an instruction embedded somewhere in the program (where the code's value happened to be 12) instead of explicitly storing a 12 somewhere. Such tinkering did shave words from the program size and milliseconds from the running time. However, most of these programs were so cryptic that analysis of the construction and behavior was inordinately difficult. For many applications this meant that the original author was needed even for small changes. If the program could not be unraveled and the author no longer was available, the change frequently was redefined as being unimportant, thereby dispensing with the matter. Alternatively, failure to push the new requirement aside frequently prompted abandonment of the program, only to have it supplanted by a new version filled with the same kind of catacombs and Byzantine mazes.

Another aspect of this drive for program "efficiency" was a tendency toward monolithic lumps of code often containing several thousand instructions. Some costly internal bookkeeping could be avoided by treating an application as a single module, wherein all information is always available. This amorphous approach to programming worked hand in hand with the exotic tricks to produce inflexible code, since a change in one part of such a program was likely to affect other areas throughout its extent (for example, the program is changed so that the operation code 12 no longer resides the same storage location).

1.1.2.3 Aggravation Through Growth   While the ad hoc approach to computerization was solidifying into standard operating procedure, the continuing rapid growth of computer usage was introducing new difficulties: As long as a particular application was relatively modest in scope, the false starts, blind alleys, and other pitfalls could be accepted as "normal occupational hazards" that come with the territory. As applications became more ambitious and their complexity grew, use of this approach became increasingly troublesome simply because it could not grow correspondingly. As a result, the lack of structure and discipline began to exert more and more stress on the application development process and costs began to rise out of proportion to the increased size of the undertaking.

In many instances the decline in effectiveness was most noticeable when a particular project was sufficiently complex to make it impossible for a single individual to deal with all of its details. The resulting need to divide programming responsibilities among several people inevitably brought with it a requirement to coordinate these activities so that all the pieces eventually fit together. With everyone rushing off to write code using his or her special incantations and secret shortcuts, it is no surprise—even in retrospect—that such coordination turned out to be inordinately difficult. The general response to this problem was to extend it by adding more or "better" programmers. These, too, were people trained in a baroque manner, each bringing his or her own dark alleys and hidden caves to add to the pot. The better programmers, by virtue of their more intimate knowledge of programming, brought deeper crevasses and more ingenious knots to the proceedings. Consequently, many struggling projects were actually slowed down by bringing in reinforcements.

The frequency of problems in implementing computer programs and the wide range of environments and applications in which they arose made it less and less plausible to view them as isolated incidents related primarily to insufficient staffing and inadequate computing machinery. Instead, a growing number of installations began to examine and evaluate their basic methods of implementing an application on a computer. At the same time, more general inquiries were undertaken to find the extent of this problem and its possible causes. Findings from a wide variety of sources made it unmistakably clear that ad hoc approaches to application development worked primarily because of the relatively limited scope of the applications undertaken. Where more ambitious projects were completed, it appeared to be sheer persistence as much as anything else that contributed to their realizations. Thus more systematic methods would be needed if computer users were to expect continuing growth in applications. Moreover, this systematic approach, whatever its characteristics, could not be merely an improved way of writing large programs. Rather, it would require a shift in emphasis from the program itself to those activities preceding and motivating the writing of the programs. As we shall see in succeeding chapters, this shift has been so dramatic that it unseated the coding process from its traditional focal position in all applications regardless of scope. In fact, one of the most significant aspects of the departure from tradition is the explicit intent to reduce the importance of programming within the larger perspective of the overall processes of conceptualization, design, and implementation.

With this background, we can begin to explore the characteristics of a structured approach as a response to the major problems just described. In doing so it will also be possible to deal with some of the issues that this methodology has evoked.

1.2 THE NEW TRADITION

As often happens when basic changes are involved, the pivotal factor in the over-throw of the mystic programming tradition is a very simple one: People began to realize that programs are (and always have been) products. They are sold, leased, and even taxed as products; as is true with other ''manufactured'' items, their users expect them to behave in certain ways that persist with every use. Yet, for the most part, the production of programs departed drastically from the preparation of other manufactured goods. This deviation is conspicuous when we note the primary emphasis traditional practice placed on ad hoc program writing. Imagine manufacturers producing goods with the same approach: They do not quite know what they want to make, but there is no need to worry; they will decide as they make it, and by the time it is finished they will know what it is.

We shall now align the computerization process more closely with that of any other manufactured product or component by explicitly and intentionally applying those design and engineering methods that characterize the development of complex products to this process. Several basic guidelines are derived from this outlook. We shall introduce them here and build on them repeatedly throughout the text.

1.2.1 A Structured Approach

We have often referred to the ad hoc characteristic of what used to be traditional practice. The essence of a structured approach is the adoption of an engineering approach, implying the imposition of a disciplined methodology in which clearly distinct, recognizable activities are begun and completed in an orderly sequence. This means that we know and agree upon each activity and how to tell when it is completed. There are no physical laws whose behavior push this approach in one direction or another. Hence, there is no natural methodology that can be sanctioned as the ''official'' approach to software design and implementation. It is crucial to institute and enforce a sequence of well-defined activities whose effectiveness has been (or can be) demonstrated. Accordingly, the approach followed in this text is not the only one that exists or is pertinent. Rather, it is one with an imposed discipline that has been found to yield good results in a wide range of projects and environments.

1.2.2   Know the Product

As self-evident as this may sound, history has shown the uncompromising importance of knowing exactly what program is to be written before starting to write it. This is nothing more than the insistence on a separate design phase, recognized as such, during which the desired outcome (the specification of the product) is carefully and completely defined. The result of this design phase is not the program. Rather, it is the conceptualization of the entire application, a way of using a computer to do something. Each pertinent module must then be viewed as a product which is part of that package. Once there is agreement on precisely what the particular package will provide, then the appropriate programming requirements can be determined. For some applications this design process is a natural progression, easily fulfilled. For more complex undertakings it will be necessary to resist the urge to plunge in and start coding. In all cases it is inherently self-defeating to contemplate programming without a design phase.

1.2.3   Reducing Apparent Complexity

We mentioned earlier that software difficulties become disproportionately acute with more complex projects. The reason for this is well understood, now that the problem has been recognized and studied: While experience with computers has enabled people to envision increasingly complex applications at some abstract level, our ability to absorb and encompass such complexity in all its details has not grown nearly as much. Moreover, there is every reason to believe that our capacity will not increase substantially, which seems to thwart our push toward greater scope and complexity.

Relief is provided by applying one of the cornerstones of engineering methodology, namely, the reduction of apparent complexity. The word *apparent* is crucial here: While we cannot reduce the complexity of a computer application without diluting its intent, we can carefully and systematically subdivide it into a collection of smaller, interconnected subproblems each with its scope comfortably within a person's absorptive capacity. At the same time, we can enhance the apparent reduction of complexity by making the interconnections as simple as possible. The idea is to burden each subproblem with its neighbors' problems only to the extent that it is absolutely necessary. As we shall see later, this general approach, which is called *decomposition,* helps determine the boundaries of subproblems when they are being defined, and it guides the subsequent implementation of their respective solutions when they take form as programs, procedures, or both.

1.2.4   Verification and Stubbornness

Another basic aspect of this product-oriented approach calls for assurance that a given step is correct before embarking on the next one. That seems straightforward enough, but there are general implications here.

First, this assurance assumes that within the solution to a given problem there is a series of recognizable steps to be followed in a certain sequence. As we shall see in the next chapter, this is emphatically the case. For instance, we should not permit ourselves to seek a solution to a problem until we are convinced that the problem, as stated, is the one we want to solve. Similarly, if we find a solution and express it as an algorithm, we should establish that the algorithm solves the problem we set out to solve before that algorithm is expressed as a program or programs.

The second implication is that we know what *correct* means. As we work our way through these concepts, it will become apparent that the idea of correctness will be tackled in a variety of ways ranging widely in rigor. What is important is the idea that verification is an unavoidable conclusion for each step in the production process.

The third implication is somewhat more subtle. If verification (however performed) is something like a rite of passage to a subsequent activity, then we can infer the existence of a mechanism that bars such entry if we are not convinced that the previous step is correct. This is where the stubbornness comes in. At a large number of computer installations where structured methodologies are successfully used, obstinacy is formalized by requiring each software design to undergo a careful review before any programming can begin. This is completely consistent with standard engineering practice, in which a review or inspection punctuates each stage in a product's development.

1.2.5 Art and Engineering

When the need for a structured approach to software first was recognized, the most serious objections pivoted around the notion that program writing was, and must remain, an art. It was argued that people who wrote programs were performing a creative activity which this new methodology surely would stifle. It is now abundantly clear that this creative activity has turned innumerable cases of what could have been straightforward programs into so many unguided missiles. People expressing such apprehension have confused the removal of art with its relocation.

The imposition of discipline on software design and implementation obligates its practitioners to concentrate the creativity where it belongs—in the design of the application, the algorithms that realize it, and the program structures that ultimately embody those algorithms. Thus, by the time the modules are ready to be coded, we should know precisely (for a given application) how many there will be, how they interface, and what each one does. These detailed specifications, when combined with rules of practice that guide the internal construction of individual modules, represent a concerted effort to reduce the actual coding process to a straightforward but not mundane task. The result, as repeated experience has amply demonstrated, is a piece of software with properties of a well-engineered product and benefiting fully from the art and ingenuity applied to its development. We shall examine some of these properties in the next section to see how they are derivable from a structured approach and, in turn, help define the ingredients of such a methodology.

1.3 PROPERTIES OF THE FINAL PRODUCT

Because a structured methodology brings the development of software more closely in line with established engineering practice, the properties of the resulting products can be expected to reflect this discipline. Three such characteristics are of special interest here because they are peculiar, though perhaps not unique, to the nature of software: clarity of major components, ease of refinement, and ease of modification.

1.3.1 Clarity of Major Components

One of the benefits of a properly engineered software product is its clarity. When the product is examined, there is no mystery about exactly what it does. Moreover, this question of function can be answered fully at any level at which it is asked because the software and its description are closely interwoven. By definition, the product is incomplete without either. We shall examine this notion of clarity from several points of view.

1.3.1.1 Software Specifications An integral component of well-engineered software is an exact description of the problem it solves. This is presented at a very abstract level in that it pointedly avoids any detail regarding implementation of the solution. Consequently, the user of such a product need go no further to determine what the product does and the resources (for example, machine type, operating environment) required to use it. At the same time, the description serves as a vehicle for determining whether or not the problem being solved is the one the user wants to solve. (*The user* in this context may be the person who asked for the software in the first place or an outsider looking at its possible acquisition.) Correctness is ensured by the fact that further work on the application cannot proceed without endorsement of the specifications.

1.3.1.2 Clarity of Algorithms Another level of inquiry about a software product seeks to determine how the particular problem is solved. Here again, the question is answered abstractly by a description of the algorithm so that the inquirer can establish the exact method being used without becoming bogged down with the details of the implementation language. For example, a computerized application may be based on one of a variety of algorithms, each using a different mathematical model requiring a different set of formulations and yielding different results. Yet all seek to solve the same problem, for example, to predict the relative prices for certain stocks at some specified time in the future. Accordingly, the description would define precisely the particular approach being used. (The effectiveness of the algorithm is a completely separate issue; in this example it is primarily an act of faith). As before, the clarity is not established merely by edict. If a structured approach is followed, this description must serve as the basis for subsequent implementation. Toward this end, rules often are defined for the form in which algorithms must be stated.

1.3.1.3 Clarity of Programs Because the definition of the algorithm selected or devised for a given application is developed and stated in abstract terms, it carries little or no predilection toward a particular programming language or other organizational consideration. Such decisions as choice of language are influenced by practical realities (such as available hardware and software resources) and, in no small measure, by personal style and ingenuity.

However, experience with structured methodologies has identified certain restrictions useful in avoiding the construction of sloppy and obscure programs. For instance, modularization (division of programs into numerous smaller subprograms) without rigid limits on the size and scope of a module makes it possible to treat each such component conceptually as a single entity. Overall structure and operation of an arbitrarily complex program can then be described as a synthesis of these "black boxes." At this level of abstraction we presume that each module does (or will do) its job properly without our knowing precisely how it does it. This enables us to concentrate on examining the overall program structure while remaining unburdened by the unnecessary complexity of subordinate details.

Other structural rules and guidelines also contribute to this concerted effort to enhance program clarity by focusing on a program's design and submerging detail that does not elucidate the design. In many cases these guidelines include some type of formal vehicle (such as a program design language) in which a program's construction must be stated. This is used for review (verification) and then serves as the written source of information for subsequent implementation.

1.3.1.4 Clarity of Modules This is the most concrete level of scrutiny because our dealings here are with the actual source-language code. Although the intent of that code follows directly from the program's structural specifications, the richness of most programming languages makes it possible to realize that intent in numerous ways. Here, as in overall program organization, the application of certain structural coding rules makes it possible to produce modules with functions that are relatively easy to discern by direct inspection. While these rules limit coding practice to specified structured programming techniques, they leave the way open for wide choice in the way these techniques are combined, without compromising the clarity of the results.

We have emphasized the notion that an orderly, step-by-step approach from the highest level of abstraction down to the actual code compels us to produce and verify specification at each step of the development; the contents of each step must be clear enough to drive the next step. Consequently, this clarity cannot be accidental; it is, in fact, an explicit objective of any structured methodology for software production.

1.3.2 Ease of Refinement

Even with the most disciplined methodologies, program errors cannot be completely controlled. However, we can exploit structured design to control the process of finding these mistakes. Specifically, we can take advantage of the fact that we must know, before coding is undertaken, how the program is to be built and what each module will do. Thus we can set up the entire application in skeletal form, systematically incorporating each module after it has been developed and corrected independently. Once incorporated, a module makes its expected contribution to the overall operation and—at least in concept—receives no further attention. Until it is ready, its place in the overall software is filled by a substitute trivial enough to preclude serious validation problems. This temporary replacement, sometimes known as a *stub,* may be designed to do nothing at all, in which case it is simply a placeholder for the appropriate module. Alternatively, it may simulate the actual module by producing the same results (for one or more known test cases) without going through the actual processing that will eventually reside within the module.

In this way, an arbitrarily complex application can be built up gradually and systematically. Perhaps the most conspicuous benefit is that this approach offers the explicit opportunity to control the refinement process so that debugging activities may focus on more local errors.

The ability to perform selective refinement is not just a nice property that we would like to have if the methodology happens to supply it to us; it is imperative that we have the ability to incrementally implement small components of large software products. It is not in any way possible to code a 50,000-line program in one sitting and have it run correctly the first time. After eliminating the syntax errors, when a given input does not produce the appropriate output, where do you start looking to identify the logic errors? In the input section? In the processing section? In the output section? The magnitude of the problem is too large. Without the ability to identify, design, implement, and debug small, functionally complete components of such a complicated software product, the project is doomed to failure before it has begun.

1.3.3 Ease of Modification

With rare exceptions, it is unrealistic to expect an unchanged software product to retain its usefulness over a prolonged time span. In many instances, new requirements arise as part of normal growth. It is very common for capabilities and features to be identified whose absence is now viewed as a serious shortcoming even though they were not considered at all when the "completely comprehensive" system was defined earlier. In other cases external factors, such as changes in the tax laws or new management policies, may impose a need for modification. Even when the application is very stable, programs may have to be changed because of secondary effects wrought by other changes (such as a new machine, compiler, or operating system).

Structured design removes much of the trauma formerly associated with change. Much of the help stems from the serious concern given to modularity during conversion from algorithms to programs and procedures. The fundamental reason for modularity is to reduce the apparent complexity of the entire product. Toward this end there is great motivation to equip the modules with the simplest possible interconnections so that their functional integrity is maintained. These clean boundaries greatly facilitate the ability to specify and implement changes. In concept, each functional change would be achieved by replacing the module embodying the old function by the new one, which embodies the new function, as it becomes available (that is, as it is designed, implemented and verified). Because of the minimal interconnections, the effects of such changes would be highly localized. Extensive experience indicates that this relatively simple idea is extremely beneficial in practice. It is easy to validate such modifications, because only a very restricted part of the software is perturbed for a given change.

While structured design is being applied successfully to a wide range of complex software projects, its features and benefits may seem to be just promises and claims. In the following chapters, we shall strive to clarify these concepts and techniques so that it is obvious the promises can be fulfilled.

1.4 SUMMARY

In the past, producers of software systems have failed to recognize the total cost of developing such software. This cost must encompass the entire lifetime of the system starting from its design, ranging through implementation and testing, and culminating with maintenance and exportation of algorithmic components. Because of the propensity to jump into the coding phase before the problem is understood, many problems surface late in the lifetime of the product. The cost of resolving these problems often significantly outweighs the cost of the original implementation. Major difficulties include the following.

- Unverified designs—implementing the wrong thing.

- Unverified implementations—inadequately tested programs.

- Poor coding practices—obscure procedures that are difficult to follow and, therefore, difficult to correct and modify.

- Poor maintainability—inadequate means for establishing and correcting errors in a program or the data on which it operates, or both.

Software engineering is a disciplined approach to developing software products aimed at eliminating these problems, or at least minimizing them so that they stay within acceptable bounds. The pertinent methods and attitudes are designed to produce software with the following properties.

- Designs and implementations that are clear and easily understandable.

- Modular components of the complexity that are easily and conveniently grasped.

- Designs and implementations that are easily verified.

- Software organization that allows convenient and straightforward modifications.

Techniques and methodologies presented in this text have been found in practice to be convenient and effective in reducing the apparent complexity of large and intricate software projects, thereby enabling them to be successfully developed systematically.

PROBLEMS

1. It is illuminating (and often surprising) to find out how large certain types of programs are. One crude measure of program size is the number of source language statements in that program; another such measure is the size of the final executable program. Using either or both of these measures, see if you can obtain information about the size of each of the following.

   a. The largest program you have ever written.

   b. A standard high-level language compiler (for example, FORTRAN, COBOL, PL/I, PASCAL).

   c. A basic assembler or macroassembler for a medium scale processor.

   d. A basic assembler or macroassembler for a minicomputer.

   e. A program that produces a company's payroll checks from its personnel file.

   f. A generalized engineering application (such as the STRUDL stress analysis program).

   g. A generalized statistical application (such as a factor analysis program or ANOVA, an analysis of variance program).

   h. A general mathematical application (such as a program for linear programming).

   i. A general discrete simulation system (such as GPSS or SIMSCRIPT).

   j. An operating system for a microcomputer, minicomputer, or large scale computer.

2. Try to obtain and examine information that enables you to contrast the sizes of programs written some time ago with those produced more recently. One way to do this might be to ask an organization (such as your computing facility) about the size of their largest programs written 10 years ago compared to the largest one written recently.

3. Check your city's daily newspaper for a period of 2 weeks and see how many references you find in which the computer is blamed for something or is involved in something in some negative way.

4. Check your city's daily newspaper (especially the advertisements) for a period of 2 weeks to see how many references you find in which something is claimed to be better or more effective in some way because the computer is involved.

5. Gather your own experiences and those of your family, friends, and associates

to determine how many of you have recently been inconvenienced or harassed by a ''computer error.''

6. Using one or more of the program types mentioned in Problem 1, see if you can determine how much such a program costs to purchase (if it was purchased), or how much it costs to lease (if it is leased). Alternatively, if it was produced locally, see if you can find out how much it cost to develop and implement. (Another way of assessing cost is to determine how long it took to develop and how many people were involved.)

7. Another indicator that companies often use as an index of program cost is an estimate of the cost per statement in the final program. Alternatively, such information may be reported in terms of the time expended per final program statement. See if you can determine these figures for various organizations.

8. An experimental investigation produces a number of data points where each point is expressed as a pair of coordinates, (x, y). Prior research already has provided strong evidence that the relationship among these points should be expressed as a straight line, that is,

$$y = a + b*x$$

List as many algorithms as you can for determining the straight line for these points (that is, how to find the values for the two coefficients). Arrange these choices in order of preference and indicate the good and bad points of each.

9. Consider the following situation: You have decided to make a trip to a city within 5-6 hours' driving distance. You will be unable to drive there yourself, and public transportation is scheduled at times that are rather inconvenient for you. However, a devastatingly boring acquaintance is planning to make the same round trip at times that are convenient to you and has offered to give you a ride. Discuss the factors that you would consider in determining how your trip is to be managed. (Remember that canceling the trip also is an option.)

10. Describe three or four algorithms for getting to your home from school or work. Select the one that is ''best'' for you. Would your selection change if you were explaining your algorithm to a visitor who is new to your city?

11. You are driving along a highway and you discover that you have a flat tire. Describe the separate actions that must be taken to solve the problem. List the sequence in which these actions should be performed. Is the sequence you gave the only one that will solve the problem? Note the level of detail at which you described the actions. Are there subactions required to complete the actions you listed? List those subactions under their appropriate actions. Is this enough detail?

12. In designing and implementing reliable and effective software products, it is very important to describe a required process with great precision. Accordingly, it is helpful to recognize the strengths and limitations of natural languages as vehicles for such descriptions. For instance, even though we all understand English, the statement, ''Use 103,'' does not make much sense as a process description unless much more information is known about it. List four or five similar statements for which it is impossible to determine the meaning without placing them in specific contexts. Are there other natural languages (Latin or German, for instance) that are less ambiguous? More ambiguous? What alternatives are there to natural languages?

13. List at least a half dozen common, manufactured products that have built-in computers.

14. List the people you know who are in no way affected by (involved with) computers. (Remember that using a credit card, depositing money in a bank, and making a phone call all involve interaction with a computer).

15. List any occupations you can think of that are in no way involved with computers.

16. The tremendous growth of computer usage and the diversity of endeavors in which they play a role must mean that they are helpful and useful. What kinds of activities, in your perception, can computers perform better than people? For what kinds of activities are computers particularly inappropriate? Why?

17. Suppose that alien invaders wanted to disrupt the earth so that they could take over, and they had the ability to disintegrate any type of manufactured item.

    a. If you were to list various types of items (such as automobiles, airplanes, telephones, electric motors, television sets, computers, electric ice crushers, and so on) in order of the effects on people, how far down the list would computers be? Why would the destruction of the other items be more significant?

    b. What would be the short-term effects (up to a year from now) be if the invaders stopped all electronic computing?

    c. What would the long-term effects be?

    d. How would the disintegration of all computers affect you and your interaction with the rest of the world?

18. Describe the process of reading and understanding the meaning or intent of a computer program. Do you think a compiler or other automatic language translator interprets the meaning in the same way? Which aspects of the process do you think are fundamentally alike? Which are different? If differences do exist and those differences are fundamental, explain how you and the compiler can arrive at the same conclusions about a given program.

The Structured Design Process

2

The basic challenge in software design is the same as that in any problem-solving situation: How can a complex problem be decomposed into smaller, more understandable subproblems so that their solutions can be "glued" back together somehow to solve the original problem? Doing this is an art that involves the concurrent application of many skills. The designer must consider the original problem specifications, possible time and space constraints on the solution, and the general capabilities and properties of the proposed implementation language, to name just a few of these skills. When the design is further complicated by the propensity to develop a monolithic solution to a complicated problem, the task becomes extremely formidable. The more the designer must juggle at one time, the more error prone his or her work will be.

The major purpose of structured design is to allow the practitioner to minimize the algorithmic complexity to be considered at one time. It has been found that a top-down stepwise refinement process is an effective method of decomposing a complex problem into subproblems, each of which can easily be understood in its entirety. It is basically this process, along with some specific tools for documenting it, that is described in this chapter.

2.1 BASIC PRECEPTS AND ATTITUDES

People can have difficulty distinguishing between the design of a software product and its implementation. For example, a person developing a product may think he or she understands the problem so well that the solution is clearly evident and no formal design effort is required. This kind of assessment often is fostered in an academic environment, where class assignments tend to be simple enough to preclude the need for a substantial design effort. A student is able to "do the design" in his or her head and immediately start coding. As assignments become more complex, however, this approach becomes less and less effective. The student may write a large segment of identical code three or four times before realizing that it is a common algorithmic component and should be collected into a separate module to be invoked whenever it is needed. If there are a large number of unanticipated, uncoordinated modifications to the implementation (the refinement that should have been done during design and not during implementation), the interfaces between modules may not be "clean," and the flow of control may not be logical or clear. An increasing number of experienced programmers have gone through this phase and have come to realize the importance of a good initial design within the larger context of the problem-solving process. A *specification language* is a vehicle for specifying the essential content of an algorithm to a person; it allows a designer to express the sequence in which specific computations are to be performed. An *implementation language* is a vehicle for describing the details of an algorithm to a computer. The intent, usage, and level of complexity of these two kinds of languages are different, and problem solvers must avoid the serious pitfall of mistaking the implementation language for the specification language. If they can keep the distinction clear, they can do what they are supposed to do at the stage during which they are supposed to do it.

Design and implementation are separate endeavors. They are *not* independent, but they are different phases of the problem-solving process. Solving a problem may, in fact, require repeated use of the two phases. Implementation details may indicate that the original design was inappropriate or inadequate. At that point in the development cycle, the design must be modified before implementation can continue.

2.1.1 Design Versus Implementation

Consider the design and manufacture (implementation) of a physical object such as a trumpet. What actions are involved in the total development process, and in what order should they occur? Should *all* parts of the trumpet be designed in complete detail before *any* of them are manufactured? This latter issue is by no means clear cut and may be affected by many considerations. For example, seasonal requirements (a great demand for end-of-year proclamations) may make it necessary to try to get the trumpet on the market by a certain date. When this constraint is juxtaposed with time lags associated with the manufacture of certain of the parts, it may not be feasible to wait until all the parts have been completely designed before any of the parts are sent off for manufacture. On the other hand, if a poorly designed part is released for manufacture and does not fit with the rest of the final assembly, then the resulting trumpet is useless unless the original part is redesigned and manufactured again.

The question of timing also comes up in software design. At what point should a software module actually be implemented? When possible, of course, implementation should be delayed until the entire design of the total software system is complete. At that point it can be determined whether or not the design considerations in other areas of the software system affect the current design of the module in question. However, time constraints may not allow implementation to be put off until the total design has been worked out in detail. In this situation, those modules that are apt to be least sensitive to the remainder of the system design are implemented first.

What tools might be available for designing our hypothetical trumpet? Probably the most important set of aids would be a series of drawings, which might include the following.

1. *Detail Drawings.*
   This collection includes a drawing of each piece of the finished product specifying the exact shape, dimensions, tolerances, and material of the specific piece.

2. *Subassembly Drawings.*
   The trumpet may be subdivided logically into functional subassemblies.

   a. Valve slides.

   b. Valve assemblies.

   c. Valve casings.

   d. Bell.

   e. Tuning slide.

   The subassembly drawings are used to show how the different pieces will fit with one another in the final product and how the components of the separate pieces will interface with one another. Such a drawing is often a compromise between clarity and completeness, however, not showing all the hidden lines where pieces fit together.

3. *Assembly Drawings.*
   The purpose of assembly drawings is to show how all the parts of the trumpet fit together. Such drawings might outline the relationship of the parts in several different ways. For example, one drawing might be a three-dimensional exploded view of the trumpet that shows how all the pieces fit together (illustrated in Fig. 2.1). Another might be a standard orthographic three-view drawing showing how the different subassemblies fit with one another. In this case, again, only enough detail is included to show the spatial relationships among the subassemblies.

Notice that this system of drawings can be viewed as a hierarchical method for describing the entire product. Depending on the level at which the mechanism of the trumpet is to be understood, the appropriate set of drawings can be extracted and studied. No one drawing enables its reader to develop a complete understanding of the entire mechanism of the trumpet, however. The overall assembly drawing pro-

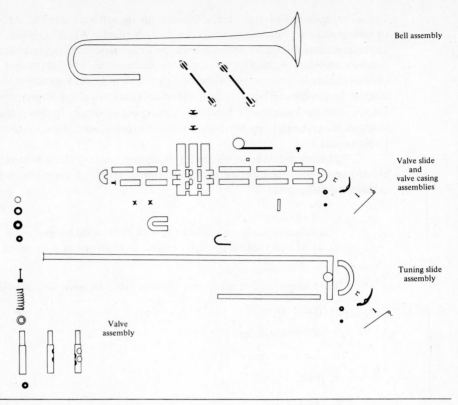

Bell assembly

Valve slide
and
valve casing
assemblies

Tuning slide
assembly

Valve
assembly

FIGURE 2.1 *Component picture of a trumpet. (Photo courtesy of Frank Holton Division of G. Leblanc Corporation)*

vides complete information about what types of parts are used and how many of each; and all the drawings, when viewed as a set, must provide sufficient information to enable the manufacture of the individual pieces, assembly of the pieces into subassemblies, and—finally—production of the entire trumpet. The set of drawings also must permit an understanding of the mechanism by which the final product functions. An analogous set of tools for a software system will be described later in this chapter.

So how do design and implementation differ from each other? In manufacturing a physical object, the distinction is clear. The design process involves the description of the individual pieces of the object and how these parts interface with each other. The implementation process deals with selecting a part of this documentation and interpreting it to produce a physical realization of what it describes.

The distinction between design and implementation in software development is equally clear. However, the nature of the final product of software design—a program—sometimes causes confusion in viewing the development process. Be-

THE STRUCTURED DESIGN PROCESS

cause a program is a description, its intent, which is to describe a set of algorithms to a *computer,* is sometimes confused with its design, the intent of which is to describe the set of algorithms to a *person.* To some, this distinction might seem small; after all, people can read computer languages (obviously, they write in them)! However, most computer languages are designed to help a *computer* understand the details of the algorithms, not to help a *person* understand the overview of the system, the conceptual logic, and the component interfaces. Many high-level languages are compromises between these two requirements, but they are just that—compromises.

Effective software development is just a question of putting first things first: One cannot do something before one knows what has to be done. Design documentation eventually will have to be produced, so it might as well be prepared in the first place. It will provide a good overview of what must be done and how the pieces fit together to form the total product.

A pitfall for many people is the misuse of the implementation language for the specification or descriptive language. Because the implementation language is known and understood, any implementation details (the absence of which might make the design incomplete) can be supplied along the way. This is the pitfall. If the implementation language is used for design, it is very difficult to resist filling in all the implementation details. This takes a significant amount of time and gets in the way of the developer's doing what should be done first, understanding the overview of the system and how the components fit together.

2.1.2 Factors Affecting Software Design

An undetermined complex of factors affects the overall design of software systems, and it is virtually impossible to list them all. The number and types of factors that must be considered depend on the particular problem being solved. A few of these factors are presented here to give a flavor of what might be involved.

2.1.2.1 Problem Specification The specification of the problem to be solved is of major importance in the design of the solution. For many reasons, the original specifications may not be very precise with regard to the required attributes of the final product. The ultimate user—who supplies the original specifications—may not know exactly what he or she wants. The user may be relying on the designer to fill in the holes that were left unspecified. Once an initial design and implementation have been done, the user may request a modified system to address new or (originally) hidden aspects of the problem to be solved. If the designer has had the foresight to develop a flexible and modifiable design, these new aspects may be incorporated easily within the original design. Otherwise, a totally new design may be required.

2.1.2.2 Algorithms Available Often, a set of low-level or intermediate algorithms designed for and implemented in another system may serve as building blocks for a new system. The properties and interfaces of these algorithms may, therefore, significantly affect the design of a new system.

2.1.2.3 Resource Limitations A variety of limitations may be imposed on a specific software system. Time or space considerations or both may be of paramount importance. For instance, if a system is to be implemented on a minicomputer or microcomputer system, the amount of main storage may be limited because of prohibitive storage cost or an inherently small address space.

If the system is a real-time system, response time may be of paramount importance. The required algorithms may have to guarantee narrowly bounded response times, which may affect storage requirements, data representations, and the methods of interfacing between modules, to name a few aspects. In turn, these aspects can exert a strong influence on the overall design of the system.

Other physical limitations also may affect algorithms and system design. For instance, specific input/output devices may have data transfer properties that constrain the overall system design. Disk or tape units may have maximum block lengths or transfer rates, and the printer has a maximum line width and cannot be "backspaced." Such constraints may affect the order in which data are collected and organized.

An implementation of the original problem specifications may not be possible within the constraints of the resources available. This should be determined as early as possible so that revisions can be made before the implementation phase is entered, if possible. A good design can be useful as an analytical tool for estimating system performance. If these performance estimates are unacceptable, the original problem specifications, the design, the resources to be used, or any combination of these can be modified.

2.1.2.4 Implementation Language
The implementation language can affect the type of algorithms chosen as the basic building blocks of the system. A given algorithm may be either easily or efficiently implemented in one language, but virtually impossible to implement in another. For instance, an algorithm that is basically recursive in nature should probably not be chosen if the implementation language does not support recursion.

2.1.2.5 Cost
There is a basic cost tradeoff over the lifetime of any software system among design, implementation, maintenance or support, and execution. If these costs can be analyzed before the system is developed, this analysis can significantly affect the design and implementation.

Assume a system is needed to produce an annual report for the next 6 years. An elegant design and implementation may result in a system that produces the report in a half hour of computer time. A more crude design and implementation may result in a system that requires a full hour of processor time. Depending on the maintenance cost and other factors, it may not be worth the extra time and effort (that is, cost) in design and implementation to produce an elegant system.

In contrast, if the report is to be run once a day for the next 6 years, there may be a significant cost advantage in applying the extra time and effort to design and implementation.

Another situation is one in which an interim system must be developed, but a new system will replace it in the near future. In such a situation it may not be of benefit to invest a large effort in design and implementation, because the lifetime of the system will be short. Thus maintenance and execution costs should be minimal.

2.1.3 Realization of the Design

No known algorithm guarantees the development of a good design. However, certain methods or approaches have been found more productive than others. One such approach, known as *top-down design,* or *stepwise refinement,* will be followed in this text.

Sometimes top-down design may be a linear process in which "good" decisions made at each step of the process produce a "reasonable" design in one pass. In other situations, an iterative process is required, in which design decisions at a given level may have to be reconsidered because of problems at lower (subsequent) levels. In any event, there is no guarantee of an optimal design (whatever that might be).

Top-down design has been applied in many areas of problem solving other than software design. It is not necessarily intrinsically better than other useful design approaches, but it is a viable approach in practice. People seem to be able to subdivide problems into component subproblems using tree structures as a natural vehicle. These tree structures are basic components of top-down software design.

2.2 ESSENTIALS OF THE TOP-DOWN DESIGN APPROACH

The basic concept in the top-down design process is to take the original problem and perform a stepwise refinement in which the problem is segmented or decomposed into smaller, functionally self-contained subproblems, each of which is simpler to solve than the original one. This must be done in such a way that when these component subproblems are "spliced" together, they correctly solve the original problem. Proper splicing of the component subproblems requires careful specification of the data and control interfaces between them.

In this decomposition process, the concept of *functional integrity* should be stressed. Associated with each subcomponent, it should be possible to make a succinct statement about the function it performs or the problem it solves: This component does "X." This function or problem solution should make sense to an interested observer and should embody a complete self-contained activity. Such decomposition makes it easy to splice the components back together and verify that the internal algorithm chosen to carry out the function is correct.

Once the stepwise refinement has been performed at a specific level (on a specific problem), each of the component subproblems can be addressed individually as a problem in its own right. Thus the process can repeatedly be applied to each of the subproblems until a desired level of decomposition is reached.

2.2.1 Advantages of Stepwise Refinement

Stepwise refinement allows a designer to think about a problem at one abstract level at a time. The details of the design never have to be coordinated on more than two levels. Thus attention can be focused on the decomposition of a given problem without having to worry about how the resulting subproblems will be decomposed. (This occurs later, at the next level of decomposition.)

Software systems can be extremely large, requiring a team of designers or implementers (or both) for their timely completion. When the stepwise refinement approach is used, each of the subproblems defined by the decomposition process can be given to an individual or subteam for further design refinements. In this way all the members of the team do not have to know the details of the other members' activities, which has been shown to be an advantage. The stepwise refinement approach relieves difficulties created by the communication of surplus information.

2.2.2 Concluding the Decomposition Process

The process of stepwise refinement should be continued until the solution to each particular subproblem is obvious. This does not imply that this refinement should be carried to extremes, for instance, until the lowest level corresponds to a single statement in the implementation language. The refinement usually stops when the resulting algorithm is predefined (such as a square root function) or well understood (such as a linear table search).

2.2.3 Problems with Stepwise Refinement

The process of stepwise refinement is not so easy and foolproof that an acceptable solution is always obtained on the first pass. It may happen that even though the decomposition of a given problem does solve the original problem, one of the resulting subproblems may not have an effective or efficient implementation.

Example 2.1

Consider the following problem: Assume a large, spherical, free-floating heavenly body is composed entirely of grains of sand. We wish to determine the approximate mass of the body. One solution to the problem might be to perform the following steps.

1. Count the number of grains of sand N.

2. Take a "representative" grain of sand and determine its mass m.

3. Multiply m and N to determine the approximate total mass.

If each of the three subproblems can be implemented, then we have a solution to the original problem. However, Subproblem 1 may not be effectively implementable. Where do we put a grain of sand after we pick it up to "check it off" in the counting procedure so that it does not get counted again? Even if we can find some effective way of keeping track of each grain as we check it off, the physical counting procedure may take so long that we cannot determine the answer within the required time frame.

What can we do at this point? One approach is to retain the original decomposition but try to modify the subproblems so that they can be implemented. In the example above, we might try to modify Subproblem 1 to something like this.

1'. Determine the *approximate* number of grains of sand N.

There may be some effective method for decomposing Subproblem 1'.

Another approach is to retreat and decompose along another dimension of the problem in order to obtain subproblems that do have acceptable solutions. For instance, another decomposition of the original example is as follows.

1. Determine the radius R of the sphere (this might be done by some indirect measure such as triangularization).

2. Determine the volume of the sphere by $V = 4/3*PI*R**3$.

3. Determine the approximate density of the sphere by the following sequential steps.

   a. Take a small sample of sand.

   b. Determine its volume v.

   c. Determine its mass m.

   d. Determine its density $D = m/v$.

4. Determine the mass $M = V*D$.

If the initial stepwise refinement of a specific problem does not yield subproblems that have effective solutions, an iterative process—which may include starting all over again—often is required to produce an effective, efficient design.

2.2.4 Interfaces

In the design process, we must know how the different components (subproblems) of the problem interface with one another, both statically and dynamically. We must also be able to determine how information (data) flows between the components. In Example 2.1, data were implicitly passed between the separate subproblems by using the same variable name in each subproblem in which the variable was either modified (assigned) or referenced. Thus the R used to represent the radius in Subproblem 2 of the second approach was the same radius, also called R, used in Subproblem 1. Similarly, the V defined in Subproblem 2 of the second approach is the same V, representing the same thing, in Subproblem 4.

2.3 DESIGN TOOLS

We need to develop a notation that will allow us to specify each of the following.

1. How a specific problem has been decomposed into component subproblems.

2. How these subproblems interact and interface with one another.

3. What data are transferred between the subproblems.

In developing this notation, we must decide how much detail should be supplied by the notation itself and how much should be transferred to external written documentation. Enough detail should be supplied within the notation itself so that the essence of the decomposition, algorithmic interfacing, and data interfacing is present. However, excess detail may result in notation so complicated that it becomes unreadable, thus defeating its original purpose.

Many notations for describing algorithms and the interfaces between them have been developed over the years. In this text we shall employ the use of two specific design tools, which will be called *structure diagrams* and *pseudocode*. Structure diagrams supply a graphical method for describing how a specific problem has been decomposed into component subproblems and how data flow between these components. Pseudocode will be used to describe the algorithmic content of the components and how they interface.

The following example will clarify these two design tools. Several solutions will be presented, along with their structure diagrams and pseudocode descriptions.

Example 2.2

The array of numbers in Figure 2.2 is commonly known as *Pascal's triangle,* and this is the form in which it is normally presented. We define $P<i,j>$ to be the entry in the ith row and the jth number from the left. For example, $P<5,3> = 6$. We define $P<i,j>$ to be $(i\text{-}1)!/((j\text{-}1)!(i\text{-}j)!)$ for $i \geq 1$, $1 \leq j \leq i$. Although this definition is sufficient to calculate any arbitrary entry of the triangle, any given row n can also be completely determined by knowing only the values in row $n\text{-}1$, without using the formula at all. Except for the two 1s on each end, any entry in row n is just the sum of the two numbers just above it (to the upper left and upper right) in row $n\text{-}1$, for example,

$$P<6,3> = P<5,2> + P<5,3>$$
$$10 \quad = \quad 4 \quad + \quad 6$$

In general, it is true that

$$P<i,j> = P<i\text{-}1,j\text{-}1> + P<i\text{-}1,j> \qquad i \geq 2, 1<j<i.$$

Assume that the problem to be solved is to print the first NROWS rows of Pascal's triangle (in the form shown in Fig. 2.2) on the line printer.

For the most part, the above statement is sufficient to define the problem to be solved, but there still are some details that are unspecifed. For instance, how many print positions should be reserved for each number printed (let us assume 10 positions)? What if NROWS is so large that an entire row will not fit within 120 print positions (so let us assume NROWS $\leq$ 11). Implicit in the original statement is the fact that we start at row 1 and center the table on the printed page. (How about blank lines in between rows?)

			1			Row 1
		1		1		Row 2
	1		2		1	Row 3
1		3		3		1	Row 4

Row 4: 1 3 3 1
Row 5: 1 4 6 4 1
Row 6: 1 5 10 10 5 1

FIGURE 2.2 *A portion of Pascal's triangle.*

Several different solutions to this problem—which will be documented later—are presented next.

Solution 2.2.1

We use the original definition of $P<i,j> = (i\text{-}1)!/((j\text{-}1)!(i\text{-}j)!)$. In a language such as PL/I (which has stream I/O), it is possible to execute many output statements and have an aggregate of the data printed on one line. In this solution we shall calculate a specific $P<i,j>$ and print it immediately. In order to have the numbers come out on the printed page in the correct positions, the values of $P<i,j>$ must be calculated in a specific order. They will be calculated starting at row 1 and working down the triangle. Within each row, they will be calculated from left to right.

Solution 2.2.2

In this solution, we shall still use the original definition of $P<i,j>$, but we shall collect the entire row (in an array) before we send any entries of the given row to the line printer. The order of calculating $P<i,j>$ will be the same as that used in Solution 2.2.1.

Solution 2.2.3

In this solution, we use the observation that the entries of row n can be determined from the entries of row $n\text{-}1$. The values of $P<i,j>$ will be collected (in an array) and printed, one row at a time. They will be calculated in the same order as in Solution 2.2.1.

2.3.1 Structure Diagrams

You may already have inferred from the description of the stepwise refinement process that it can be represented by a treelike structure. The structural representation is actually a flow graph, because a specific subproblem may be a component of more than one problem. A structure diagram is precisely that—a treelike (graph) structure that describes how each problem is decomposed into its component subproblems.

Structure diagrams are analogous to the assembly and subassembly drawings of the manufacturing design process. The purpose of these drawings was to specify these items.

1. Parts present in the assembly or subassembly.

2. Physical orientation of these parts in relation to one another, that is, how they interface.

The purpose of structure diagrams is similar; they specify the following.

1. Decomposition of problems into their constituent subproblems.

2. Data interface between component subproblems.

Just as assembly drawings do not supply all the details, neither will structure diagrams. They are intended to impart an approximation of the overall structure of the software system. This includes specifying the logical components of the system, indicating which of the components interact with which other components and conveying how the interacting components interface with one another, that is, their data interface.

A structure diagram consists of a set of boxes connected by unidirectional arcs (arrows). Each box represents a separate logical module of the system. The arcs emanating from a given module point to modules produced in the decomposition process. The arcs are labeled with the data that are passed across the modular boundaries and indicate the direction in which the data flow.

We shall take a specific problem and show a sample structure diagram for a possible solution. Consider Example 2.2 using Solution 2.2.1.

In any problem there is almost always some initialization to be performed. In this case, the determination of NROWS, the number of rows to be printed, is the only initialization required. The initialization might be done by an assignment statement (using a constant or some formula), or the value might be read in. The two major components of this problem are to determine the value of each $P<i,j>$ and to print each specific $P<i,j>$ in the correct position on the output page. Thus our first level of decomposition could be represented by the structure diagram shown in Figure 2.3(a).

The notation indicates that NROWS is an output parameter of module B; i and j are input parameters of module C; $P<i,j>$ is an output parameter of module C; and $P<i,j>$ and POS are input parameters to module D. We enclose POS in parentheses to indicate that some information is to be transferred about where $P<i,j>$ is to be printed. This might be the position of the units digit of $P<i,j>$ on the printed page, or it might be i and j, from which module D might calculate the appropriate print position.

This brings up some interesting questions. To what do the names of these parameters refer? Variables in a program? Not really; at this point, there is no program. It may turn out that names similar to these will be picked for the implementation (which is advantageous for clarity), but this is a decision to be made later. These parameters usually correspond to quantities to which we refer in the original

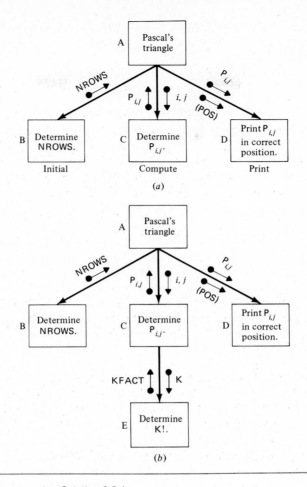

FIGURE 2.3 *Structure diagram using Solution 2.2.1.*

problem specifications; they may also correspond to "internal" quantities required by algorithmic components not present in the problem specifications. In any event, all parameters should be well documented, leaving no doubt about what information the variable logically contains.

Each box corresponding to a separate subproblem should contain a brief description of the function performed within the subproblem. (An alternative is to place a mnemonic name inside the box and document the functional content externally.) The details of how the function is performed are not included. For instance, module B does not present the details of how NROWS is determined: NROWS might be read in from a card or assigned a constant value, but the structure diagram does not indicate how it gets its value.

Another level of decomposition can be performed. In determining $P<i,j>$, three factorials must be calculated. Thus module C might be decomposed one more level to reflect this algorithmic component. The total decomposition is shown in Figure 2.3(*b*).

From this discussion, we can make the following observations.

1. Structure diagrams describe the conceptual decomposition of a problem into its component subproblems and indicate the data interface between them.

2. Structure diagrams do not present detailed information on how each function is performed.

3. Parameter names usually come from the problem specifications and need not be used in the subsequent implementation.

The decomposition indicated in the structure diagram does not lock the implementer into a specific style of implementation. It simply indicates the algorithmic decomposition of the problem. For instance, in this example it is possible to produce a PL/I implementation that has five separate procedures, each one corresponding to one of the boxes in Figure 2.3(*b*). However, this same design can be used to implement just one procedure with straight-line code. A compromise probably is preferable. Assuming the implementation language is block structured and each module is actually implemented as a procedure, the parameter-passing notation does not necessarily imply actual parameters in a formal parameter list. Such information may be passed globally or through function names.

Consider the decomposition of Solution 2.2.2. A structure diagram is shown in Figure 2.4(*a*). Now we must compute (module G) and print (module H) an entire row at a time. Note that modules B, C, and E of Figure 2.4(*a*) are logically the same as those of Figure 2.3(*b*). We could decompose module H further; such a decomposition would probably include module D of Figure 2.3.

Finally, consider the decomposition of Solution 2.2.3. The structure diagram shown in Figure 2.4(*b*) is similar to that shown for Solution 2.2.2. However, the calculation of row *i* is so simple that no decomposition (of module L) is necessary.

2.3.2 Pseudocode

Now that we have a way of describing the algorithmic components involved in the solution to a specific problem, we need a way of describing the details of how these components are spliced back together to solve the problem. Pseudocode is such a tool.

Pseudocode is analogous to the detail drawings of the manufacturing design process. In the same way that these drawings describe the shape and substance of each individual part of a physical product, pseudocode describes the algorithmic content of the components identified by the stepwise refinement (decomposition) process.

Pseudocode is a notational way of presenting six specific structured constructs for flow of control: SEQUENTIAL (concatenation), WHILE, IF-THEN-ELSE,

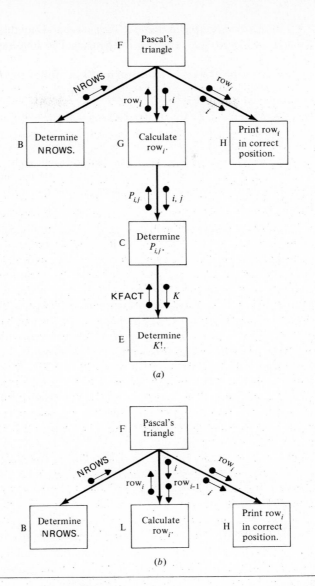

FIGURE 2.4 *Structure diagram comparing Solutions 2.2.2 and 2.2.3.*

REPEAT-UNTIL, DO, and CASE. The notation is designed so that any of these constructs can easily be embedded inside any other construct. There are many different forms of pseudocode. The specific form presented in this text is one such form; it is straightforward enough so that you can easily adapt to any other form you might encounter in the future.

2.3.2.1 Definition and Notation It has been proven[1] that three basic constructs for flow of control are sufficient to implement any "proper" algorithm.

- SEQUENTIAL (concatenation) is the operation of performing one task sequentially after another.

- WHILE is a simple conditional loop with the test at its beginning.

- IF-THEN-ELSE is a simple decision in which one code sequence is performed if a Boolean condition is true and an alternative code sequence is performed if it is false.

Although these constructs are sufficient, it often is useful to include three more constructs.

- REPEAT-UNTIL is a simple conditional loop with the test at the bottom.

- CASE is a multiway branch (decision) based on the value of an expression (a generalization of the IF-THEN-ELSE).

- DO is a special form of the WHILE loop in which an index variable is "automatically" initialized, incremented, and tested.

The meaning of and notation for each of these constructs will be discussed in this section.

SEQUENTIAL

Sequential control is indicated by writing one action after another. The actions are performed in the sequence in which they are written, for example,

Example 2.3
    Drive to store.
    Do shopping.
    Drive home.
    Unpack groceries.

IF-THEN-ELSE

Binary choice on a given Boolean condition is indicated by use of four keywords: IF, THEN, ELSE, and ENDIF. The general form is:

---

[1]*C. Bohm and G. Jacopini, "Flow Diagrams, Turing Machines and Languages with Only Two Formation Rules," Communications of the ACM 9(5):366-71 (May 1966).*

```
IF <Boolean condition> THEN
        <statement list 1>
ELSE
        <statement list 2>
ENDIF
```

The ELSE keyword and <statement list 2> are optional. Note that DO-END or BEGIN-END keywords do not delimit the statement lists. If the <Boolean condition> is true, the THEN clause is performed; otherwise, the ELSE clause is performed.

Example 2.4
```
IF A > 3 THEN
        Print that A is greater than 3.
ELSE
        Print that A is not greater than 3.
ENDIF
```

WHILE

The WHILE construct is used to specify a loop with a test at the top. The beginning and ending of the loop are indicated by the two keywords WHILE and END-WHILE, respectively. The general form is

```
WHILE (<Boolean condition>)
        <statement list>
ENDWHILE
```

The loop is entered only if the <Boolean condition> is true. At the conclusion of each iteration, control is transferred to the top of the loop, and the loop continues only if the <Boolean condition> is still true.

Example 2.5
```
WHILE (there are still more data)
        Get some data.
        Process the data.
ENDWHILE
```

CASE

A CASE construct indicates a multiway branch based on conditions that are mutually exclusive. Four keywords, CASE, OF, ELSE, and ENDCASE, and conditions are used to indicate the structure showing flow of control. The general form is

```
CASE <expression> OF
<condition 1>:
        <statement list 1>
<condition 2>:
        <statement list 2>
        ⋮
<condition n>:
        <statement list n>
ELSE:
        <default statement list>
ENDCASE
```

The ELSE clause with its <default statement list> is optional. Conditions are normally numbers or character strings indicating the value of the <expression>, but they can be English statements or some other notation that specifies the condition under which the given statement list is to be performed. A given statement list may be associated with more than one condition.

Example 2.6

```
CASE I OF
=1:
        Print that I is 1.
=2:
        Print that I is 2.
≥ 3:
        Print that I is greater than or equal to 3.
ELSE:
        Print that I is less than 1.
ENDCASE
```

REPEAT-UNTIL

This loop is similar to the WHILE loop except that the test is performed at the bottom of the loop instead of at the top. Two keywords, REPEAT and UNTIL, are used. The general form is

```
REPEAT
        <statement list>
UNTIL (<Boolean condition>)
```

This type of loop always is executed at least once, because the test is performed at the end of the loop. At the conclusion of each iteration, control is transferred to the top of the loop only if the <Boolean condition> is false. That is, the activity exits from the loop when the <Boolean condition> becomes true.

DO

A DO construct is a special form of a WHILE construct in which an index variable is incorporated. There are four keywords: DO, = , TO, and ENDDO. The general form is

DO <index> = <expression 1> TO <expression 2>
    <statement list>
ENDDO

This is exactly equivalent to the following WHILE construct (with I the index variable, <index>).

I ← <expression 1>.
TEMP ← <expression 2>.
WHILE (I ≤ TEMP)
    <statement list>
    Add 1 to I.
ENDWHILE

Example 2.7

DO I = 1 TO 100
    Read X(I).
ENDDO

The description of the processes embedded in the pseudocode are often in a terse form of English. Because processes may involve evaluation of expressions and assignment of results, such descriptions may appear in a shorthand form that resembles many implementation languages. However, these descriptions should be language independent. Bear in mind that the purpose is to convey a message to *people*, not *computers*. Whatever notation best meets this end is the one that should be used.

2.3.2.2 Presentation The notation just described is used to specify the sequence of actions to be taken by an algorithm. However, there are other aspects of an algorithm that must also be presented. The general presentation of an algorithm will have the following components.

- *Name*.
  Name of the algorithm.

- *Input Parameters*.
  Data supplied to the algorithm.

- *Output Parameters*.
  Data extracted from the algorithm.

- *Functional Definition*.
  English description of what the algorithm does.

- *Definition of Terms*.
  Definitions and commentary on variables or phrases (or both) used in the pseudocode.

- *Specification of the Algorithm.*
    Actual pseudocode.

Example 2.8

NAME: IS_POWER_OF_2

INPUT PARAMETER: NUM, an integral value.

OUTPUT PARAMETER: The answer, either yes or no.

FUNCTION: Given a value, NUM, the algorithm determines whether or not it is a power of 2. It answers yes if it is a power of 2 and no otherwise.

DEFINITIONS: TEMP is a temporary value corresponding to NUM divided by successive powers of 2. Answer denotes a return.

ALGORITHM:

```
IF NUM ≤ 0 THEN
    Answer no.
ENDIF
TEMP ← NUM.
WHILE (TEMP > 1)
    IF TEMP/2 is an integer THEN
        Divide TEMP by 2.
    ELSE
        Answer no.
    ENDIF
ENDWHILE
Answer yes.
```

2.3.2.3 Examples The pseudocode corresponding to the modules shown in Figure 2.3(*b*) (Solution 2.2.1) is shown in Figure 2.5. Notice that some of the modules (B, C, and D) are very sparse. Depending on the calling configuration and the external utility, such modules may not be primary candidates for implementation as distinct procedure.

A PL/I implementation corresponding to this design is shown in Figure 2.6. Notice that only two of the modules (A and E) were actually implemented as separate procedures, because modules B, C, and D all could be implemented with *one* PL/I statement. Names used in the design documentation are carried over to the programming whenever possible. But, for instance, the notation $P<i,j>$ used in

```
NAME: A

FUNCTION: This module prints a portion of
    Pascal's triangle.

DEFINITIONS: NROWS is the number of rows of
    Pascal's triangle to be printed; I indicates
    the row, J indicates the (slant) column, and
    P is the entry to be printed.
```

FIGURE 2.5 *Pseudocode for Solution 2.2.1.*

```
ALGORITHM:
     Invoke B(NROWS).
     DO I = 1 TO NROWS
          Print a blank line.
          DO J = 1 TO I
               Invoke C(P,I,J).
               Invoke D(P,I,J).
          ENDDO
     ENDDO
     Stop.
```

NAME: B

OUTPUT PARAMETERS: NROWS

FUNCTION: This module supplies the value of NROWS.

```
ALGORITHM:
     NROWS <- 11.
```

NAME: C

INPUT PARAMETERS: I, J

OUTPUT PARAMETERS: P

FUNCTION: This module calculates the value to be
     printed as a function of I and J.

DEFINITIONS: P1, P2, and P3 are intermediate factorials
     used to calculate the value to be printed.

```
ALGORITHM:
     Invoke E(I-1,P1).
     Invoke E(J-1,P2).
     Invoke E(I-J,P3).
     P <- P1/(P2*P3).
```

NAME: D

INPUT PARAMETERS: P, I, J

FUNCTION: This module prints the value of P in the
     appropriate position.

```
ALGORITHM:
     Print P in position (I,J).
```

NAME: E

INPUT PARAMETERS: K

OUTPUT PARAMETERS: K_FACT

FUNCTION: This module implements the factorial
     function.

```
ALGORITHM:
     K_FACT <- 1.
     DO I = 2 TO K
          K_FACT <- I*K_FACT.
     ENDDO
```

FIGURE 2.5 *(continued)*

```
PASCAL:PROC OPTIONS(MAIN);
    DCL (
         I,          /*  ROW OF TRIANGLE  */
         J,          /*  COLUMN (SLANT) OF TRIANGLE  */
         P,          /*  ENTRY OF TRIANGLE  */
         NROWS       /*  NUMBER OF ROWS TO BE PRINTED  */
         ) FIXED BIN(31);
    FACT:PROC (K) RETURNS(FIXED BIN(31));
        DCL (
             K,          /*  FIND FACTORIAL OF K  */
             K_FACT,     /*  INTERMEDIATE FACTORIAL  */
             I           /*  INTERMEDIATE COUNTER  */
             ) FIXED BIN(31);
        K_FACT = 1;
        DO I = 2 TO K;
            K_FACT = I*K_FACT;
        END;
        RETURN(K_FACT);
    END FACT;
                    /*  START OF MAIN PROCEDURE  */
    PUT PAGE;
    NROWS = 11;
    DO I = 1 TO NROWS;
        PUT SKIP(3);
        DO J = 1 TO I;
            P = FACT(I-1)/(FACT(J-1)*FACT(I-J));
            PUT EDIT (P)  (COL(51+10*J-5*I),F(10));
        END;
    END;
    STOP;
END PASCAL;
```

FIGURE 2.6 *PL/I code for Solution 2.2.1.*

the structure diagram did not imply or require the use of an array in the implementation.

Figures 2.7 and 2.8 contain the pseudocode and PL/I implementation, respectively, for the structure diagram of Figure 2.4(*b*) (Solution 2.2.3). Note again the flexibility of an implementation corresponding to a given design. The design specifies only the overall structure and form of the final product; it does not prevent the implementer from making a variety of qualitative implementation decisions, which—of course—is his or her job.

The example (printing Pascal's triangle) chosen here to show a specific exploitation of these software design tools was chosen for its simplicity so that the use and content of the structure diagrams and pseudocode could be presented without a lengthy discussion of the problem itself. The designs presented could be done mentally. However, as problems become more complex, this will not continue to be the case, and the use of these design tools becomes an undeniable aid in the development of a well-engineered product.

2.4 INSPECTION AND VERIFICATION

Verification means to ascertain that whatever has been produced (design, documentation, program code, and so on) is correct. At each step in the development proc-

```
NAME: P

FUNCTION: This module prints a portion of
     Pascal's triangle.

DEFINITIONS: NROWS is the number of rows of the
     triangle to be printed.  I indicates a row.
     ROWN is a vector containing the Nth row of the
     triangle.  ROWNM1 is the N-1st row of the triangle.

ALGORITHM:
     Invoke B(NROWS).
     ROWN 1  <- 1.
     IF NROWS >= 1 THEN
          Invoke H(ROWN,1).
          DO I = 2 TO NROWS
               ROWNM1 <- ROWN.
               Invoke L(ROWNM1,I,ROWN).
               Invoke H(ROWN,I).
          ENDDO
     ENDIF



NAME: H

INPUT PARAMETERS: ROWN, I

FUNCTION: This module prints a row of Pascal's triangle.

DEFINITIONS: J indicates the position within the row.

ALGORITHM:
     DO J = 1 TO I
          Print ROWN J  in correct position.
     ENDDO



NAME: L

INPUT PARAMETERS: ROWNM1, I

OUTPUT PARAMETERS: ROWN

FUNCTION: This module calculates the Nth row as a
     function of the N-1st row.

DEFINITION: J indicates the position within the row.

ALGORITHM:
     ROWN 1  <- 1.
     DO J = 2 TO I-1
          ROWN J  <- ROWNM1 J-1  + ROWNM1 J .
     ENDDO
     ROWN I  <- 1.
```

FIGURE 2.7 *Pseudocode for Solution 2.2.3.*

ess, we want to check the correctness of what has been produced. There is no reason to enter the implementation phase if the design phase has produced an incorrect (or in some other way unacceptable) product design. The sooner flaws are detected within the total development process, the more effective the process will be.

```
PASCAL:PROC OPTIONS(MAIN);
     DCL (
          I,              /* ROW OF TRIANGLE */
          J,              /* COLUMN (SLANT) OF TRIANGLE */
          NROWS           /* NUMBER OF ROWS TO BE PRINTED */
          ) FIXED BIN(31);
     DCL (
          ROWN(11),       /* ROW TO BE CALCULATED */
          ROWNM1(11)      /* ROW ABOVE ROWN */
          ) FIXED BIN(31);
     NEXT_ROW:PROC(ROWNM1,I,ROWN);
          DCL (
               ROWN(*),   /* ROW TO BE CALCULATED */
               ROWNM1(*), /* ROW ABOVE ROWN */
               I,         /* ROW NUMBER */
               J          /* TEMPORARY COUNTER (COLUMN) */
               ) FIXED BIN(31);
          ROWN(1) = 1;
          DO J = 2 TO I-1;
               ROWN(J) = ROWNM1(J-1) + ROWNM1(J);
          END;
          ROWN(I) = 1;
          RETURN;
     END NEXT_ROW;
                    /* START OF MAIN PROCEDURE */
     PUT PAGE;
     NROWS = 11;
     ROWN(1) = 1;
     IF NROWS >= 1 THEN DO;
          PUT SKIP(3) EDIT(ROWN(1)) (COL(56),F(10));
          DO I = 2 TO NROWS;
               ROWNM1 = ROWN;
               CALL NEXT_ROW(ROWNM1,I,ROWN);
               PUT SKIP(3) EDIT((ROWN(J) DO J=1 TO I))
                    (COL(51+10*J-5*I),F(10));
          END;
     END;
END PASCAL;
```

FIGURE 2.8 *PL/I code for Solution 2.2.3.*

Most of the verification that a given product will fit together and have the desired properties can be done by inspection of the design documentation. One of the major purposes of the design phase is to detect and eliminate problems before the manufacturing (implementation) begins.

In the case of drawings produced as part of the manufacturing design process, we can confirm that parts are of the required shape and fit together correctly; for instance, we can inspect dimensions supplied in the drawings. In the case of software design, it can be verified that all the required algorithmic components are present, that each component has sufficient input data to complete its task, and that each component returns the required values.

Within the theory and practice of software engineering, there are formal program-proving techniques that can sometimes be used to verify the correctness of an algorithmic component. The description and use of these formal techniques are beyond the scope and intent of this text. However, there are informal methods of verifying algorithmic correctness in which simple everyday logic is the major vehicle for the verification. These informal methods are enhanced by the fact that, within the stepwise refinement process, problems are decomposed into functionally self-contained components (as opposed to using some other criteria). When the decomposition produces components with well-defined functions, it becomes relatively easy to develop statements of purpose or function (semantics) for each component. Each component can be taken separately and its semantics verified. Once this is done, the component can be assumed to be correct and used as an entity in the verification of higher-level components.

Because the verification is done informally by hand, human error can occur. Moreover, these verification techniques can indicate only the algorithmic correctness of the components and do not resolve implementation questions about, for instance, time and space requirements. However, reasonably close estimates concerning even these parameters can be developed using only the design documentation and a minimal knowledge of the implementation language.

2.5 DOCUMENTATION

Documentation is a method of describing a product to the world. Who is "the world"? Within our context, we shall define the world as any set of people who want to do one of the following.

- Manufacture the product.

- Modify the product.

- Redesign the product.

- Analyze the product.

The world includes the original designer. After designing (and possibly implementing) a product and then leaving to design other products, the designer will not be able to remember the details (or even the intent) of the original design without sufficient documentation, which is necessary to reproduce a complicated line of thought.

What might the world want to know about the product? It might want to know these facts.

- Constituent parts of the product.

- Function of these parts.

- How the parts relate and interact with one another.

- Why the specific design was chosen as opposed to another.

The total design documentation must supply enough information so that each part can be manufactured (implemented) and the parts can be put together to make the final product. It should also include a description of how the product is used either by itself or in conjunction with other products.

The world may want to have information about this product at many different levels. Depending on how complex the product is, there may be many different levels of decomposition. Each of these levels must be documented both conceptually and in detail.

Well-thought-out, complete documentation is useful for more than describing the original product. Components of the original product may be useful in developing other products. If the design and function of these components have been well documented, then the evaluation of these components for other uses is relatively easy; moreover, the documentation is already done for the secondary product. A well-documented design approach can also help in the design of future products.

Sparse documentation may be inappropriately produced because people feel (often subconsciously) they are documenting for themselves alone. Important conceptual information is omitted because people understand the concepts at the time they are documenting, failing to realize that others may not have that understanding or that they (the authors) may need a reminder when they come back to look at it. This attitude is self-defeating, and we shall continue to stress the need to document for public (rather than private) consumption.

In the same way that drawings form the basic set of documentation within the manufacturing process, structure diagrams and pseudocode can be used as the core of the documentation in software design. The structure diagrams supply the conceptual information about how the problem has been decomposed at each level and indicate the major control and data interfaces. Pseudocode supplies the details of the algorithmic content of the components.

In addition, a narrative description of each algorithmic component should be included to indicate the intent, general logic, control interface, and data interface. Structure diagrams and pseudocode are graphical representations of the content and interfaces between the components. While a picture may be very effective, words will certainly help to clarify the picture. A description of each parameter and any major data structures should also be included.

In the same way that the drawings form a basic set of documentation for the trumpet, the manufacturing of the trumpet cannot be completed successfully without specification of the tolerances to which the parts should be machined, the materials to be used, and instructions for assembly. These still are part of the design. Similar supplementary information also must be supplied in software design.

2.6 SUMMARY

What is involved in the process of software design? The process involves the decomposition of the original problem into functionally self-contained subproblems, the specification of the algorithmic content of the subproblems, and a description of the interaction between them in terms of both control and data flow.

Structure diagrams offer a means of describing the results of the decomposition and specifying the control and data-flow interaction. Pseudocode conveys the algorithmic content of the component subproblems.

The purpose of such a design phase is to produce a final product with certain desired properties; it must be flexible, modifiable, understandable, and verifiable. If possible, the design of the entire system should be completed before the implementation phase is entered to avoid production of duplicate segments of code for which one common generalized module would have sufficed, thus producing a larger and more complicated system than needed. In trying to optimize and modify the code, the control and data interfaces can become very complex.

The decomposition of the problem into functionally self-contained modules helps the designer and implementer understand the interaction between the modules and makes it easy to check the correctness of each module separately, as well as of the system as a whole. It also tends to produce modules that may be useful as building blocks of other software systems. Thus they may be exported and have multiple utility.

The software-design process is always part of the development of any program. It may be done implicitly in the developer's head, or it may be documented by use of ad hoc descriptions—but it is always done. The tools and techniques presented in this chapter simply provide a more orderly approach to presenting the design documentation.

PROBLEMS

1. Discuss the use and importance of the size and speed of main memory, secondary sequential storage capacity (for example, magnetic tape), and secondary direct access storage capacity (for example, magnetic disk) in each of the following systems.

   a. An airline reservation system.

   b. A monthly payroll preparation system.

   c. A single-user word processing system.

   d. A system to check and process income tax returns.

2. There are occasions where it is useful to describe a collection of numerical values in terms of certain basic statistical characteristics. Among these are the following.

   (1) *Arithmetic Mean.*

   $$\text{XMEAN} = \frac{\sum\limits^{N} X}{N}$$

(2) *Median*. That value XMED such that there are equal numbers of X's above it and below it (once the X's have been sorted).

(3) *Mode*. Member(s) of the collection XMODE1, XMODE2, and so on, that occur most frequently.

(4) *Maximum and Minimum*. Largest (XMAX) and smallest (XMIN) values in the collection.

(5) *Range*. Difference between XMAX and XMIN plus 1.

(6) *Variance*.

$$VAR = \frac{\sum_{}^{N} (X - XMEAN)^2}{N - 1}.$$

(7) *Standard Deviation*.

$$STDEV = \sqrt{VAR}$$

We want to develop a software product that computes and prints these statistics for an arbitrary collection of values submitted in any order. The following assumptions are applicable.

(1) The fractional part of each X has no more than three decimal places.

(2) A given collection has only one mode.

(3) There is sufficient main storage capacity to accommodate any collection in its entirety.

An initial decomposition for a possible design is shown in Figure 2.9.

a. Extend the decomposition to one more level.

b. Using the decomposition developed in *a*, show how it would change if we could not impose Assumption 2.

c. Discuss some of the changes or restrictions (or both) that you would have to impose on your design if Assumption 3 did not apply.

3. Write pseudocode representation for the processing in ST_MAIN (Fig. 2.9) using Assumptions 1, 2, and 3 given in Problem 2 and assuming that all the data are read and stored before any processing is done.

4. Write pseudocode representation for the processing in ST_MAIN as in Problem 3 with the exception that Assumption 3 from Problem 2 no longer holds.

5. Business organizations often find it useful to compare performance figures

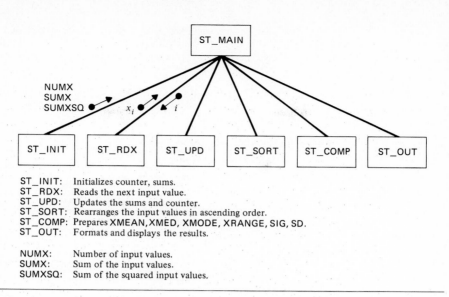

ST_INIT: Initializes counter, sums.
ST_RDX: Reads the next input value.
ST_UPD: Updates the sums and counter.
ST_SORT: Rearranges the input values in ascending order.
ST_COMP: Prepares XMEAN, XMED, XMODE, XRANGE, SIG, SD.
ST_OUT: Formats and displays the results.

NUMX: Number of input values.
SUMX: Sum of the input values.
SUMXSQ: Sum of the squared input values.

FIGURE 2.9 *Initial decomposition for Problem 2.*

compiled for each month of the year. A particularly convenient way to display such data is in a bar chart like the one shown in Figure 2.10.

A company requires a software product that will produce such displays for an arbitrary number of input data sets. Each set consists of 12 pairs of values (month, performance figure) and labeling information to identify the types of figures being presented on a particular display. Assuming that a display of fixed size will be used for all cases (that is, the scale of the ordinate will be adjusted to suit the range of the particular figures being shown), show a structure diagram for this product using at least two levels of decomposition.

6. Prepare a structure diagram for the situation described in Problem 5 with the following change in requirements: Instead of being presented in summary form (a single performance figure for each month of the year), an input data set consists of an arbitrary number of value pairs in which each pair consists of a month designation and a performance figure that contributes to the overall total for that month.

7. *Stylistics* is an area of inquiry in which various statistics are gathered and used to help describe the characteristics of a literary text. Basic information developed for this purpose includes the following.

   (1) Words themselves, accompanied by their frequency distribution.

   (2) Number of words in the text.

   (3) Number of different words in the text.

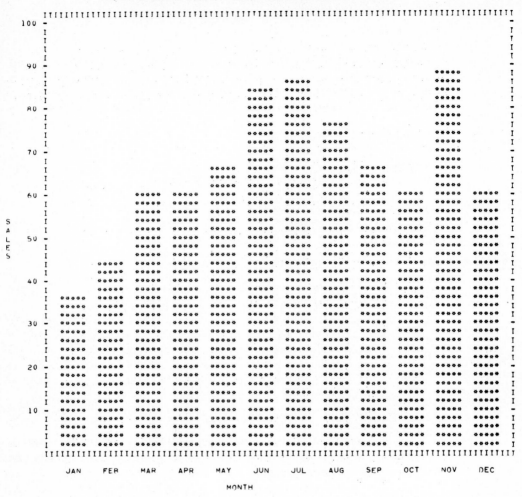

FIGURE 2.10 *Use of the line printer for histogram display.*

(4) Number of sentences in the text.

(5) Average sentence length (number of words per sentence).

(6) Average word length (number of letters per word).

(7) Frequency distribution of the word lengths.

(8) Frequency distribution of the sentence lengths.

(9) Frequency of certain word combinations.

(10) Number of hyphenations.

(11) First and last words of the sentences.

Design a software product that reads a text of arbitrary length (in natural form) and prepares (and prints) the information listed above. In addition, the product is to print the input text with each sentence being numbered and starting on a new line. The following assumptions are acceptable.

(1) A given text may be arbitrarily long, but it will not contain more than 1000 different words.

(2) There is enough room in main storage to accommodate all of the different words, associated counters, and other supporting data and data structures, but there is not enough room to contain the entire text.

Describe your design in terms of a structure diagram that includes at least three levels of decomposition.

8. It is often useful to display an entire set of data as a graph. When no line or curve is drawn through these points, such a graph is called a *scattergram* (Fig. 2.11). The line printer is a particularly convenient device for preparing large numbers of scattergrams quickly and economically. These scattergrams can be examined to determine which displays might be of sufficient interest to warrant their production in a more elaborate form (for example, on a computer-driven, high-quality graph plotter).

Figure 2.12 shows an initial structure diagram for a software product designed to produce a set of basic displays such as the one shown in Figure 2.11. The major components defined in Figure 2.12 are based on the following assumptions.

(1) Each scattergram is produced using a fixed frame having a capacity of 50 (ordinate) x 100 (abscissa) points.

(2) The scale is fixed at one unit per division in either direction.

(3) The origin always is at (0,0) so that all input points are expected to have positive X and Y-values. More specifically, X-values will range from 0 through 100 and Y-values from 0 through 50.

(4) Each scattergram will have an arbitrary number of (X,Y) points, and there is no guarantee that each point will have a unique pair of coordinate values.

(5) The names (labels) for the ordinate and abscissa variables are fixed.

(6) Labeling at the top of a scattergram consists of one fixed line and up to three lines that can be submitted as input.

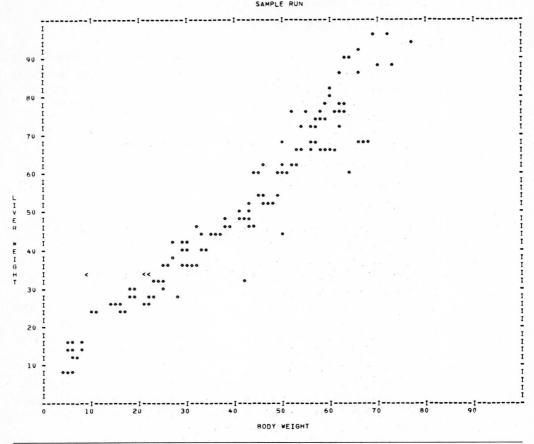

FIGURE 2.11 *Use of the line printer for scattergram display.*

(7) The presence of one or more points at a particular place on the scattergram is denoted by a fixed symbol.

(8) There is sufficient room in main storage to accommodate an entire scattergram.

a. Without imposing any further decomposition, complete the structure diagram in Figure 2.12 by showing the flow of major data items between the main module and the five subsidiary components.

b. Extend the decomposition one more level. State all of the assumptions required to do this.

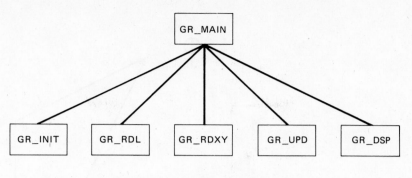

GR_INIT: Initializes the basic scattergram template.
GR_RDL: Reads labeling information (if present) for a scattergram.
GR_RDXY: Reads (x, y) data.
GR_UPD: Converts (x, y) data to appropriate graphical representation.
GR_DSP: Produces the output scattergram.

FIGURE 2.12 *Initial decomposition of a scattergram design.*

    c. Describe how you would set up the input data stream. How does this affect the design? How will it affect the subsequent implementation?

    d. Briefly list the types of errors that the implemented product will have to address.

9. As a modification to Problem 8, assume that the *X* and *Y*-values no longer lie in a constrained interval (that is, *X*-values are not restricted to the range 0-100, and *Y*-values are not restricted to the range 0-50). Accordingly, it is necessary to scale the *(X,Y)*-points to fit within the available 50 x 100 output frame.

    a. How would this modification affect your design?

    b. List the design options that you think are applicable to this new set of requirements and indicate the assumptions that would have to be made in support of each of these options.

    c. Indicate the scaling information that would be printed along the axes.

    d. Nobody likes to look at a graph that uses awkward scales. Define a ''nice'' scale and list criteria that can be used to identify such a scale.

    e. Specify an algorithm for determining a nice scaling factor for a given set of data values.

10. An airplane in flight does not always travel in the direction it is headed. The effects of the prevailing winds may cause the aircraft to drift off course. For instance, the aircraft in Figure 2.13(*a*) is headed north at 200 miles per hour.

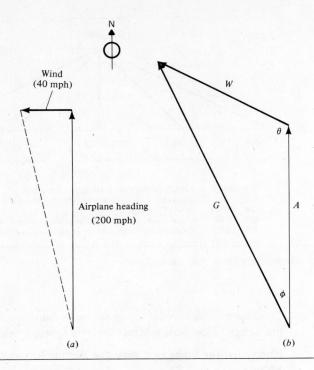

N

Wind
(40 mph)

W

Airplane heading
(200 mph)

θ

G

A

ϕ

(*a*)   (*b*)

FIGURE 2.13 *Representation of requirements for*
Prob. 10.

There is a wind blowing due west at 40 miles per hour. In 1 hour, the aircraft
will travel 200 miles north and 40 miles west.

To prevent getting lost, pilots solve the triangle in Figure 2.13(*b*), where
A is the speed of the aircraft through the air, *W* is the wind speed, and theta (θ)
is the angle between the aircraft's heading and the wind direction. The unknown *G* (the ground speed of the aircraft) and the drift angle phi (ϕ) may be
determined by using the law of cosines and the law of sines, respectively. (The
third angle in the triangle is irrelevant.)

$$G = \sqrt{A^2 + W^2 - 2AW \cos \theta}$$

$$\frac{G}{\sin \theta} = \frac{W}{\sin \phi}$$

Input consists of an arbitrary number of data cards with each data card containing *A*, *W*, and θ, in that order. A software product is needed to compute and
print *G* and θ (the latter in degrees) for each input set.

$$\text{radians} = \text{degrees} \left(\frac{\pi}{180} \right)$$

$$\text{degrees} = \text{radians}\left(\frac{180}{\pi}\right)$$

Develop a structure diagram for this software product showing at least two levels of decomposition beyond the main module.

11. Data are frequently reported as sequences of yes-no, on-off, or true-false responses, all of which are called *two-valued, binary-valued,* or *bistable data.* The following string is an example of such data.

01110010

(Here, 1 stands for *true, yes*, or *on,* and 0 represents the alternative). We are interested in a software product that reads such strings and calculates the length of the longest consecutive sequence of 0s and the longest consecutive sequence of 1s. In the above example, for instance, the maximum length of consecutive 1s is three, and that of 0s is two.

Each input string is punched on a separate card containing the string starting in Column 1. Maximum string length is 25, with the last 1 or 0 being followed immediately by a single 9. Any number of input strings may be processed during a given run. For each string, the output is to show the string itself and the maximum number of consecutive 1s and 0s in it.

Devise a structure diagram for such a product, showing at least two levels or decomposition beyond the main module.

12. Referring to Figure 2.14, we see that points $(X1,Y1)$, $(X2,Y2)$ and $(X3,Y3)$ lie on a straight line, while points $(X1',Y1')$, $(X2',Y2')$ and $(X3',Y3')$ do not. (They form a triangle.) A software product is needed that reads and processes a set of cards, each containing the coordinates of three points $(X1,Y1)$, $(X2,Y2)$, and $(X3,Y3)$ (in this order, in free format). If the points are *not* on a single straight line, the software product is to report this by setting a variable L to a value of zero and reporting the area of the triangle thus produced in a variable named AREA. If the points *do* lie on a straight line, L is to be set to a value of 1 and AREA to a value of zero.

   a. Using pseudocode, describe an algorithm that you might use to determine whether or not a particular set of input points lie on a straight line.

   b. Produce a structure diagram for this product.

13. The software product required here is similar to the one in the previous problem with the following extension: Each input data card now contains four pair of coordinates, $(X1,Y1)$ through $(X4,Y4)$. As before, we are to determine whether or not the first three points lie on a single straight line. If they do, L and AREA are to be set as in Problem 12 and the fourth point is to be ignored. An additional variable, T, is to be set to -1 to indicate that the fourth point is irrelevant. If the three points do not lie on a straight line, L and AREA are to be set as in

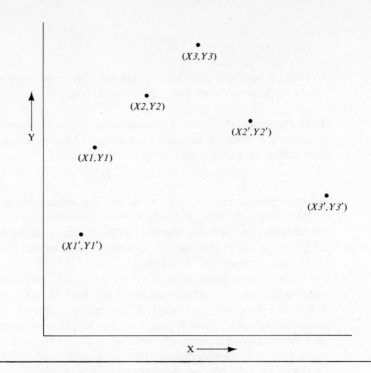

FIGURE 2.14 *Representation of requirements for*
Prob. 12.

the previous problem. In addition, T is to be set to zero if the fourth point lies
inside the triangle formed by the other three points and 1 if it does not.

a. Describe an algorithm (using pseudocode) that would be suitable for determining the relation of the fourth point to the other three.

b. Devise a structure diagram for this product.

For Problems 14–20, express the indicated activities using pseudocode.

14. Given a rectangular solid with dimensions L, W, and H, we can compute the
following:

```
FRONT = L * H
SIDE  = W * H
TOP   = L * W
VOLUME = L * W * H
```

Read L, W, and H. Print the input, followed by FRONT, SIDE, TOP, and
VOLUME.

15. Compute and print the results described in the previous problem for twelve
input sets of L, W, and H.

16. Read a value NUMBRK that specifies how many rectangular solids are to be described during a particular run. Then read and process the data (as in the previous two problems) for the appropriate sets of L, W, and H (as specified by NUMBRK).

17. Read and process dimensional data for an arbitrary number of rectangular solids, with each set handled as in Problem 14. The last set is followed by a special set (not to be processed) in which one of the dimensions is zero.

18. Read three sets of input values for L, W, and H. Process the data (and print the same results as in Prob. 14) for each of the three input sets in the reverse order in which they were read (that is, last set first).

19. Read 36 sets of input values for L, W, and H; process and print them in reverse order.

20. Read and process 36 sets of input values for L, W, and H as in Problem 19. For this problem, however, the results are to be printed in descending order, with largest volume first. Output for each set is to include an integer value SEQ indicating the order in which the data were read. For instance, the 29th set to be read in will have a SEQ value of 29. (This has nothing to do with the set's position in the output; that is determined by the computed volume).

21. Refer to the specifications in Problem 5 and recall that it required a display of performance data for a 12-month period spanning a calendar year (that is, January through December). However, not all reference years start and end that way. For example, many companies have a fiscal year that starts in July. Accordingly, this particular company would like to display a set of performance figures over *any* 12 consecutive months. The first month (the reference month) is to be submitted as part of the input specifications. Accordingly, the 12 sets of input values, still the same as in Problem 5, are to be preceded in this version by a single integer value (1-12) indicating which of the 12 months is to be treated as a reference month.

22. Modify the structure diagram of Problem 21 to accommodate the requirement described in Problem 6.

23. A more challenging version of Problem 22, presented to us by a more challenging company, is as follows: While it is handy to be able to look at consecutive months, there are many occasions where it is more valuable to look at a shorter or longer time span. Consequently, you are to devise a structure diagram for a product in which the first input card now contains three data items: The month (1-12) to be used as the reference month, the year in which the reference month occurs, and the number of months to be shown on that display. Each individual performance card, then, contains the month, year, and performance figure.

(*Note:* As the main chief designer, it will be up to you to define the maximum and minimum number of months that your product will accept for a given display.)

24. A dash of reality from the hard-boiled software world: As soon as you think you have provided the users with everything they could want, they define yet another requirement. Although the version of the performance display software in Problem 23 is quite flexible, there are two more requirements that will be introduced. These are fairly independent of each other, so that either or both may be included in a revised design.

    a. Performance figures are not always positive; they may be zero or negative. Accordingly, include provisions in your design for an arbitrary mixture of positive, negative, and zero entries for a given display.

    b. It is possible for performance data to be missing completely for one or more months of a given display. This does not have a particularly serious effect on the preparation of the display, but a good software product should notify the user that the data, in fact, are not available. That way, everyone is assured that the software did not overlook some input. Consequently, modify the design to make note of months in a specified span with no available data, so that appropriate messages can be printed.

25. Write a pseudocode description for the main procedure identified in your structure diagram for each of the following.

    a. Problem 5.

    b. Problem 6.

    c. Problem 21.

    d. Problem 22.

    e. Problem 23.

26. One of the data manipulation techniques that is commonly employed for comparative purposes is that of *normalization*. The basic idea is to represent a set of related values as fractions of a single reference value. For example, the value of a dollar during any given year often is normalized by dividing it by the value of the dollar in some reference year. In the same general way, the company requesting the display of Problem 5 would like to see the performance figures for each month reported as a percentage of the maximum monthly value. Thus the maximum itself (by definition) would be reported as 100 percent.

    a. Modify the structure diagram (in Probs. 5, 6, 21, 22, 23, or 24) to reflect this change in requirements.

    b. Modify the corresponding pseudocode for the main procedure.

27. Prepare a pseudorepresentation for the main procedure identified in your structure diagram for Problem 7.

28. Describe the processing for the GR_MAIN module (Prob. 8) using all of the assumptions given in that problem.

29. Consider the requirements of Problem 8 with Assumption 5 removed.

   a. Modify the structure diagram given in Figure 2.12 to accommodate this change.

   b. Prepare a pseudocode representation for the main procedure consistent with this modification.

Case Study—A Design

3

This chapter presents a specific problem, a design decomposition of the problem, and a description of the algorithmic components used in the solution. An implementation for this design is given in Chapter 5. Generality of the solution is emphasized so that the modules motivated by this problem can be applied to a wider range of problems.

3.1 THE PROBLEM—CHEMICAL FORMULA EVALUATION

The problem motivating this software design is a very real one faced by people working in chemistry and related areas. A wide variety of scientific and technical information has been published on millions of chemical compounds, and this information is being supplemented and updated at a rapid rate. In addition, thousands of new compounds are being formulated every year, providing an additional source of growth for this ever-expanding base. Because the value of such information lies in its accessibility to those people seeking to make use of it, it is not surprising that thousands of people throughout the world are dedicated to organizing and maintaining this information within a systematic framework.

The heart of such an organizational system is its *index,* the vehicle that serves as the key for the system users and managers alike. For chemical compounds, this presents some severe problems and a unique challenge: The appropriate entry in a chemical information system is the compound itself. This means that, unlike other types of information, conventional means of organization are irrelevant; there is nothing (of meaning) to alphabetize. Thus the obvious expedient of indexing according to chemical composition is not very effective. Even for a formulation as simple as C_3H_8O, for instance, there are three distinctly different, common compounds matching it.

Compound 1:

```
    H   H   H   H
    |   |   |   |
H———C———C———C———O
    |   |   |
    H   H   H
```

Compound 2:

```
        H
        |
    H   O   H
    |   |   |
H———C———C———C———H
    |   |   |
    H   H   H
```

Compound 3:

```
    H   H       H
    |   |       |
H———C———C———O———C———H
    |   |       |
    H   H       H
```

In other words, although the formulation C_3H_8O gives some information about the compound (the number of atoms of each element), it is ambiguous because it does not contain structural information about how the atoms are configured. The situation worsens with molecular size, as the number of possibilities grows exponentially. Consequently, it is a combination of structure and formulation that constitutes an appropriate entry in a chemical index. The basic difficulty lies in the fact that input to a conventional digital computing system is inherently one-dimensional (a sequential string of characters, numerical values, individual bits, and so on), while two dimensions are often inadequate for representing even simple molecular structures.

Numerous attempts have been made to reconcile this fundamental incompatability by devising coding schemes in which a particular molecule can be represented unambiguously by a (one-dimensional) character string without loss of structural information. Once such a notation is defined, it constitutes a viable basis for constructing a computer-based chemical information system in which indexing, searching and maintenance operations can exploit computational speed and effectiveness.

One of the most successful coding systems of this type is the Wiswesser notation.[1] That notation serves as a basis for the product to be designed here.

Using a relatively modest subset of simple organic chemicals, we shall design a software product that will read chemical formulas (in linear form) from cards, translate them to some internal representation, produce certain useful statistics about the molecule thus described, and print the molecule in a two-dimensional form similar to what a chemist might write on a chalkboard. As we go through the design process, it is helpful to keep in mind that many of the algorithmic components identified by the analysis embody techniques whose utility extends far beyond the manipulation of formula representations. Consequently, we seek explicitly to encourage general designs that will enable a module to function (often without change) in environments quite different from the particular one that motivates it. For instance, a module that extracts a symbol from a larger string need not be tied inexorably to the idea that the symbol represents an atom and the string represents a molecule. Using the precepts introduced in the previous chapter, the design of such a module could enable it to extract dipthongs from phrases, expressions from mathematical equations, keywords from program statements, or theme motifs from a musical score.

Before a design of such a software product can be developed, we must understand clearly the form and meaning of the linear formulas to be analyzed, the analysis and output that is to be performed, and the internal representation to be used. It should also be realized that the solution to the specific problem presented here probably will be only a component of a much larger system (for example, a chemical database system), and the design must be flexible enough that components of the system can be extracted easily and placed in different contexts.

3.1.1 The Input—Line-Formula of the Molecule

A *structural-formula* is a two-dimensional graphical form of the molecular structure; for example,

$$\begin{array}{c}
\text{H} \quad \text{O} \quad \text{H} \quad \text{Cl} \\
| \quad || \quad | \quad | \\
\text{H}-\text{C}-\text{C}-\text{C}-\text{C}-\text{H} \\
| \quad \quad | \quad | \\
\text{H} \quad \quad \text{H} \quad \text{H}
\end{array}$$

A *line-formula* is a structurally equivalent, one-dimensional representation of the molecular structure, as defined below.

Our system is interested only in certain elements and functional groups. Although the original implementation will be limited to the elements and groups listed below, the product should be flexible enough to allow the convenient addition of

---

[1]E. G. Smith, The Wiswesser Line-Formula Chemical Notation, *McGraw-Hill, New York, 1968.*

TABLE 3.1 ELEMENTS OF INTEREST TO THE LINE-FORMULA SOFTWARE

Element	Symbol	Bonds	Atomic Number	Atomic Weight
Hydrogen	H	1	1	1.00797
Carbon	C	4	6	12.01115
Nitrogen	N	3	7	14.00670
Oxygen	O	2	8	15.99940
Fluorine	F	1	9	18.99840
Sulfur	S	2	16	32.06400
Chlorine	G	1	17	35.45300
Bromine	E	1	35	79.90400
Iodine	I	1	53	126.90440

other elements and groups. The elements of interest, along with certain relevant information, are listed in Table 3.1. Besides these specific elements, certain functional groups will be represented by single letter identifiers.

1. *Q:* Hydroxyl group, —O—H.

2. *V:* Carbonyl connective,
$$-\overset{\overset{\displaystyle O}{\|}}{C}-\ .$$

3. *W:* Nonlinear (branching) dioxo group, as in $-N\overset{O}{\underset{O}{\diagup\!\!\diagdown}}$.

The symbol W is not used for linear (unbranched) structures, such as CO_2.

4. *M:* Imino or imido group,
$$-\overset{\overset{\displaystyle H}{|}}{N}-\ .$$

5. *Z:* Amino or amido group,
$$-\overset{\overset{\displaystyle H}{|}}{\underset{\underset{\displaystyle H}{|}}{N}}\ .$$

6. *U:* A double bond (*UU* indicates a triple bond, and so on).

7. *Numerals:* The number of carbon atoms in an unbranched alkyl chain or segment.

Example 3.1

Line-formula   Structural-formula

1V1

Q2Q

WN101NW

3US

1UU1   H—C≡C—H

    The line-formula has a form that can easily be read by the computer, from which the structural-formula of the molecule can be reconstructed. Note that the line-formula notation suppresses the explicit use of the H atom. The hydrogen atom will be used as a default atom wherever an unused bond is present.[2]

3.1.2 The Output

The output will consist of certain statistics about the molecule, along with its two-dimensional structural-formula. In the remainder of this section, each output item

---

[2]*A more detailed definition of the notation can be found in Chapter 1 of Smith,* The Wiswesser Line-Formula Chemical Notation.

will be discussed in detail. The line-formula 1V1 will be used as an example to provide continuity throughout the different statistics developed.

3.1.2.1 *Statistics*   A table is to be printed showing the following data.

1. For the molecule:

   a. The molecular weight.

   b. The molecular number (total number of protons in the molecule).

2. For each element:

   a. The number of atoms.

   b. The percent molecular weight.

   c. The percent molecular number.

Table 3.2 shows an example for the compound 1V1.

The ratio of unsaturated to total bonds is to be calculated and printed. A *bond* is defined to be a sharing of electrons between any two carbon, nitrogen, oxygen, or sulfur atoms (elements that share more than one electron). An *unsaturated bond* occurs when more than one electron is being shared. In 1V1, for instance, there are four atoms of interest (three carbons and one oxygen) and three bonds between them (Fig. 3.1). The bond between the "middle" carbon atom and the oxygen atom is a double (unsaturated) bond. Thus the ratio is 1/3.

The output also includes a table giving the ratio of the number of atoms of each element to each other element in the molecule. This can be printed in rectangular or triangular form (Table 3.3). (The entries above the main diagonal are the reciprocals of the elements below the main diagonal).

3.1.2.2 *Two-Dimensional Structural-Formula*   Because the two-dimensional structural-formula is to be printed on a line printer, the presentation must be some-

TABLE 3.2   ELEMENT TABLE FOR THE COMPOUND 1V1

Element Percentage Table

Element	Number of Atoms	% Weight	% Number
Hydrogen	6	10.413	18.750
Carbon	3	62.040	56.250
Oxygen	1	27.547	25.000
Total	10	100.000	100.000

Molecular Weight is   58.081
Molecular Number is   32

```
        H    O    H
        |    |2   |
   H  - C  - C  - C  - H
        |         |
        H         H
```

FIGURE 3.1   *Structural-formula for* 1V1.

what restricted. For instance, the use of subscripts and multiple bars (for multiple bonds) is not feasible.

We shall use a rectangular display model in which an atom can be placed only to the right, left, above, or below any other atom. (This causes problems if elements that can bond to more than four other atoms are introduced.) A bond will be indicated by a bar (either vertical or horizontal); if the bond is a multiple bond, its multiplicity will be printed next to (or below) the bar, as illustrated in Figures 3.1 and 3.2.

Another problem with this rectangular display model occurs when trying to print molecules that contain an NW or a WN. Ordinarily, with more elaborate output facilities, we would want to represent such groups as shown in Figure 3.2(*a*). In the absence of such features, a notation using the symbol + can be used to alleviate this problem, and the structural formula for WN1U1O1U1NW could be shown as in Figure 3.2(*b*).

An alternative solution using the symbols \ and / also can be used (if the symbol \ is available), and the presentation of WN1U1O1U1NW might look like Figure 3.2(*c*).

TABLE 3.3   ELEMENT RATIO TABLE FOR COMPOUND 1V1

Element Ratio Table (B/A) A ->	H	C	O
B			
Λ			
V			
H	1.00		
C	0.50	1.00	
O	0.17	0.33	1.00

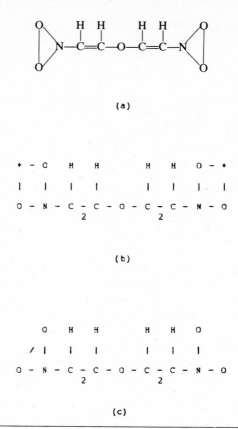

(a)

(b)

(c)

FIGURE 3.2 *Two-dimensional representations of WN1U1O1U1NW: (a) typeset display; (b) line-printer display; (c) alternative line-printer display.*

3.1.3 The Internal Representation

The design of any software project requires an analysis of the objects to be manipulated and the data structures that will represent them. In other words, once the objects of interest have been identified, it is necessary to decide on the internal encodements to be used. This step in the design is trivial if the objects have a simple structure. Thus the step often is performed without the designer's awareness.

The decision about which internal representation to use need not actually be made as part of the first phase of the design process. A general top-level design can be performed independent of the internal representations that will be used. However, the final design cannot be completed until they are chosen. An advantage of selecting these structures early in the design process is that "natural" algorithms may become evident as a result of this choice. In other words, a concrete data structure with which to evaluate trial algorithms may facilitate the selection of the appropriate algorithms. A disadvantage of selecting the data structures early is that an inappropriate choice may complicate the design by prompting the use of (ultimately) unsuitable algorithms.

The data structures chosen here have well-known properties, and we know from experience that they are reasonable for this type of application. However, there are many alternatives which would give the final product different properties. We shall discuss them prior to performing the top-level design to make the design more concrete.

In this application, there are four major objects of interest: the line-formula, the symbols extracted from the line-formula, the elements, and the molecule.

3.1.3.1 The Line-Formula
The line-formula is extracted from an input card and can be thought of most simply as a character string. In the implementation (Chap. 5), the line-formula will consist of three components.

1. The original source character string read from the card.

2. A translated form of the line-formula categorizing the characters into specific classes.

3. A pointer to the current character being scanned.

The last two components are not necessary, but they facilitate processing.

3.1.3.2 The Symbols
Symbols are to be extracted from the line-formula for subsequent interpretation. A *symbol* is nothing more than an object of interest that must be processed. In this application the symbols are very simple. Most of the symbols contain only one character (representing an atom or a group); the only symbol containing more than one character is a number, which may contain multiple digits.

A uniform way of internally representing all symbols extracted from the line-formula is to form a *token* for each symbol. A token contains two components: a *type* and a *value*. (Such general representations are called *2-tuples*). The first component (type) designates the category of the symbol (for example, an atom, a group or a carbon chain); the second component designates the specific object within the category (such as an oxygen atom within the atom category). Thus the token for a hydrogen atom might be <atom,hydrogen>, a hydroxyl group might be <group, hydroxyl> and a carbon chain of three carbon atoms might be represented as <chain,3>. In an implementation, both components of the token would probably be encoded with numeric values.

Using the concept of a token, all symbols extracted from the line-formula can be handled uniformly. Another advantage is that internally generated tokens (those not corresponding to symbols extracted directly from the line-formula) can also be handled easily. For instance, in processing a hydroxyl group, it may be advantageous to generate a hydrogen token and an oxygen token internally. Moreover, this provides the opportunity to define and generate special system tokens, such as an error token or an end of line-formula token, for use in transferring pertinent information.

3.1.3.3 Elements
The elements can be represented conveniently by use of a

one-dimensional array of structures. Each separate element corresponds to a single integer value that serves as an index to the attributes of the element, the latter being the components of the structure (Table 3.1).

3.1.3.4 The Molecules

A straightforward way of thinking about a molecule is as a graph. For instance, the molecule with line-formula 1V1 (Fig. 3.1) can be represented by the graph in Figure 3.3. In this representation, each atom appears as a *node,* and each bond between two atoms appears as an *edge*. This type of notation seems natural and gives virtually the same information as the structural-formula.

Although this form of a graph is easy for people to understand and manipulate, there is an alternative form, known as a *connection matrix,* which is more useful for manipulation by a processor. In this notation, a square matrix is constructed with each row and column corresponding to an atom of the molecule (node of the graph). Each entry in the matrix indicates the number of bonds between the corresponding atoms. For example, the molecule in Figure 3.3 can be represented by the connection matrix shown in Figure 3.4.

Note that the matrix is symmetric (the upper triangular part is a reflection of the lower triangular part), and the entries on the main diagonal are always zero (indicating that no atom is bonded to itself). Because there is no reason to make the correspondence of the rows and columns with the atoms different from one another, we choose the convention of making these correspondences the same.

The order in which the atoms should be placed in the matrix will probably depend on the algorithm used to create the matrix from the line-formula. From the standpoint of the structure of the molecule, it really makes no difference. Depending on what we want to do with the data structure, however, it may make a difference.

There is more information in Figure 3.4 than just the number of bonds between the atoms in the molecule. To the top and side of the matrix, there are designations of the type of element to which the rows and columns correspond. There is also an indication of the size of the matrix. In the implementation (see Chap. 5), this information will be embodied in a structure containing the following three components.

1. The connection matrix itself.

2. An array indicating the correspondence between the rows and columns with the specific elements.

3. A scalar value that indicates how much of the matrix has been "filled in."

FIGURE 3.3 *Graphical representation of line-formula* 1V1.

	C	O	C	C	H	H	H	H	H	H
C	0	0	1	0	1	1	1	0	0	0
O	0	0	2	0	0	0	0	0	0	0
C	1	2	0	1	0	0	0	0	0	0
C	0	0	1	0	0	0	0	1	1	1
H	1	0	0	0	0	0	0	0	0	0
H	1	0	0	0	0	0	0	0	0	0
H	1	0	0	0	0	0	0	0	0	0
H	0	0	0	1	0	0	0	0	0	0
H	0	0	0	1	0	0	0	0	0	0
H	0	0	0	1	0	0	0	0	0	0

FIGURE 3.4 *Connection matrix for the line-formula* 1V1.

3.2 THE DESIGN

Now that we have an idea what the major data structures look like, we can turn to the design. As described in Chapter 2, this process starts by performing a stepwise refinement of the problem and then writing pseudocode for the modules thus identified. The process is often iterative in nature. That is, the development of pseudocode for modules already identified by the stepwise refinement may reveal the need for new modules. As this process continues, the structure diagram is refined to lower levels.

3.2.1 Top-Level Design

The stepwise refinement process often proceeds in a series of phases. To understand the steps in the process, let us examine an initial decomposition of the original problem, as shown in Figure 3.5(*a*). In order to process a compound, the system must do the following.

1.1. Obtain the formula.

1.2. Analyze the formula.

1.3. Print the results of the analysis.

Assuming we have a rough idea of how to obtain the formula and print the results, we may choose to focus on how the system will analyze the formula. In order to analyze the molecule (Fig. 3.5(*b*)), the system must do the following.

1.2.1. Build an internal representation of the molecule.

1.2.2. Compute the desired statistics.

Assuming we perceive that the computation of the statistics is straightforward, we can refine the process of building the internal representation of the molecule. There are two actions necessary to build an internal representation of the molecule (Fig. 3.5(*c*)).

1.2.1.1. Scan the line-formula to extract the "spine."

1.2.1.2. Fill in the unused bonds with hydrogen atoms.

Filling in the unused bonds seems possible, so we can focus on scanning the line-formula. In order to scan the line-formula [Fig. 3.5(d)], the system must:

1.2.1.1.1. Extract a symbol from the line-formula, and

1.2.1.1.2. Interpret the meaning of the symbol by placing the appropriate atom(s) in the internal representation of the molecule.

Notice that each step in the decomposition is performed independently of all others. After the decomposition has been performed to whatever level of refinement is desired, the identified components must be spliced back together. The combined refinement is shown in Figure 3.6.

The process of recombining the components identified during the stepwise refinement is important because it is during this process that *common* subcomponents are identified. Although no common subcomponents occur in the decomposition shown in Figure 3.6 (because the refinement was stopped after four levels of decomposition), it is possible for the decomposition of two distinct modules to identify identical (or, at least, similar) submodules. For instance, looking ahead to the final structure diagram (Fig. 3.13), the decomposition of the two modules EXEC_SYM and INSERT identified three common submodules, CREATE, LINK and CHANGE_CONTEXT.

Although we may have implied that separate structure diagrams are produced for each step in the refinement process (as shown in Fig. 3.5), this is not normally done in practice. As more refinement is desired, the lowest level of the current structure diagram is simply refined further (as exemplified in Figs. 3.6 and 3.14).

Table 3.4 gives a brief description of the modules and the data that flow between them. This is a prototype of the kind of description that should be included in the documentation of the final product.

Notice that this design is very general. No details are included about how a symbol is extracted from the line-formula. Moreover, there is no information about the internal data structures. (Even though Sec. 3.1.3 discussed data structures, this design is not predicated on the selection of *those* structures.) Not even the nature of the statistics to be computed is included. Many different implementations with very diverse properties can be produced from this design.

We might ask if the modules specified in this design are functionally independent. Specifically, is the analysis of a line-formula dependent on how the line-formula was obtained? Is the interpretation of a symbol's meaning dependent on how that symbol was extracted from the line-formula? The stepwise refinement shown here *does* decompose the problem into functionally independent modules. Each is a self-contained computational entity, which can be extracted and replaced with a functionally equivalent counterpart. For instance, in the original specification the line-formulas to be analyzed are obtained from a card reader. However, if we choose to obtain the line-formula from a disk, a terminal, or an optical scanner,

TABLE 3.4 MAJOR COMPONENTS OF THE DESIGN

Variables and Data Structures

Variable	Meaning
FORM	A data structure embodying the line-formula of the molecule (Sec. 3.1.3.1).
MOL	A data structure representing the molecule (Sec. 3.1.3.4).
SYM	A symbol (token) extracted from the line-formula (Sec. 3.1.3.2).
STATS	Statistics about the molecule (Sec. 3.1.2.1).

Processing Modules

Module	Semantic Action
COMP	Coordinates the analysis of the separate compounds.
GET_FORM	Retrieves the formula from the medium upon which it resides (probably cards).
ANAL	Analyzes the line-formula by building an internal representation of the molecule and computing the desired statistics.
PRINT	Prints statistics about the molecule and a two-dimensional graphical form of the molecule.
BLD_MOL	Builds an internal representation of the molecule.
COMPUTE	Computes statistics about the molecule.
SCAN_FORM	Coordinates the extraction of the next symbol from the line-formula and the interpretation of the meaning of that symbol.
FILL	Attaches hydrogen atoms to those atoms with extra bonds not yet accounted for.
GET_SYM	Extracts a symbol (or token) from the line-formula.
EXEC_SYM	Performs the elementary action indicated by the symbol extracted in GET_SYM.

GET_FORM can easily be extracted from the system and replaced by a functionally equivalent module that supplies the required information.

3.2.2 Algorithmic Content

It would be unproductive to present the pseudocode for all the modules in the structure diagram in Figure 3.6. (In the exercises, you will be asked to fill in the

---

THE DESIGN **71**

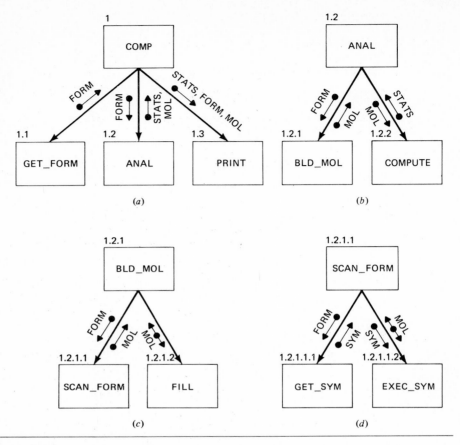

FIGURE 3.5 *Stepwise decomposition of the problem.*

content of some of these modules.) However, it is instructive to present the pseudo-code for a few of these modules and to indicate different kinds of modules that are often useful in the design of software.

At the two extremes of the computational spectrum, there are modules containing "active" computational content and modules that simply coordinate access to these active algorithms and "glue" their activities together in the proper context. In the middle of the spectrum, there are modules containing a varying amount of these two activities. There is a loose but helpful analogy between a module's position in this spectrum and its level in a structure diagram: Modules at the bottom of the structure diagram in the final design are purely computational. The module at the top and the drivers used during development normally provide coordination services only. Modules in the middle tend to be coordination modules, with some computational content.

3.2.2.1 Coordinating Modules Coordinating modules are exemplified by the

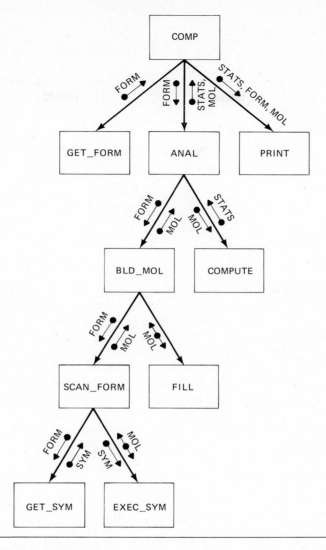

FIGURE 3.6 *Decomposition of the problem.*

pseudocode for COMP, ANAL, and BLD_MOL, as shown in Figures 3.7, 3.8, and 3.9, respectively. Notice that each of these modules simply glues other algorithmic components together:

COMP invokes GET_FORM, ANAL, and PRINT.

ANAL invokes BLD_MOL and COMPUTE.

BLD_MOL invokes SCAN_FORM and FILL.

```
NAME: COMP

FUNCTION: This module coordinates the aquisition,
    analysis, and printing of information about
    the line-formula.

DEFINITIONS: MOL designates a molecule.
    FORM designates a line-formula.
    STATS designates statistics about the
    molecule.

ALGORITHM:

    WHILE (there is still more data)
        Get a formula (FORM).
        Analyze the formula (obtaining MOL
            and STATS).
        Print information about the formula
            (FORM, MOL and STATS).
    ENDWHILE
```

FIGURE 3.7 *Pseudocode for* COMP.

This type of decomposition facilitates implementation in parts: functionally equivalent modules can be extracted easily and replaced in the final product.

3.2.2.2 Computational Modules As examples of computational modules, we shall examine the pseudocode for GET_SYM, EXEC_SYM, and modules refined from them. Analysis of the pseudocode for GET_SYM (Fig. 3.10) indicates that a new algorithmic component corresponding to ''extract the value of the number'' must be resolved. In PL/I, this function is handled easily with the GET STRING feature. However, to keep the design independent of any programming language, this algorithm will be encased in its own module (Fig. 3.11).

The pseudocode in Figure 3.12 identifies a number of new algorithmic components.

```
NAME: ANAL

INPUT PARAMETERS: FORM, the formula.

OUTPUT PARAMETERS: MOL, the molecule.
    STATS, statistics about the molecule.

FUNCTION: This module takes a formula, builds
    an internal representation of the
    corresponding molecule and calculates
    pertainent statistics.

ALGORITHM:
    Build an internal representation of
        molecule (MOL).
    Compute the statistics (STATS).
```

FIGURE 3.8 *Pseudocode for* ANAL.

```
NAME: BLD_MCL

INPUT PARAMETERS: FORM, the formula.

OUTPUT PARAMETERS: MOL, the internal representation
    of the molecule.

FUNCTION: This module builds the internal
    representation of the molecule (MOL) given
    a line-formula (FORM).

ALGORITHM:


    Scan the formula (FORM), extracting the spine
        of the molecule (MOL).
    Fill in the unused bonds with hydrogen atoms.
```

FIGURE 3.9   *Pseudocode for* BLD_MOL.

```
NAME: GET_SYM

INPUT PARAMETERS: FORM, the line-formula.

OUTPUT PARAMETERS: TOKEN, a tokenized representation
    of the next symbol scanned.  TOKEN contains
    two components, TYPE and VALUE.

FUNCTION: This module scans from the current
    position in the line-formula for the next
    symbol and returns the corresponding TOKEN.

ALGORITHM:

    Determine the TYPE of the symbol.
    CASE TYPE OF

    illegal character:
        VALUE <- error code.

    atom:
        Determine specific element.
        Assign to VALUE the corresponding code.

     group:
        Determine specific group.
        Assign to VALUE the corresponding code.

    number:
        Extract the value of the number.
        Assign the value to VALUE.

    blank:
        Indicate "end of line-formula."

    ENDCASE
```

FIGURE 3.10   *Pseudocode for* GET_SYM.

```
NAME: NUMBER

INPUT PARAMETERS: FORM, the line-formula.

OUTPUT PARAMETERS: NUM, the number.

DEFINITIONS: NUM is an accumulator into which the
    numeric counterpart will be placed.

FUNCTION: This module translates a number
    in the form of a character string to
    its numeric (value) counterpart.

ALGORITHM:

    NUM <- 0.
    Look at first character.
    WHILE (character is a digit)
        Determine numeric counterpart of digit.
        NUM <- 10*NUM + numeric counterpart.
        Look at next character.
    ENDWHILE
```

FIGURE 3.11 *Pseudocode for* NUMBER.

1. How do we create a new atom?

2. How do we link a new atom into the molecule?

3. How do we change the context?

Each of these computational entities will correspond to a separate module as the design is continually refined (Fig. 3.13). To show how groups can be handled easily, the pseudocode for the module that inserts groups into a molecule is presented in Figure 3.14.

3.2.3 The Final Design

Once the design specified by the structure diagram in Figure 3.6 is understood, pseudocode is written, and appropriate data structures have been selected, a more complete design can be formulated. Such a design is presented in the structure diagram in Figure 3.13.

After reading the pseudocode in Section 3.2.2, it should be clear how the new modules were identified. In scanning the pseudocode, certain common phrases or concepts become evident. A phrase written in the pseudocode does not present the details of what is to be done. Rather, it simply brings to mind the designer's intent. As a specific concept is identified for placement in a separate module, additions can be made to the pseudocode to reflect this refinement. For instance, a line such as

Link the atom into the molecule.

can be modified to become

Link the atom into the molecule (invoke LINK(ATOM,MOL)).

```
NAME: EXEC_SYM

INPUT PARAMETERS: TOKEN, the tokenized symbol
    containing two fields, TYPE and VALUE.

INPUT-OUTPUT PARAMETERS: MOL, the molecule.

DEFINITIONS: I, a loop parameter.

FUNCTION: This module performs the action
    indicated by the TOKEN.

ALGORITHM:

    CASE TYPE OF
    atom:
        Create an atom of type VALUE.
        Link this new atom into MOL.
        Change the context for new insertions.

    group:
        Insert the group into MOL.

    number:
        DO I = 1 TO VALUE
            Create a carbon atom.
            Link this new atom into MOL.
            Change the context for new insertions.
        ENDDO

    ENDCASE
```

FIGURE 3.12 *Pseudocode for* EXEC_SYM.

Table 3.5 gives descriptions of the additional modules and the data that flow between them. (Refer to Table 3.4 as well.)

Before the implementation is started, the functions of each of these modules must be described in greater detail. For instance, what action does GET_SYM take if it cannot extract a symbol (for example, if it encounters an illegal character)? What action does BLD_MOL take if it is impossible to build a "legal" molecule from the line-formula? These seemingly unimportant details can significantly affect the implementation.

The structure diagram in Figure 3.13 is a summary produced after the final product was completed. Such a completed design often is not available before the implementation phase is started. However, it must be available prior to the completion of the implementation. A graphic representation of how the design, implementation, and testing phases often intertwine over time is presented in Figure 3.15.

PROBLEMS

The problems in this chapter describe software design projects whose scope encompasses the entire range of issues addressed in this text. Applications have been selected to provide a wide range of size and complexity. Specifications for each

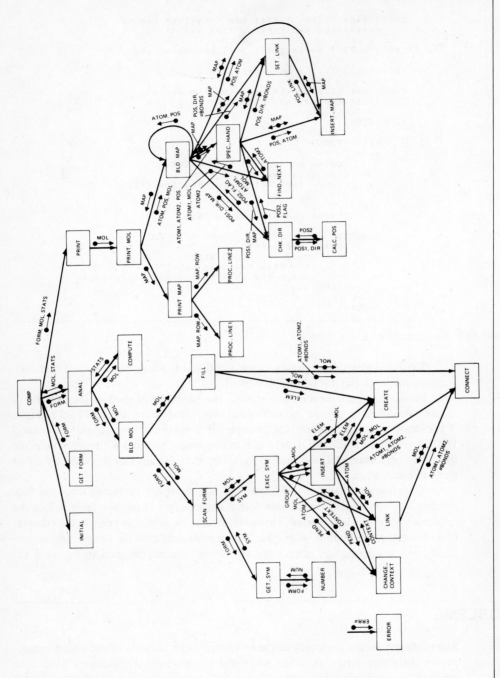

FIGURE 3.13 *Total decomposition of the problem.*

```
NAME: INSERT

INPUT PARAMETERS: GROUP, the group to be inserted.

INPUT-OUTPUT PARAMETERS: MOL, the molecule.

FUNCTION: This module inserts the given group
    into the molecule.

ALGORITHM:

    CASE GROUP OF
    Q:
            Create an oxygen atom.
            Create a hydrogen atom.
            Connect these two atoms with a bond of one.
            Link the oxygen atom into the molecule.
            Change the context.

    V:
            Create an oxygen atom.
            Create a carbon atom.
            Connect them with a bond of two.
            Link the carbon atom into the molecule.
            Change the context.

    W:
            Create two oxygen atoms.
            Create a "connect" atom.
            Connect the two oxygen atoms to the
                "connect" atom with a bond of one.
            Link the oxygen atoms into the molecule.
            Change the context.

    M:
            Create a nitrogen atom.
            Create a hydrogen atom.
            Connect the nitrogen and hydrogen atoms
                with a bond of one.
            Link the nitrogen atom into the molecule.
            Change the context.

    Z:
            Create a nitrogen atom.
            Create two hydrogen atoms.
            Connect each hydrogen atom the nitrogen atom
                with a bond of one.
            Link the nitrogen atom into the molecule.
            Change the context.

    U:
            Add one to #BONDS.

    ENDCASE
```

FIGURE 3.14 *Pseudocode for* INSERT.

project are given in terms of a basic version; it can be extended or enhanced in a variety of ways. Suggestions for such augmentation are included as supplementary specifications. These components have been chosen so that they can be incorporated singly or in any combination. If the basic project is designed systematically, in accordance with the precepts emphasized thus far, inclusion of these features—

either as part of the initial design or as subsequent extensions—will not cause any serious disruption of the project's structure.

Many of the extensions involve the use of processing modules that are components of other projects or entire projects in themselves. Wherever it does not interfere with the overall structure or flow of a project, an effort is made to promote such multiple usage. This reaffirms that the emphasis on functional isolation in the design of a processing module extends the utility of that module beyond the immediate application for which it is being designed. In fact, with sufficient care, it is possible to move a module from one application to another without changing that module.

These project descriptions are intended to serve as starting points for the entire design, implementation, and evaluation process. At this point, however, the selected project(s) should be taken through the decomposition stage, so that the resulting product (for a given project) is a complete, detailed structure diagram. Later, as additional concepts and techniques are discussed, the designs produced at this stage will guide subsequent steps.

TABLE 3.5 ADDITIONAL COMPONENTS OF THE PROBLEM

Variable and Data Structures

Variable	Meaning
ATOM(1,2)	A specific atom within the molecule.
ELEM	A specific element (one of nine).
GROUP	A specific group (one of six).
#BONDS	The number of bonds between two specific atoms.
PEND	A set of atoms to become the new pending atoms.
CONTEXT	The context in which a new atom is to be inserted into the molecule.
MAP	An internal array representing what will be printed on the line printer.
POS(1,2)	A position in the MAP array.
DIR(1,2)	A direction to move in the MAP array. (In the implementation, there will be four possible directions: up, down, right and left).
NUM	A number. (In the implementation, this number corresponds to the number of atoms in a carbon chain).
LINK	A link (between two atoms) to be inserted into the MAP array.

TABLE 3.5 *(continued)*

ERR#	A number indicating which error message to print.
ROW	A row of the MAP array.

Processing Modules

Module	Semantic Action
NUMBER	Converts a character string of digits to its numerical counterpart.
INSERT	Processes a specific group and inserts it into the molecule.
CREATE	Creates a new atom of a specific element type in the molecule.
LINK	Links a given atom into the molecule within the appropriate context.
CONNECT	Connects two atoms together with the correct number of bonds.
CHANGE_CONTEXT	Changes the context in which the next symbol extracted from the formula will be processed.
ERROR	Prints a specific error message on the line printer. This general utility is accessed from various modules (not indicated in the structure diagram).
PRINT_MOL	Prints the two-dimensional structural-formula of the molecule.
BLD_MAP	Builds a representation (in MAP) of what will be printed on the line printer. Note that this module is recursive in nature.
SPEC_HAND	Handles the special case of the W group.
CHK_DIR	Checks to see if the entry in MAP moving in a specific direction is available (does not already have an entry in it).
CALC_POS	Calculates a new position in MAP as a function of an old position and a direction to move.
FIND_NEXT	Determines the next unprocessed atom which is bonded to a specific, given atom.
INSERT_MAP	Inserts a value into the MAP array.
PRINT_MAP	Prints the information contained in MAP on the line printer.
PROC_LINE1	Processes a row of the MAP array for the first time. Atoms and bonds are printed.
PROC_LINE2	Processes each row of the MAP array for the second time. Multiplicity of horizontal bonds is printed.
SET_LINK	Inserts a link (or bond) into the MAP array.

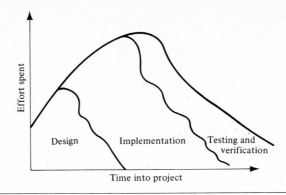

FIGURE 3.15 *Development time distribution.*

1. A BASIC POLYNOMIAL INTEGRATOR

Functional Description

This software product is to compute and print a value V, where V is defined by the following definite integral.

$$V = \int_{XL}^{XR} P(x)\, d(x)$$

where $P(x)$ is a polynomial of the form

$$P(x) = \sum_{i=0}^{m} a_i x^i$$

with *m* not exceeding six. In the most general terms, input for a given computation of V consists of a complete specification for $P(x)$, and for XL and XR, the two limits defining the extent of the desired interval.

Applicable Algorithms

The computation of V is to be done analytically: if we characterize a term in $P(x)$ as

$$a_i x^i$$

then the corresponding integral for that term can be expressed as

$$\left(\frac{a_i}{i+1}\right) x^{i+1}$$

Accordingly, V can be computed as

$$\sum_{i=0}^{n} \left(\frac{a_i}{i+1}\right) XR^{i+1} - \sum_{i=0}^{m} \left(\frac{a_i}{i+1}\right) XL^{i+1}$$

where XR and XL have their previous meanings.

Input Requirements

In this basic version, each input set consists of two cards (or card images). The first one contains a value for m, followed by the m coefficients for $P(x)$, and the second card contains XR and XL, in that order. Any number of input sets may be submitted in a given run. For example, the following values represent the description of a fourth-order polynomial with coefficients 1.0, 2.0, 3.0, 4.0 and 5.0. The value V is required between XL = -18.8 and XR = 25.5.

```
4    1.0    2.0    3.0    4.0    5.0
25.5    -18.8
```

Output Requirements

Output for each set is to consist of three lines: A representation of $P(x)$ as a high-level language expression—for example,

```
1.0 + 2.0*X + 3.0*X**2 + 4.0*X**3 + 5.0*X**4
```

the input values for XL and XR, and the value of the integral V. A blank line separates the output sets and a terminating message concludes the run.

Data Structures

Because of the relatively straightforward nature of this project, data structure requirements are modest. The only pertinent data aggregate is one to accommodate the list of coefficients for $P(x)$. The suggested data structure for this purpose is a simple one-dimensional array.

Enhancements to the Polynomial Integrator

The following extensions are not specified in any particular order. Rather, they are intended to be mutually independent.

1A. *Default input function.* This feature enables the user to request a succession of integral values for several (XL,XR) ranges applied to the same polynomial. Although the basic version makes this possible, the user must submit the same set of coefficients each time, even though they do not change. This enhancement, then, keeps a particular set of coefficients in force until a new set is submitted. (It is up to the user to design a method for expressing this in the input.)

1B. *Default integral range.* This represents a complementary feature to the default input function. Its incorporation in the polynomial integrator would enable the user to specify a variety of polynomials, each of which would be integrated over a given (XL,XR) range.

1C. *Input expression processor.* This enhancement enables the user to submit a description of $P(x)$ as an arithmetic expression rather than a list of coefficients. For instance, the polynomial used to illustrate input for the basic version of this software product is entered as

1.0 + 2.0*X + 3.0*X**2 + 4.0*X**3 + 5.0*X**4

The additional processing analyzes the expression and produces pertinent information about the polynomial to interface with the rest of the integrator. Note that incorporation of this feature obviates the need for m, the degree of the polynomial. (This information is discernible from the input expression.) Each input expression appears in its entirety on a single card, and it always will use X as the independent variable. The symbols +, −, *, and ** have the same meanings as in FORTRAN or PL/I, and any number of blanks may appear where a single blank may appear. (If list-directed input format is to be used, the expression may be delimited by apostrophes.) Since the software must determine the input values from an analysis of the expression, there no longer is any reason to require the user to submit a coefficient for every power of X. Thus, for example, if there is no X**2 term, there is no reason to submit a (vacuous) 0.0*X**2 as part of the expression. We shall impose the restriction, however, that limits the input expression to one term for each pertinent power of X. However, the terms need not appear in any specific order.

1D. *Comparative integration.* This enhancement extends the integrator to include two numerical algorithms that can be used to approximate V. The first of these methods, called *trapezoidal rule,* divides the range (XL,XR) into a set of n equal intervals, each of width w. The portion of the functional curve in each interval is approximated by treating it as a straight line segment (see Fig. 3.16.). Thus, if $x[j]$ is the value of x at the beginning of one of these intervals and the ordinate value (the y-value at $x[j]$) is called $f[j]$, then $(x[j],f[j])$ is a point on the curve at the beginning of one of these intervals. Correspondingly, $(x[j + 1],f[j + 1])$ is the point at the other boundary of that interval. Thus the trapezoidal rule approximates the area under the curve between $x[j]$ and $x[j + 1]$ as

$$A_{j, \, j+1} = \frac{w}{2} \, (f(j) + f(j + 1))$$

The second method to be considered here is known as *Simpson's rule.* As with the trapezoidal rule, this method divides the range (XL,XR) into n equal intervals. It seeks to improve on the approximation of each part of the functional curve by approximating it with a parabola rather than a straight line segment. For this purpose, each of the n intervals is subdivided into two equal halves. As a result, we identify a third point on the curve, midway between $x[j]$ and $x[j + 1]$. As Figure 3.17 shows, we refer to that point as $(x[j + 0.5],f[j + 0.5])$. By char-

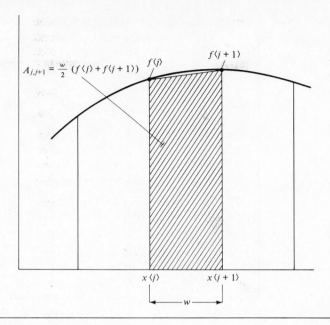

$$A_{j,j+1} = \frac{w}{2}\left(f\langle j\rangle + f\langle j+1\rangle\right)$$

FIGURE 3.16 *Numerical integration via the trapezoidal rule.*

acterizing the parabola drawn through the three points, we can approximate the area under the curve in the range $(x[j], x[j+1])$ as

$$A_{j,\,j+1} = \frac{w}{6}\left(f(j) + 4f(j+0.5) + f(j+1)\right)$$

It turns out that application of Simpson's rule produces exact results for any third-degree (or less) polynomial. Thus, to obtain any variation between analytic integration and that obtained by using Simpson's rule, the target polynomial must be of fourth-degree or above.

For both the trapezoidal rule and Simpson's rule, we can approximate V by adding the n areas together. For this version of the project, the value of n will be fixed (in the software) at 20.

To acknowledge the incorporation of the additional integration methods, the output now will include three values for V labeled ANALYTICAL V, TRAPEZOIDAL V, and SIMPSON'S V. In addition, it will show the difference between the analytical result and each of the approximations.

1E. *Interval-size specification.* This feature enables the user to override the integrator's default value for n and replace it with one of his or her own choosing. The new value then can serve for one or more subsequent input sets, after which the user can specify a new value or instruct the integrator to revert to its built-in value.

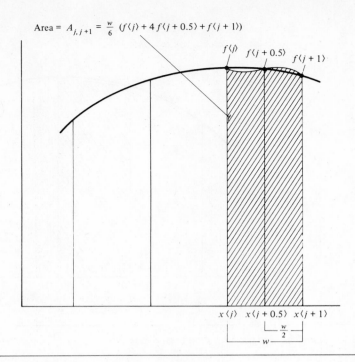

$$\text{Area} = A_{j,j+1} = \frac{w}{6}\ (f\langle j\rangle + 4f\langle j + 0.5\rangle + f\langle j + 1\rangle)$$

FIGURE 3.17 *Numerical integration via Simpson's rule.*

1F. *Self-adapting integration.* In this version, operations of trapezoidal and Simpson's rules no longer are governed by some predefined number of intervals. Instead of using a fixed value of n given by the user or set by the software, this design is to perform an initial approximation (for each method) using n equal to 4. The resulting V should be no more than 0.0001 different from the value computed analytically. If that is true, the integration is complete for that particular method. If not, n should be increased by 2 and V should be recomputed on that basis. This continues until the above-mentioned criterion is met or until n reaches 64. Note that the value of n required for trapezoidal integration will not necessarily be the same as that needed for Simpson's integration in a given situation. (In fact, it is highly likely that they will differ.)

The output will show one value for the analytically determined V and a series of values for each of the other two methods, along with the corresponding values of n used to compute those results. The output also should print an explicit message after the integration terminates to indicate which halting criterion stopped the iteration.

1G. *User-defined epsilon.* This version is similar to the one described previously with the additional flexibility that enables the user to specify EPSILON, the maximum acceptable difference between an approximation to V and the analytically determined value. Facilities should be included so that the user-defined EPSILON can remain in force over several cases or the software can revert to the 0.0001 default.

1H. *Context-free integration.* Comparison of a numerical approximation against an analytically determined result reveals useful information about the behavior of the numerical method. However, the very reason for using a numerical approximation lies in the fact that the analytical solution is unavailable. Consequently, the accuracy of a particular approximation must be compared with a previous approximation.

A technique that finds frequent use in such situations compares a particular result with one obtained in a previous attempt. With specific regard to integration, for instance, a result would be computed based on the division of an (XL,XR) range into some number of intervals. Then the number of intervals would be increased, the integral recomputed, and the new result would be compared with the previous one. If the absolute difference between them fell below some predetermined maximum value EPSILON, the last result would be accepted; if it did not, another computation would be performed with an even larger number of smaller intervals.

Even though we have access to an analytical solution in the case of polynomials, it will be useful to design a version of this software product in which the computations are regulated by the type of comparison described above. Accordingly, start with $n = 4$ and compute respective values of V for each of the two numerical methods used above. Then increase n by 2 and recompute V for each method until the value for V thus obtained falls within EPSILON of the previous value or an n of 64 has been used. EPSILON can be constant at 0.0001 (as in 1F) or it may be supplied as an input item (as in 1G). Note that, for a given polynomial, we can expect the two numerical methods to behave differently, so that their computations must be handled independently of one another.

For each polynomial processed, the output shows EPSILON, the analytical result (since it is easily computed), and a set of tabulated results for each of the two methods showing the value of V for each n and, after the first n, the difference between that V and the previous value. An appropriate message indicating why the process terminated (either it was successful or the maximum n had been reached) is included.

2. DISCRETE SIMULATION—A SLOT MACHINE SIMULATOR

Functional Description

One of the areas in which growth has been accelerated considerably by computer science and its applications is discrete simulation. This is the representation of systems in which individual events affect the state of the systems and the behavior of these systems in response to subsequent events. An example of such a system is a two-lane vehicular tunnel fed by (and feeding into) four traffic lanes. Entry of a vehicle represents an event in such a system, and when it is simulated on a computer, the controlling software is designed to provide answers to a wide variety of questions. For example, what if we hold constant the rate at which vehicles arrive at the tunnel entrance from each lane, but close off one of the lanes feeding the tunnel? Similarly, this type of simulation might be used to assess the effects of, say, a 20 percent increase in the number of vehicles (per unit time) approaching the tunnel.

A less elaborate but still realistic system is a simple slot machine in which each event consists of a bet (money fed into the machine), and the outcome of each event is a display of three items (plums, oranges, bars, or a similar array). Certain combinations result in a "win," in which case the player's "account" is credited with some multiple of the bet; otherwise, the account is depleted by the amount of the bet. A simulation, in this context, starts with an account set at a predefined level (either by default or by reading an input value) and consists of a series of bets applied to that account. The placement of the bet generates an outcome (based on the machine's predefined set of behavioral properties) and the player's account balance is updated to reflect the outcome of that event. The events continue until the player's account is completely depleted or (much less likely) until the system completes a predetermined number of events. Each event is reported, along with its outcome and its effect on the player's account. The slot machine never runs out of money.

For purposes of this project, the outcome of a given event is tied to the slot machine's three wheels, each of which is equipped with a collection of display items. Some of the items are present only once (on a given wheel), while others may be present several times.

These items are built into the machine: bar (1), bell (2), cherry (3), orange (4), and plum (5). Each wheel contains a sequence of items as shown below:

Left wheel: 1,2,3,4,5,3,4,3,5,1,3

Center wheel: 3,4,5,3,1,2,4,1,5,2,5

Right wheel: 5,3,2,4,1,3,5,4,3,3,4

In this basic version, the actual amount of each bet is irrelevant. Rather, we are interested in the fact that this machine takes a fixed amount for each bet. For convenience, we shall call that amount 1 coin. In this context, the machine pays off as shown on page 89.

In each simulation, the player begins with a 50-coin account, and each wheel is at a randomly determined initial position. The process continues automatically, with each play causing random shifts in the positions of each of the three wheels. Besides defining the outcome of the play, these resulting positions serve as the starting positions for the next play. If the (infinitely wealthy) slot machine does not succeed in emptying the player's account, the simulation stops after 100 plays.

Left	Center	Right	Amount of Payoff
X	X	Cherry	2 Coins
X	Cherry	Cherry	5 Coins
Cherry	X	X	2 Coins
Cherry	Cherry	X	5 Coins
Plum	Plum	Plum	10 Coins
Orange	Orange	Orange	14 Coins
Bell	Bell	Bell	20 Coins
Bell	Bar	Bell	25 Coins
Bar	Bar	Bar	50 Coins (jackpot)

Input Requirements

The simulator is to be restartable for any number of simulations. Input consists of the player's name and a positive integer specifying the number of simulations to be performed for that player. (A limit of 100 might be prudent for this number.)

Output Requirements

Each simulation starts on a new page and gives the player's name, the simulation number, and the number of simulations requested; for example:

```
BIGWINNER, ELMER G.      NO. 2 OF  4  SIMULATIONS
```

After each play, the printout is to display the play (bet) number, the outcome, the amount of payoff (if any), and the updated balance in the player's account. Here is a sample of suggested output.

```
BET NO. 7:
**************************
*        *        *        *
*ORANGE *  PLUM *  BELL *
*        *        *        *
**************************
SORRY; NO PAYOFF THIS TIME
CURRENT BALANCE:    43 COINS
```

Each simulation is to end with an appropriate terminating message.

Random Numbers

The heart of this software product, and of many other discrete simulation systems, is a mechanism for generating numbers which appear to have a random sequence.

Very few systems have the physical facilities for actually producing random numbers; instead, they content themselves with the more practical alternative of computing a sequence of numbers that exhibit many of the mathematical properties of random numbers. Such numbers are called *pseudorandom numbers,* and there are various ways of computing them. A relatively simple procedure that is suitable for most types of simulators is shown in Figure 3.18. This technique finds frequent use for computers of the IBM 360/370 type. (Some of the constants must be adjusted when other types of computers are used; your instructor will indicate these as necessary.)

Each number developed by this procedure is a 9-digit (decimal) positive fraction in floating-point form. Accordingly, it needs to be adjusted to fit its intended use. For example, if we were throwing a die and wanted pseudorandom integer values from 1 to 6, a value VRAND taken from the generating procedure would have to be converted to an integer in the range (1,6). Accordingly, multiplication by 6 brings VRAND within the range (0.000000,6.000000), and a last addition of 1 produces the last adjustment:

```
VRAND6 = TRUNC(6*VRAND + 1)
```

Following this same general approach, the output of the pseudorandom number generator can be regulated so that its magnitude and range are appropriate for the movements of each wheel. Note that the RAND function, built into the PL/C compiler, produces the same basic processing as that shown in Figure 3.18.

Enhancements to the Slot Machine Simulator

2A. *User-controlled batch simulations.* The simulator can be generalized by permitting the user to define the number of coins available to the machine. Maximum flexibility, of course, is obtained in an interactive simulator where the user can specify the size of the slot machine's hoard at the beginning of each simulation just before it is undertaken. In a batch-oriented simulator, however, flexibility can be provided by means of the options listed below.

(1) The user specifies the number of simulations (as in the basic simulator) along with a starting number of coins for each of these simulations.

(2) Instead of specifying a starting number of coins for each simulation, the user specifies a single starting value for the simulator to use (and reset) in each simulation. This value would be an alternative to the simulator's default amount, the latter being used in the absence of an explicit specification.

(3) In this option, the user specifies a single starting value (for the first simulation), and all subsequent simulations are driven by that value. Thus the amount available to the machine for the jth simulation with that player is that remaining after the $(j-1)$th simulation. Of course, if no coins remain, the simulator would shut itself off after printing an appropriate message.

CASE STUDY—A DESIGN

```
/**********************************************************/
/*                  PSEUDORANDOM NUMBER GENERATOR          */
/**********************************************************/
/*  RND IS A FUNCTION THAT RETURNS A FLOATING POINT BETWEEN */
/*  0 AND 1. IN ORDER TO USE IT IN A PL/I PROCEDURE, THE IN-*/
/*  VOKING PROCEDURE SHOULD INCLUDE THE DECLARATION        */
/*                                                        */
/*                  DECLARE RND RETURNS (FLOAT);           */
/*                                                        */
/**********************************************************/


        RND: PROCEDURE;
            DECLARE I FIXED BINARY(31) STATIC INITIAL (131067);
        (NOFIXEDOVERFLOW):
            I = I*2083;
            RETURN (I*(1E-31B));
            END RND;
```

FIGURE 3.18 *PL/I code for a pseudorandom-number generator.*

As indicated above, this enhancement now raises the possibility that the player can ''break the bank'' during a given simulation. Accordingly, the simulator's design must include this contingency.

2*B*. *User-controlled initial stake.* This enhancement is similar to the one described above because it would enable the user to vary the size of his or her stake. The various ways in which this could be specified are the same as described before.

2*C*. *User-controlled betting sequence.* The user can vary the number of bets comprising a given simulation in this enhancement. As in the basic version, this would serve as an override that would terminate that simulation if both machine and player still have coins left after the betting had gone that far. Here again, as in the previous two enhancements, the user could set this limit for a single simulation or for an entire sequence.

2*D*. *Enhanced output displays.* While the output display described for the basic simulator is reasonably informative, it is rather plain. A more garish format might be more in keeping with the device being simulated. Accordingly, you are invited to produce a more suitable frame in which the positions of the three wheels are shown pictorially, rather than by name. In keeping with the overall spirit of such displays, the software might include facilities for (random) production and display of snide remarks, messages of encouragement, stars, comets, or other exclamatory ejaculations.

2*E*. *User-defined slot machine.* Each group of simulations (specified with or without any or all of the options described above) in this more elaborate enhancement would be preceded by a description of the machine to be simulated. If such specifications are present, the simulator is to depart from the default machine built into its design and substitute the behavioral properties defined by the user. Types of definitions could include the following.

(1) The number of wheels in this particular machine. (To keep things more or less realistic, the design could impose a minimum of three and a maximum of five.)

(2) A description of the items (and their positions) on each wheel. (We shall impose the restriction that the five types of items given in the basic specifications are the only ones available and that each wheel can have between 11 and 17 positions; the number of positions must be the same for all the wheels in a given slot machine.)

(3) A description of the payoff schedule (a list of all winning output displays along with the amounts of the respective payoffs). Note that if the information in (1) is specified, then (2) and (3) both must be present.

2F. *User-defined betting amounts.* Because some people approach a slot machine with a predetermined sequence of betting amounts, this version of the software accepts and uses a betting sequence predetermined by the player. For a given simulation, the user is to supply an amount (an integral number of coins) to be used for each bet in succession. If this sequence is not long enough, the user is to have the option of specifying either the last value in the sequence or the software's default (for instance, 1 coin) as the fixed amount for the rest of the simulation.

2G. *Heuristic strategies.* There are players who believe in hot and cold streaks. This software enables the user (if he or she wishes) to specify the details for a betting approach, in which the amount of a bet may vary, based on one or more previous outcomes.

(1) If the player wins at least NUMWIN bets in succession, then the next bet is to be NMORE coins more than the most recent one. This process is to continue (as long as the bettor keeps winning) until the ceiling MAXBET is reached and the betting stabilizes at that level for subsequent wins. NUMWIN, NMORE, and MAXBET are to be specified by the bettor for each simulation. To illustrate, suppose NUMWIN, NMORE, and MAXBET are set at 2, 2, and 10, respectively, the current bet is 1 coin, and the player has won the first bet. Accordingly, the next bet still is 1 coin. Now, the bettor wins again. Because the NUMWIN criterion has been met, the next bet is 3 coins. Another win for the bettor satisfies the NUMWIN criterion, so the next bet is 5 coins. Another win would raise the bet to 7 coins (and the bettor's pulse rate to who knows what), and so on.

(2) The same type of information covers losing streaks: If the player loses at least NUMLOSS bets in succession, the bet is reduced (if applicable) by NLESS coins; and this process continues until the bet size MINBET is reached, at which point the bet stabilizes. NUMLOSS, NLESS, and MINBET can be specified by the bettor.

(3) This simulator provides two additional features: The bettor may specify an integer value BIGWIN. If the number of consecutive wins should reach this

value, the simulation terminates abruptly. In effect, this is a "take the money and run" option. Another override provides escape at the other extreme: The player may specify an integer value BIGLOSS. Then, if the number of consecutive losses should reach this value, the simulation terminates abruptly. In effect, this is the "get out while you can" option.

3. A DATA-FILE GENERATOR

Functional Description

Very often, the evaluation of a software product or component requires the availability of a rather extensive collection of data with certain properties. Actual data, to be processed when the software ultimately becomes operational for production (day-to-day) use, frequently cannot be released for debugging purposes because the data are too sensitive, the risk of inadvertent change to the data is unacceptable, and so on. This type of situation occurs often enough so that many installations develop (or purchase) software products with the sole purpose of generating arbitrarily large collections of organized data to provide a basis for realistic, yet risk-free, tests.

Typically, this product follows a set of specifications consisting of a combination of data characteristics explicitly defined by the user and defaults built into the software. The result is a file (stored on some specified medium) containing a specified number of records. Each record, in turn, consists of a defined sequence of data items whose types and values fall within certain respective domains. Because the organization and contents of a data file encompasses virtually an infinite array of possibilities, it is not far-fetched to think of the user's description of a desired output file as a set of statements in a specification language.

The file generator described for this project is relatively modest, in that we shall impose several basic restrictions on the range of specifications that the user can submit and on the variety of files the software can produce. Nonetheless, it will be helpful to think of the communication from the user to the software in terms of "language statements." We can define these restrictions as follows.

1. This product will generate files consisting of a specified number of 80-character records (punched cards or card images).

2. All the records in a given file will be organized identically. The product will generate as many as 50 variables (fields) for a given record.

3. The product will be capable of developing three types of variables.

    (a) *Continuous variables*. These may be integers or numbers with fractional components. For the latter type, all values for a given variable will have the same precision (that is, the number of decimal places) in accordance with the user's specifications.

(*b*) *Discrete variables*. The values of these variables, represented as single characters, are selected from a predetermined set specified by the user. For example, the user might wish to define a discrete variable representing "student status," whose value can be one of the four choices 1, 2, 3, or 4. (Note that although these appear to be numeric designations, there is no intrinsic numerical value attached to these designations. They could just as easily have been designated, for example, by, F, S, J, and G.) The product will accept as many as 15 such designations for each discrete variable.

(*c*) *Identification variables*. These are character strings with a maximum length of four characters. Since they are intended to provide distinctive labels for a file's records, the software will generate a unique value for a particular identification variable on each record. For instance, if the user specifies a three-character identification variable, the software will simply assign 001 to the first record's value, 002 to the second record's value, and so on. Only one identification variable can be supplied for each file.

4. For continuous and discrete variables, the distribution of values (within a given variable) will be uniform. For instance, if a variable representing *subject's sex* has as its two choices M and F, a collection of N generated records will have approximately $N/2$ records with a value of F in that variable.

5. All unused positions in the 80-character record will be filled with blanks.

Input Requirements

The user must supply the following information.

1. Number of records to be generated.

2. Number of variables.

3. Information about each variable:

   (*a*) Position in the record.

   (*b*) Variable type (continuous, discrete, or identification)

   (*c*) Domain (precision and range for continuous variables, an explicit list of one-character choices for discrete variables, and number of characters for the identification variable).

Output Requirements

Because the assignment of an output medium or device is a very straightforward process, it will not contribute appreciably to this particular project. Accordingly, the generated file will be printed, one record per line.

Another Use for the Pseudorandom Number Generator

As described in the slot machine simulation project, a basic pseudorandom number generator will produce, on demand, a floating-point number between 0.0 and 1.0. Subsequent adjustment, then, can place that generated value in a desired domain. In this project, it may be necessary to develop and apply a separate (different) adjustment for calculating each variable in the record (except the identification variable). Thus it is reasonable to envision the basic pseudorandom number generator as the heart of the data-generation process, supplemented by an appropriate collection of operations that mold the standard number given to it.

Data Structures

There is no reason to store the generated file internally (in fact, there are compelling reasons not to do this), so the overall preparation process can be envisioned as a loop that cycles once for each record to be generated. Each cycle consists of a systematic examination of the specifications for each variable, followed by an execution of the process (or processes) prompted by that examination. Thus a straightforward way of constructing an appropriate structure is to make a table in which an entry consists of an (encoded) indication of the action(s) to be taken to generate a value for a specific variable, accompanied by restrictions and adjustments that apply for that variable. For example, if a particular variable is to be continuous, its entry in this table would indicate that fact, along with its precision and its upper and lower limits. These controls would govern adjustments to the pseudorandom value and subsequent rounding of that adjusted value.

With these considerations in mind, the implementation of a table may take a number of convenient forms, depending on the implementation language. (For example, it may be a PL/I structure, a PASCAL record, or a set of coordinated one-dimensional FORTRAN arrays.)

Enhancements to the Data-File Generator

The following additions to the basic project extend its versatility in terms of the size and complexity of the files it can generate, and in terms of the precision and detail with which the user can describe a file's organization and contents.

> 3A. *Multiple identification variables.* This enhancement removes the limit of a single identification variable and extends the possibilities for the definition of such variables. Specifically, the user is now permitted to specify as many independently defined identification variables as desired. The positions of these identification variables do not have to be consecutive, nor is it necessary for all of them to have the same length. (Obviously, all values for a given identification variable will have a consistent length throughout the file.) Minimum specifiable length is two characters, and the maximum is eight characters.

In order for identification variables to convey their basic intent, there must be a way to prevent the assignment of the same values to several identification variables in the same record. That is, it would make no sense if the file had three identification variables, each four characters long, and the software assigned '0001' to all three of them on the first record, '0002' to all three of them on the second record, and so on. Accordingly, the user must be able to specify a starting value for each variable. The software will then sequence automatically from that value. Such values need not consist solely of numeric characters. The software will use the system's collating sequence in generating subsequent values. For instance, if an identification variable is specified to be three characters long starting with the value 'AAA', the next value will be 'AAB', then 'AAC', and so on. (As a safety precaution, the collation should be done in a wraparound fashion, so that the character following the ''highest'' one starts the sequence again. Recall also that not all the characters in the collating sequence have visible printed counterparts. Consequently, some care has to be taken in restricting the repertoire of characters to the visible subset.)

3B. *Distribution of discrete variable values.* As pointed out in the basic project specifications, the software assumes a uniform distribution across each of the alternative values defined for a discrete variable. In this enhancement, that feature is retained, but it is available as a default that can be upset by the user for any and all discrete variables. Accordingly, when the user defines a discrete variable for this version, the user will be able to list the available choices for values as before. In addition, for each value, the user can specify the percent (or fraction) of the records that are to receive that value. (Note that in adapting one's design to accommodate this feature, it is *not* appropriate simply to assign a particular value to a discrete variable for some number of consecutive records and then switching to another value for the next group of records. Note also that it will be necessary for the software to make sure that the distribution figures add up to 100 percent.)

3C. *Continuous variable distributions.* This enhancement is similar to the previous one, but it applies to continuous variables. A feature like this can be carried to almost any extent, so we shall limit it specifically for our purposes here: The user will be able to specify a continuous variable's distribution of values in terms of 10 specifications, each corresponding to one-tenth of that variable's range. Accordingly, a continuous variable will be described in terms of its precision, range, and percentages (or fractions) for each of the 10 intervals. As in the last enhancement, uniform distribution will be available as a default in the absence of explicit specifications.

3D. *Flexibility in record length.* This enhancement removes the 80-character record-length restriction but retains the restriction that limits the file to fixed record lengths. Because the output will be printed, this version imposes a maximum record length of 132 characters. Accordingly, the user must specify a record length in addition to the other file descriptors. The software must check to make sure that the cumulative lengths of all the variables do not exceed the specified record length.

3E. *Flexibility in discrete variable encodement.* This enhancement removes the restriction with regard to the number of characters used to express a value for a discrete variable. While the number of possible designations for a discrete variable still is limited to 15 (as described in the basic project specifications), the designations may be 1, 2, or 3 characters long. (The length must be fixed for any given variable.) To provide this flexibility, note that the input specifications must be expanded to include information about the length of each discrete variable. (It is up to you to determine how this is to be expressed.)

---

4. A GENERALIZED FREQUENCY ANALYZER

Functional Description

One of the most dramatic effects that computers have had on the collection and manipulation of data manifests itself as a great variety of convenient aids for summarizing and displaying large amounts of information. The software product described in this project is one such vehicle.

There are many data collections in which discrete variables play a significant role. (As described in Project 3, a discrete variable may take on a value selected from a predefined set of encoded designations, each representing a mutually exclusive state or condition.) Replies reported on well-designed survey questionnaires and multiple-choice examinations are examples of discrete variables. This analyzer examines an arbitrary collection of data and, for each discrete variable specified by the user, displays the number of occurrences of each value reported for that variable. These frequencies are presented in two ways:

1. Absolute frequencies, the actual number of occurrences for each value.

2. Relative frequencies, the ratio of the number of occurrences for a given value to the total number of occurrences for all values of that variable.

The analyzer is general in the sense that there are no restrictions on the homogeneity of the discrete data presented to it. Specifically, there are only three restrictions.

1. A given run will report on a maximum of 50 variables. Note that this does not restrict the number of discrete variables in a particular data collection; all it means is that larger numbers of variables must be subdivided into several runs.

2. A given discrete variable may have as many as 50 different encoded values defined for it. These may be completely arbitrary. That is, each set of coded designations for a discrete variable is completely independent of that used for any other variable in the collection. Moreover, the number of different values assignable to a variable

has nothing to do with the variable's length, the number of characters used to report a value.

3. The software imposes a maximum length of 6 characters on any discrete variable regardless of the number of choices from which a value may be selected. The set of values for a given variable all must be the same length.

The frequency analysis for each variable is to be reported on a separate page headed by the general name assigned to the data collection and by the name of that particular variable. (For instance, the former might be 1982 NATIONAL TELEVISION PREFERENCE SURVEY and the latter might be 12: TYPE OF NEWS REPORTAGE.) These headings are to be followed by the total number of values reported for that variable. Then for each value, the analyzer is to list the name assigned to that value or condition, the encodement representing that value, the absolute frequency, and the relative frequency.

```
          1982 NATIONAL TELEVISION PREFERENCE SURVEY
                 12: TYPE OF NEWS REPORTAGE
                   NO. OF RESPONSES: 685

    VALUE          MEANING              FREQ     PCT OF TOTAL
      1            LOUD AND BREATHLESS   104       15.18
      2            AUTHORITATIVE         211       30.80
      3            LOW-KEYED              68        9.93
      4            PERSONAL, INTIMATE    287       41.90
      5            DON'T CARE             15        2.19
```

Note: In this version of the analyzer, we assume that all values are recorded and submitted accurately. However, it is *not* assumed that the data are complete. Thus, if we happen to be analyzing 42 questions from a clinical drug test involving 293 subjects, for example, there is no guarantee that each of the subjects answered all 42 questions. Accordingly, one of the conditions defined for a discrete variable is likely to be *missing data* or *no response*. This is usually represented by blank data. (Some installations make it a practice to assign an explicit code for missing data, thereby guaranteeing that something visible is entered for each variable all the time.)

Input Requirements

From the requirements described in the previous section, it is clear that the input for an analyzer must consist of two basic sections:

1. *A description of the input data.* This must include the name of the collection and the number of discrete variables to be analyzed during this run. In addition, each variable must be defined in terms of its name, appearance (its length and position in the overall collection), and encoding (the name and encodement assigned to each value).

2. *The input data.* Its format must be consistent with the description given for it. In this version of the software, each record is restricted to a single punched card or

card image. There is no particular limit to the number of records comprising a given data collection.

(As part of the designer's requirements, note that you are responsible for the formulation of the detailed input and output specifications.)

Applicable Data Structures

While the amount of summary information to be accumulated can become rather extensive, its organization is relatively straightforward. The counters, labels, and other display-related information organize conveniently as structures (PL/I), records (PASCAL), or coordinated collections of arrays (FORTRAN). Use of adjustable dimensions (in PL/I) will avoid the necessity of predefining storage allocations designed to accommodate the limiting number of variables and codes.

Enhancements for the General Frequency Analyzer

These enhancements, which may be introduced singly or in any combination, are designed to extend the versatility of the analyzer. In this regard, a simple increase in system capacity is considered to be of secondary importance. Note that each enhancement may require adjustments to the input specifications. Thus the designer is well advised to examine those specifications in conjunction with the enhancement's characteristics.

4*A*. *Arbitrary record length.* This enhancement removes the restriction with regard to 80-character records. Although all of the records in a given collection still must have the same length, that length (which may be anywhere from 10-500 characters) now becomes an input item, specifiable for each run.

4*B*. *Error-handling enhancement.* The basic version permits missing data but assumes that all available data are recorded correctly. This enhancement removes that restriction, thereby requiring the software to recognize and report erroneous values. An *error,* in this context, is a value that differs from any of the assignable encodements defined for that variable. Strictly speaking, this error could be an oversight (a failure to define that value as an acceptable encodement) rather than an erroneous transcription. The software cannot make this distinction. Accordingly, the software is to include an OTHER subcategory for each variable, and the number of occurrences is to be displayed as part of that variable's frequency analysis.

4*C*. *Additional error-handling.* This is an extension of the enhancement described in 4*B:* Instead of displaying a single frequency for all erroneous values, this version reports separate frequencies for each unrecognizable encodement that is encountered. (Protection is a good thing; in this case it is suggested that a limit be placed on the number of ''illegal'' codes that the software will handle for each variable. If that limit is exceeded, the software reverts to the treatment of Enhancement 4*B* for that variable.)

4D. *More flexible encodement definition.* In certain instances, it is useful to develop frequency distributions in which several encoded values for a given variable are grouped together and treated (at least for purposes of that particular analysis) as a single value or condition. This enhancement supplies that capability. Thus the user now would be able to specify (for any or all discrete variables) any desired grouping. (For example, a variable named CIRCUIT_TYPE, originally defined as having one of 11 possible values, may be redefined as one of, for instance, 5 possible values.) Note that this is a little more insidious than it first appears: The software must make sure that the new definition still provides mutually exclusive values. That is, we should not leave it to the user to guarantee that a particular encodement will be assigned to only one group. Also, it is necessary for the software to make sure that a particular grouping does not reduce that variable to a single-category item. (The frequency distribution for such a variable is not very useful.)

4E. *Extension to continuous variables.* By its very nature, a continuous variable (as defined in Project 3) is not particularly suitable for analysis via frequency distribution. However, there are numerous occasions when such distributions are useful. For this reason, continuous values are often grouped into categories defined for particular subranges, thereby creating (temporary) discrete variables. The resulting loss in precision is intolerable for other types of analyses, but this transformation can be quite adequate for a variety of objectives.

This enhancement provides the product's users with the capability of describing a continuous variable in terms of its position in the record, length, and precision. In addition, the user than can define subranges and corresponding group names. (It should not be necessary for the user to specify group codes; these can be assigned and used internally.) To illustrate, we shall pick a continuous variable and describe a hypothetical transformation for it. The description will be somewhat narrative; it will be up to you to design a precise, compact specification scheme.

```
VARIABLE NAME:        LATITUDE
POSITION:             21-26
DESCRIPTION:          SIGNED, PRECISION IS (6,1)
GROUPING:
            LATITUDE <  -66.5  = SO. FRIGID
 -66.5 <=   LATITUDE <  -23.5  = SO. TEMPRT
 -23.5 <=   LATITUDE <    0.0  = SO. TORRID
   0.0 <=   LATITUDE <   23.5  = NO. TORRID
  23.5 <=   LATITUDE <=  66.5  = NO. TEMPRT
            LATITUDE >   66.5  = NO. FRIGID
```

4F. *Sorted frequency display.* In the project versions described thus far, no mention was made of the order in which the frequencies for the encodements of a given variable are to appear. (A reasonable assumption is to use the order given in the input specifications.) In this enhancement, the user is given the option of requesting the frequencies in decreasing order (that is, the encodement with the greatest number of occurrences appears first). The software's default is to leave the data unsorted, so that the user must request this option explicitly. You may choose one of the following approaches.

1. A single specification activates the sorting option for all of the discrete variables specified in the input.

2. Sorting may be enabled or suppressed for each of the variables individually.

3. A combination of (1) and (2) may be used. That is, each variable is individually controllable. However, if the user wishes sorted frequencies for all the variables, he or she should not have to include a specifier for each of them; one grand, sweeping indicator should suffice.

5. AN INFIX-TO-POSTFIX CONVERTER

Background

An operation frequently used in a wide variety of computer science endeavors is the evaluation of expressions. Perhaps the most well-recognized context in which such evaluations take place is in programming language compilers. The ability to deal with arbitrarily complicated strings of arithmetic operators and operands pivots around a software mechanism capable of examining these expressions, recognizing their individual components, and defining appropriate processing based on these findings. A variety of mechanisms exist for doing this, some more complicated than others. For example, it is possible to isolate the ingredients of an expression such as

$$B - A / (D + C) \div 19$$

by scanning the expression repeatedly and applying a set of predefined rules that determine the order in which arithmetic operations are to be performed. This procedure, already awkward for an expression as simple as the one shown above, becomes increasingly cumbersome with more intricate constructions.

Considerable simplification is possible by taking advantage of an alternative form for presenting expressions. Unlike the traditional *infix notation,* in which a binary operator is placed between its two operands (as in A*B), alternative forms place the operator before its operands (*prefix notation*) or after them (*postfix notation*); A*B is *AB in the former scheme and AB* in the latter. The two systems are referred to collectively as *Polish notation* in acknowledgement to their originator, Jan Lukasiewicz. Using either prefix or postfix notation, it is possible to represent any arithmetic expression uniquely without parentheses, even though such parentheses were indispensable in conveying the intent of the expression when written as an infix expression. More significantly, from the point of view of its subsequent analysis, an expression in Polish notation can be dissected completely with only a single scan. Moreover, such dissection includes the ability to distinguish between valid expressions (those that follow a predefined set of structural rules) and invalid ones.

This does not alter the fact that Polish notation is relatively inconvenient for people to use. The tradition of infix notation is so long established that asking people to change for the sake of more efficient automatic expression analysis is unrealistic. Instead, high-level language processors generally reconcile this difficulty by including a component that converts an expression from infix to Polish notation (and checks its validity in the process). It is this converter that occupies our attention here.

Functional Description

Our specific interest will be in conversion from infix to postfix notation (also called *reverse Polish notation*, or RPN). Thus we shall be starting with an infix expression which is valid or not (in accordance with a set of precisely defined rules), and the outcome will be an equivalent postfix expression or a signal noting that the expression is not valid. It is necessary, then, to state the rules explicitly. For this basic version of the converter, an infix expression is characterized as follows.

1. An expression consists of a combination of operators and operands in strict alternation; that is, two operators or two operands cannot appear in succession.

2. An operator is either + (addition), − (subtraction), * (multiplication), or / (division). The only way an operator can appear in a legal expression is by placing it between two operands. Thus the expression A-B is legal while the expression -A+B is not. In other words, only *binary* + and − are allowed; *unary* + and − are excluded.

3. An operand may be one of two types: It may be a symbolic name consisting of a single uppercase letter (A-Z). Alternatively, it may be an unsigned (positive) number, with or without a decimal point and with or without a fractional portion. (If there is a fractional portion, there must be a decimal place.) Thus the only characters that can be used in a constant are the ten decimal digits (0-9) and a single decimal point.

4. The simplest expression consists of a single operand. Implied in this rule is the fact that an expression consisting of more than one term must begin and end with an operand.

5. Any number of blank characters (including zero) may be placed between an operator and an operand.

6. The operations * and / have the same precedence. They are performed before + and −, which share the same (second-level) priority.

7. The precedence of operations indicated in Rule 6 can be upset by the use of parentheses. A subexpression enclosed in parentheses is evaluated in its entirety even though there may be higher priority operations outside the parentheses. For in-

stance, division would precede addition in the expression B+A/C-D, but the reverse would be true in the expression (B+A)/C-D.

8. Operations associate from left to right.

Note that the priority of operations is important, even in this basic infix-to-postfix converter. Essentially, the thing that makes such conversions consistent is the fact that Polish notation retains the order in which the operands were presented originally; the change from one notation to the other (in addition to the removal of parentheses) is in the order in which the *operations* are presented, and this new sequencing reflects the priorities of those operations.

In the next section, we shall discuss an explicit algorithm for effecting such conversions. However, in preparation for that discussion, Table 3.6 gives several examples of valid infix expressions and their postfix representations.

Applicable Data Structures

With regard to this project, it is especially useful to discuss appropriate data structures prior to considering the algorithms for the actual conversion. This is true because the effectiveness of these algorithms depends heavily on proper exploitation of the *stack* and the operations associated with it. A stack is an arbitrarily long collection of data items in which each *item* (that is, each member of the stack) may be arbitrarily defined. (Thus far, it sounds like a lot of other data collections.) The following crucial property helps characterize a stack: The *top* of a stack is its only directly accessible position. Thus, if a new member is to be added to a stack, it cannot be inserted arbitrarily; it must be *pushed* onto the top of the stack, becoming the new top. As expected, every stack is equipped with some mechanism that keeps track of (and makes available) the current location of the top of the stack. A member can be removed (*popped*) from a stack only if that member is positioned at the top of the stack. The member just below this element then becomes the new top of the

TABLE 3.6 INFIX-TO-POSTFIX CORRESPONDENCE

Infix	Postfix
(A−B) / (C+D)	AB−CD+/
A−B/C+D	ABC/−D+
A−(B/C+D)	ABC/D+−
B✲B−4✲A✲C/2✲A	BB✲4A✲C✲2/A✲−
B✲B−4✲A✲C/(2✲ZA)	BB✲4A✲C✲2A✲/−
(B✲B−4✲A✲C) / (2✲A)	BB✲4A✲C✲−2A✲/
A/B/B✲(C+2/D)/7+2✲(D+6)/A	AB/B/C2D/+✲7/2D6+✲A/+

stack. For this reason, the characteristic of *last in first out* (LIFO) is implicit in the name *stack*.

We mentioned earlier that a stack may be arbitrarily long. This is conceptually true, but practical factors may compel certain implementations to place an explicit limit on the extent of a stack (its *depth*). Accordingly, a stack with this imposed limitation will include a mechanism for detecting (and reporting) the fact that the stack is full. This will prevent attempts to perform a push operation until one or more pop operations have been performed.

By the same token, an empty stack is a plausible condition regardless of the stack's capacity. Consequently, the data structure includes an intrinsic mechanism that detects (and reports) the fact that the stack currently is devoid of occupants. This prevents any attempts to perform a pop operation until one or more push operations have provided the stack with something to pop.

Another data structure that helps greatly in infix-to-postfix conversion is the *queue*, an arbitrary collection of items which, like the stack, is characterized by specific rules for accessibility. As its name implies, the queue has a *front* and a *rear*, the former containing the member that has been in the queue the longest, and the latter containing the member whose addition to the queue has been most recent. The only member that can be removed from a queue is the one at the front, and the rear is the only point of entry. Thus, the characteristic of *first in first out* (FIFO) is intrinsic to this data structure. (Note that in special cases, a queue and a stack may be supported by facilities that enable their users to refer to and examine any member. However, this does not change the fact that addition to and removal from these data structures still adhere to the restrictions described before.)

Conceptually, a queue may be infinitely long (and to people waiting in queues, many may have seemed so). However, practical considerations in a given situation may place a specific upper limit on a queue's extent. In any case, the locations of the front and rear are always available so that the fundamental operations of addition (ENQUE) and removal (DEQUE) can be performed routinely. If the queue does have a predefined maximum length, it will need a supporting mechanism to prevent attempts to add an item to a full queue. Of course, all queues require a mechanism that detects an empty queue, thereby making it possible to foil attempts to remove items when there is nothing to remove.

Applicable Algorithms

The basic approach to the infix-to-postfix conversion process involves the isolation of each token in an expression so that it can be characterized (for example, operand or operator). Once its type has been established, we can determine how it will be manipulated, based on what type it is and under which set of circumstances it was encountered. This process is performed repeatedly as the procedure works its way through the input (infix) expression, systematically building the output (postfix) expression. Even before we examine the details of this process, four basic dispositions are obvious.

A1. *Attachment of a component to the output expression:* Available evidence (the type of component or the type of the previous component) prompts the inescapable conclusion that this is to be the next component in the output expression.

A2. *Detention of a component for addition to the output expression later on:* When postfix notation was characterized earlier in the discussion, it was pointed out that the notation retains the original order of the operands but alters the sequencing of operators based on their respective priorities. Typically, it is this reordering that necessitates the retention of some components so that their placement in the output expression can be delayed. (As we begin examining the procedural details, we shall see that the stack is a particularly convenient vehicle for handling such delays.)

A3. *Removal of a component:* This applies most specifically to parentheses (which are not present in postfix notation) and, secondarily, to blanks. Handling of the latter has less to do with the intrinsic conversion process than it does with the formatting rules adopted for a particular implementation.

A4. *Rejection of a component or expression:* Unless we are living in Disneyland, we must include provisions for dealing with illegal input expressions. Detection is simple enough: An illegal expression contains an unrecognizable component (one that does not fit any of the criteria defined earlier) or a recognizable component that does not belong where it was found.

We can begin filling in the details of this approach by thinking of the conversion system in terms of four structural data components.

D1. The input string (the infix expression to be converted).

D2. The output string (the converted postfix expression).

D3. A receptacle for temporary storage of those components that are not transferred immediately from the input string to the output string.

D4. A mechanism that embodies (and makes available) the rules describing the behavior of the conversion process. More specifically, the system needs a set of directives, each of which says, in essence, "When you find this particular component under these specific circumstances, then the action to be taken is the one defined here."

There is little difficulty in relating each of the first two components to a queue: The first (leftmost) token of the infix expression represents the front of the input queue, and the corresponding postfix representation is assembled the same way, that is, with each component taking its place in the queue as it is identified. The component listed in D3, the place for diverting parts of the infix expression, is represented very nicely as a stack. These three ingredients set the stage for characterizing the behavior of the conversion process.

P1. A component (the next one) is isolated from the input expression for scrutiny. This activity will be referred to as NEXT, and the component so isolated will be referred to as CURRENT.

P2: CURRENT will be PUSHed onto the top of the stack or it will disappear (as in the case of a right parenthesis). In some cases, PUSH will occur immediately; in others, one or more members of the stack will be removed (POPped) prior to the PUSH. TOP will refer to the newest (most recent) entry in the stack.

P3. Because the POP operation (as used here) removes TOP and does nothing else, POP must be combined with another activity if the value of TOP to be preserved. For example, POP and ENQUE remove the top of the stack and add it to the output queue.

The fourth component, the set of behavioral rules mentioned in D4, defines the relationships among the input queue, the stack, and the output queue. More specifically, it directs the use of the PUSH, POP, ENQUE, and NEXT operations as influenced by the contents of CURRENT and TOP. To make the examination of

TABLE 3.7 RULES FOR INFIX-TO-POSTFIX CONVERSION: BASIC PROJECT

NEXT:	Get next token from infix expression
PUSH:	Contents of CURRENT become new TOP
POP:	Remove top of stack
ENQUE:	Append to rear of postfix string
TOP:	The (present) top of the stack
CURRENT:	The infix token most recently obtained

Top	Current	Action
$	operand, (	PUSH, then NEXT.
	;	End of conversion; terminate.
	+,−,*,/,)	Error; unexpected token.
operand	)	PUSH, then NEXT.
	+,−,*,/,),;	POP, then ENQUE.
	operand	Error; unexpected token.
*,/	(, operand	PUSH, then NEXT.
	+,−,*,/,),;	POP, then ENQUE.
+,−	(, operand,*,/	PUSH, then NEXT.
	+,−,),;	POP, then ENQUE.
(	(, operand, +,−,*,/	PUSH, then NEXT.
	)	POP, then NEXT.
	;	Error; unexpected token.

```
NAME: INFIX_TO_POSTFIX
INPUT PARAMETER: A (valid or invalid) expression in infix form.
OUTPUT PARAMETER: An equivalent expression in postfix form or
                  an error message.
FUNCTION: The converter finds and categorizes each token in the
          input expression. Based on the nature and relative positions
          of these tokens, together with a prescribed set of operator
          precedence rules, the converter then removes all parentheses
          and reorders the operators to produce an equivalent postfix
          expression.
ALGORITHM:
        Initialize the stack (set TOP to $).
        Append ';' to the rear of the input queue.
        Initialize output queue (set to null or empty).
        Obtain the first input component (perform NEXT).
        WHILE ('$' and ';' do not occur simultaneously in
                TOP and CURRENT, respectively)
                CASE F(CURRENT,TOP) of
                1:    PUSH, NEXT;
                2:    POP, ENQUE;
                3:    POP, NEXT;
                4:
                      ERROR; invalid expression.
                ENDCASE
        ENDWHILE
        Stop.
```

FIGURE 3.19   *Pseudocode for infix-to-postfix conversion.*

these rules easier, we shall introduce two more items: the dollar sign ($) and the semicolon (;). Strictly speaking, these are not really part of an expression, but will serve as aids in the processing. The dollar sign is a special designator that signals an empty stack. Accordingly, we can use $ to initialize the stack. The semicolon is not part of the actual infix expression, but is placed (by the conversion process) at the end of the input expression so that we can guarantee that the expression has an explicit conclusion (for which we can test).

Recall that the tokens (as defined for this project) consist of operands (constants or variable names), high-priority operators (* and /), low-priority operators (+ and −), left parenthesis ((), and right parenthesis ()). We can now define the operating rules in complete detail. These are summarized in Table 3.7 and illustrated with an example in Table 3.8. (The actual implementation of these rules is left to you; Table 3.7 is intended merely to specify the controls that the software must provide.)

With the infix-to-postfix algorithm as described, it is not possible to detect *all* syntax errors in an infix expression submitted to the software. For instance, the input expression A+ will be accepted without an error being detected. If such error detection is required, some other mechanism must be supplied. However, many syntax errors can be detected (and even corrected).

We can now use these operational rules as a nucleus and combine them with the three data structures to construct an overall conversion algorithm. The pseudocode representation of this algorithm is given in Figure 3.19. The undefined function F in the pseudocode is defined by the actions specified in Table 3.7.

TABLE 3.8 (a) INFIX-TO-POSTFIX CONVERSION: VALID EXPRESSION

Infix	Stack	Current	Postfix	Action
(A+B)/(C+D);	[$]	[ ]	[ ]	NEXT
A+B)/(C+D);	[$]	(	[ ]	PUSH,NEXT
+B)/(C+D);	[(] $	A	[ ]	PUSH,NEXT
B)/(C+D);	[A] ($	+	[ ]	POP,ENQUE
B)/(C+D);	[(] $	+	A	PUSH,NEXT
)/(C+D);	[+] ($	B	A	PUSH,NEXT
/(C+D);	[B] + ($	)	A	POP,ENQUE
/(C+D);	[+] ($	)	AB	POP,ENQUE
(C+D);	[(] $	)	AB+	POP,NEXT
(C+D);	[$]	/	AB+	PUSH,NEXT
C+D);	[/] $	(	AB+	PUSH,NEXT
+D);	[(] / $	C	AB+	PUSH,NEXT
D);	[C] (/ $	+	AB+	POP,ENQUE
D);	[(] / $	+	AB+C	PUSH,NEXT
);	[+] (/ $	D	AB+C	PUSH,NEXT

TABLE 3.8 (continued)

	Stack	Current	Postfix	Action
;	[D] + (/ $	)	AB+C	POP,ENQUE
;	[+] (/ $	)	AB+CD	POP,ENQUE
;	[(] / $	)	AB+CD+	POP,NEXT
□	[/] $	;	AB+CD+	POP,ENQUE
□	[$]	;	AB+CD+/	TERMINATE

(b) INFIX-TO-POSTFIX CONVERSION: INVALID EXPRESSION

Infix	Stack	Current	Postfix	Action
(A+B/(C+D);	[$]	□	□	NEXT
A+B/(C+D);	[$]	(	□	PUSH,NEXT
+B/(C+D);	[(] $	A		PUSH,NEXT
B/(C+D);	[A] ($	+	□ □	POP,ENQUE
B/(C+D);	[(] $	+	A	PUSH,NEXT
/(C+D);	[+] ($	B	A	PUSH,NEXT
(C+D);	[B] + ($	/	A	POP,ENQUE
(C+D);	[+] ($	/	AB	PUSH,NEXT

TABLE 3.8 *(continued)*

	Stack		Output	Action
C+D);	[/] + ($	(	AB	PUSH,NEXT
+D);	[( ] / + ($	C	AB	PUSH,NEXT
D);	[C] (/ + ($	+	AB	POP,ENQUE
D);	[( ] / + ($	+	ABC	PUSH,NEXT
);	[+] (/ + ($	D	ABC	PUSH,NEXT
;	[D] + (/ + ($	)	ABC	POP,ENQUE
;	[+] (/ + ($	)	ABCD	POP,ENQUE
;	[( ] / + ($	)	ABCD+	POP,NEXT

TABLE 3.8 (continued)

☐	/̲	;	ABCD+	POP,ENQUE
	+			
	(			
	$			
☐	+̲	;	ABCD+/	POP,ENQUE
	(			
	$			
☐	(̲	;	ABCD+/+	error; invalid expression
	$			

Enhancements to the Infix-to-Postfix Converter

These enhancements to the converter extend its flexibility and power in two basic directions: first, they enlarge the possibilities for legal operators; second, they increase the number of acceptable types of operands.

5A. *Multiple letters for operand names.* This extension removes the one-letter restriction on operand names. A legal operand name now may consist of up to eight letters.

5B. *More flexible operand names.* This extension enables the converter to recognize and accept operand names consisting of alphanumeric characters. Specifically, a legal name in this version may consist of any number of characters. The first character must be a letter, but subsequent characters may be letters, numeric digits, or any of the special characters $, #, and _. Embedded blanks still are prohibited.

5C. *Acceptance of exponential forms.* This enhancement extends the domain of acceptable operands to numerical constants in exponential form. These numbers may be signed or unsigned and they may or may not include an integer portion. The exponent (always implied to be applied to a base of 10) is denoted by the letter E, followed by a signed or unsigned integer value. Thus, for example, 32E4, +32E4, 32.0E4, 32.E+4, 32.0E+04, and 32E04 all are included among the acceptable forms.

5D. *Acceptance of unary operators.* This extension increases the repertoire of acceptable operators by adding unary + and −. A unary operator precedes its single operand and its priority is higher than * or /. Note that the addition of unary operators changes one of the structural rules set down for the basic version of the converter: Legal expressions may now start with + or −, as additional alternatives to the operand and left parenthesis.

5E. *Acceptance of exponentiation.* This version adds the exponentiation operator, denoted by two consecutive asterisks (**). Blanks are prohibited between the asterisks, but they may or may not appear on either side of the operator. Priority is higher than * or /, but lower than that of the unary operators. (Inclusion of ** is independent of the unary operators.) Associativity of consecutive exponentiations is such that A**B**C always is interpreted as A**(B**C).

5F. *Acceptance of the assignment operator.* This enhancement extends the basic expression to include the assignment operator, denoted by =. When the assignment operator does appear in a (legitimate) input string, it appears only once, at the beginning of the expression, preceded by a symbolic operand, that is, by a variable name. Assignment has the lowest priority.

5G. *Acceptance of additional "operators".* This enhancement extends the spectrum of operators that can be included in a legitimate expression. Although these additions will be treated (thought of) as operators, the processing implied by the operations is more extensive than that associated with +, −, *, and /. Specifically, the additional capability corresponds to a collection of built-in functions provided by many high-level programming languages. For this project, it does not matter what the exact nature of the processing happens to be, because the expressions are being converted but not evaluated. Nor is it necessary to include a particularly rich set. The purpose of this project is served quite nicely with a relatively small number of such operators, each of which is recognized by a unique, predefined name and each of which requires a predefined number of arguments. The argument(s) always must be parenthesized and the functions take precedence over all other operations. Each function name is reserved; that is, it cannot be used for any other purpose in an expression. Following is a list of such names to be used for this project.

SQRT   (One argument)

LOG   (One argument)

SIN   (One argument)

COS   (One argument)

MOD   (Two arguments, separated by a comma)

ROUND   (Two arguments, separated by a comma)

In this context, the arguments, the items on which the functions are to operate, are restricted to numerical constants or symbolic operand names.

5H. *Extended function argument capabilities.* This enhancement broadens the converter's facilities for handling the additional operators described in Enhancement 5F. The list of functions remains the same, but each argument now can be any expression, as defined by any combination of the given enhancements. We shall rule out full assignments, so that the = operator and the variable to which an assigned value is destined are illegal.

5I. *Error correction facilities.* This enhancement enables the software to perform certain types of error correction for the user. As always, an error message should be printed. However, if the error can be corrected, the software also should issue a message describing the nature of the correction.

A variety of corrections are possible, and some are exemplified below. It is up to you to determine the types of services to be provided in your particular enhancement.

(1) *Missing operator.* An infix expression such as 2A, while meaningful in mathematical terminology, lacks the * operator specified in the rules given before. Thus the need for an asterisk could be detected and rectified.

(2) *Missing operand.* An infix expression such as (A+B)/(C*), when analyzed, could signal a missing operand. While the software cannot read the user's mind, insertion of 1 after * or / or 0 after + or − would correct the illegality.

(3) *Missing parenthesis.* An infix expression such as (A+B)/(C+D lacks a right parenthesis; a left one is missing from LOG 2*A). In both cases, the converter can spot these deficiencies and insert the necessary parentheses.

6. A GENERAL TWO-DIMENSIONAL FREQUENCY ANALYZER

Functional Description

One of the most useful data reduction processes that a computer can perform is the preparation of summaries in the form of two-dimensional frequency tables. It is virtually impossible to list all the applications in which such summaries find routine use.

In the interest of brevity, we shall take advantage of a project specified earlier (Project 4) in which a simple frequency analysis was described. In a sense, the type of frequency distribution requested in that project is a one-dimensional table, and the type of summary required here is a direct extension. Given a collection of discrete variables (see Project 4 for a definition that still applies here), this software product develops and displays a joint (two-way) frequency distribution for each pair of variables specified by the user. As a simple illustration, let us say that a particular collection includes two discrete variables, MAJOR and ACADEMIC_YR. The former has seven subcategories (ENGLISH, LANG, HIST, PHYS, CHEM, BIOL, and OTHER, encoded as 1 thru 7, respectively); the latter has four subcategories (FRESH, SOPH, JUNIOR, and SENIOR, encoded as 1, 2, 3, and 4, respectively). Suppose the collection contains data for 1116 subjects, and the user requests a joint distribution of ACADEMIC_YR versus MAJOR. As Table 3.9 indicates, the basic display includes the actual frequencies for each of the 28 resulting subcategories. Summary information includes the row and column totals and the single grand total. Table 3.10 shows the corresponding relative frequencies.

TABLE 3.9   (a) TWO-WAY FREQUENCY DISTRIBUTION—ABSOLUTE

	English	Lang	Hist	Phys	Chem	Biol	Other	Total
	Row Var: Academic Yr			Col Var: Major				
FRESH	26	29	18	30	19	36	117	275
SOPH	31	29	20	36	19	38	108	281
JUNIOR	38	31	21	22	17	32	134	295
SENIOR	21	18	22	24	16	26	138	265
TOTAL	116	107	81	112	71	132	497	1116

(b) TWO-WAY FREQUENCY DISTRIBUTION—RELATIVE

Row Var: Academic Yr   Col Var: Major
Total No.: 1116

	English	Lang	Hist	Phys	Chem	Biol	Other	Total
FRESH	0.0232	0.0260	0.0161	0.0269	0.0170	0.0323	0.1048	.2463
SOPH	0.0278	0.0260	0.0180	0.0323	0.0170	0.0340	0.0968	.2519
JUNIOR	0.0341	0.0278	0.0188	0.0197	0.0152	0.0287	0.1201	.2644
SENIOR	0.0188	0.0161	0.0197	0.0215	0.0144	0.0233	0.1236	.2374
TOTAL	0.1039	0.0959	0.0726	0.1004	0.0636	0.1183	0.4453	1.0000

Input Requirements

The data themselves are organized as in Project 4. However, the description of the services for a particular run needs to be somewhat more intricate because of the two-dimensional nature of the output. Specifically, for this project the user must define the particular tables that he or she wishes to see. The reason is simple: For instance, a data collection containing 10 discrete variables produces 10 simple (one-way) frequency tables. However, that same collection processed to produce all possible two-way tables bombards the user with 45 tables. (For N discrete variables, there are $N*(N-1)/2$ two-way tables.) As there is no upper limit on the number of subjects (data records), the software design cannot count on storing all the data internally. Consequently, we must impose some rather severe restrictions on the product's capacity. For the sake of convenience, we shall use the following limits.

1. A maximum of 20 tables in any one run.
2. A maximum of 10 subcategories in any discrete variable. (This will help keep each table to a single page of printout.)

It will be up to you to impose additional restrictions (as appropriate) on maximum lengths of variable and subcategory names. Note that the design of the output display represents a substantial part of the overall effort here.

In this project, the user receives absolute and relative frequencies by default. Accordingly, the "front end" of the software should include provisions for accept-

TABLE 3.10 OPERATION CODES OF THE MACHINE FOR PROJECT 7, ENHANCEMENT B

HALT	00	Stop execution.
POP	01	Pop operand off stack. $\{SP \leftarrow SP - 1;\}$
SETS	02	Set the stack pointer to N. $\{SP \leftarrow N;\}$
FETCH	03	Get contents in address that is at top of stack and stack the value found there. $\{A \leftarrow (SP); (SP) \leftarrow (A);\}$
LDA	04	Load address onto stack. $\{SP \leftarrow SP + 1; (SP) \leftarrow N;\}$
STOR	05	Store top of stack into memory. $\{VAL \leftarrow (SP); SP \leftarrow SP - 1; ((SP)) \leftarrow VAL; (SP) \leftarrow VAL;\}$
NEG	06	Negate top of stack. $\{(SP) \leftarrow - (SP);\}$
AND	07	Add top two entries of stack. $\{VAL \leftarrow (SP); SP \leftarrow SP - 1; (SP) \leftarrow (SP) + VAL;\}$
SUB	08	Subtract. $\{VAL \leftarrow (SP); SP \leftarrow SP - 1; (SP) \leftarrow (SP) - VAL;\}$
MULT	09	Multiply. $\{VAL \leftarrow (SP); SP \leftarrow SP - 1; (SP) \leftarrow (SP)*VAL;\}$
DIV	10	Divide. $\{VAL \leftarrow (SP); SP \leftarrow SP - 1; (SP) \leftarrow (SP)/VAL;\}$
EXP	11	Exponentiate. $\{VAL \leftarrow (SP); SP \leftarrow SP - 1; (SP) \leftarrow (SP)**VAL;\}$

ing specifications that suppress the relative (or absolute) frequencies for selected tables or for the entire run.

Applicable Data Structures

As is true for the case of the one-way frequency analyzer (Project 4), arrays can be used very effectively here to represent the various counters that comprise the substance of these analyses. This is also true for the collections of names that must be positioned carefully in order to produce a clear, easily understood display.

Enhancements to the Two-Dimensional Frequency Analyzer

In many ways, these enhancements parallel the ones described for the one-dimensional frequency analyzer described under Project 4. Thus, each addition extends the range of capabilities offered by the software without compromising the fundamental design of the product. In addition, there are suggested enhancements that pertain specifically to the two-dimensional frequency distribution.

6A. *Arbitrary record length.* See Enhancement 4A.

6B. *Error-handling enhancement.* See Enhancement 4B.

6C. *Additional error-handling.* See Enhancement 4C.

6D. *Code regrouping capabilities.* See Enhancement 4D. Note that the regrouping facilities (described in the enhancement cited above) now must apply to either or both participants in a two-way table. In effect, then, it should be possible to compress the number of rows or columns or both in a given table.

6E. *Extension to continuous variables.* See Enhancement 4E. 4. As in the case of Enhancement 6D, the feature should be applicable to either or both variables in a given two-way table.

6F. *Sorted frequency display.* This is similar (but not identical) to Enhancement 4F. The similarity lies in the fact that the user is given the capability of specifying that the frequencies be displayed (for a given table) in descending order (highest frequency first). However, the idea of completely sorted frequencies loses its meaning in a two-dimensional table. (It is possible to sort all the cells in a two-dimensional table, but the resulting display would be atrocious.) Consequently, the facility is adjusted in the following way: When sorting is requested for a given table, the row subcategories will be displayed in order by decreasing row sum frequencies and the column subcategories in order by decreasing column sum frequencies. For instance, suppose our row variable was SEX (subcategories MALE and FEMALE) and our column variable was RESIDENCE (subcategories LOCAL and AWAY). Suppose further that the population under scrutiny consisted of 82 local males, 101 away males, 118 local females, and 49 away females. Thus for SEX, the first row would be MALE (because there are more males than females); for RESIDENCE, the first column would be LOCAL, because there are more people local than away.

```
       TWO-WAY FREQUENCY DISTRIBUTION--ABSOLUTE

   ROW VAR: SEX              COLUMN VAR: RESIDENCE

                 LOCAL        AWAY         TOTAL
         MALE       82         101           183
       FEMALE      118          49           167

       TOTAL      200         150           350
```

6G. *Increased row and column capacity.* The basic version of this project placed a limit on the number of subcategories (for both row and column variables) based on the underlying restriction that each table should be contained on a single page of printout. This enhancement lifts that restriction, leaving it to you (the designer) to set arbitrary limits. The adjustments that are necessary with regard to the internal data organization and computations are quite straightforward—more tables and more counters. Corresponding modifications to the output mechanisms are far from straightforward. Basically, what is necessary is a generalized output formatting capability that enables the user to partition a particular two-dimensional table into contiguous segments which, when fitted together, would form one (potentially enormous) "page." As it happens, the benefits of functional isolation and forward-looking design make themselves felt yet again: Such a problem arises when displaying the connection matrix of arbitrarily large chemical structures. In that connection, there is some pertinent material to be found in Chapter 5, and a little thought will help focus that information directly on this problem.

6H. *Statistical enhancement.* One of the most powerful statistical aids in characterizing a frequency distribution is chi-square (χ^2). This is a measure of the probability that a particular difference between an observed and an expected distribution of values occurred by chance. There are many ways in which it is computed and used. For our purposes, chi-square is

$$\chi^2 = \sum_{r=1}^{R} \sum_{c=1}^{C} \frac{[O\,(r,\ c) - E\,(r,\ c)]^2}{E\,(r,\ c)}$$

where $O(r,c)$ is the observed number of occurrences for a given cell (that is, a given row and column combination), $E(r,c)$ is the expected number of occurrences for that cell, and chi-square is obtained by summing the indicated ratio over all the cells (R rows by C columns). When information about the expected frequency distribution is undefined or unavailable, a common practice is to assume a uniform expected distribution. We shall do that here, so that the expected number of occurrences for a given cell, $E(r,c)$, is

$$E\,(r,\ c) = \frac{T\,(r)T\,(c)}{T}$$

where $T(r)$ is the total number of observed occurrences for row r, $T(c)$ is the total number of observed occurrences for column c, and T is the total number of occurrences.

Thus we have enough information to compute chi-square. Once computed, we can determine the probability of obtaining at least that value by chance in one of two ways: We can compute the value directly or we can obtain it from a table. In either case, the probability is obtained in conjunction with another value called the *degrees of freedom.* For a two-dimensional table with R rows and C columns, the value for degrees of freedom (DF) is $(R-1)*(C-1)$. To illustrate, suppose we use the illustrative frequencies in Enhancement 6F as an example. Chi-square for those four cells is

(82-96)**2/96 + (118-95)**2/95 + (101-78)**2/78 + (49-72)**2/72

or 21.74. In this case, DF is $1((2-1)*(2-1))$. At one degree of freedom, the standard chi-square table (available in any statistics text or handbook) tells us that chi-square at a probability of 0.01 is 6.63. Thus our computed chi-square needs to be at least 6.63 if we are to infer that there is no more than 1 chance in 100 that the observed difference is purely accidental. Because our chi-square is well above 6.63, we can infer that the chances of the difference being purely accidental are considerably less than 1 in 100. (More precise tables could tell us exactly what the probability is; for many situations, it is enough to know that it is below 1 percent.)

Chi-square for a given probability p also can be approximated numerically as follows:

$$\chi^2 \approx DF\left(1 - \frac{2}{90\ F} + Z\sqrt{\frac{2}{90\ F}}\right)^3$$

In this formulation, DF has its previous meaning and $Z(p)$ is the value of the normal error associated with the probability p. (In PL/I, it happens that the relation between p and $Z(p)$ is such that

$$p = 0.5 - ERF(Z(p)/SQRT(2))/2.$$

Thus, through a series of iterations, it is relatively straightforward in PL/I to compute a probability associated with a value for chi-square resulting from a particular distribution. In other languages, it may be more desirable to store a table of chi-square values and use a procedure to look up these values. Using either these computations or table, this enhancement provides the user with the option of requesting the chi-square determination (and the associated probability) for any or all tables in a given set.

---

7. A POSTFIX EVALUATOR

Functional Description

This project is related to Project 5, An Infix-to-Postfix Converter, and it will be described as a "back end," or post processor, to that project. It does not do much good to translate an expression to its postfix form if you cannot evaluate the expression in that form. Thus, as the basic foundation for this project, we shall evaluate postfix expressions derived from infix expressions as described in Project 5 with Enhancements 5E and 5F included. (Enhancement 5F is included to supply a mechanism for assigning a value to a variable. It makes no sense to evaluate an expression containing a variable if the variable does not have a value.) The intent of this project is to evaluate a series of expressions sequentially, each evaluation depending on previous evaluations. An example is shown in Figure 3.20.

Infix	Postfix	Output
X = 3	X 3 =	3
Y = 4	Y 4 =	4
R = (X**2+Y**2) **.5	R X 2**Y 2**+.5** =	5
X*2	X 2*	6
R + X + Y	R X + Y +	1 2

FIGURE 3.20 *Expression evaluation.*

Background

We translate an infix expression to postfix form because this form is easy to evaluate by use of a simple stack mechanism. There is no ambiguity in the expression; no parentheses are present and precedence of operators is irrelevant. The exact order of evaluation is explicit in the postfix form. The pseudocode for evaluating a postfix expression (held in the form of a queue) is shown in Figure 3.21. In the pseudocode, PUSH and POP have standard meanings (see Project 5), and DEQUE extracts a token from the front of the queue. (ENQUE inserts a token at the rear of the queue. DEQUE is analogous to POPping information from a stack.) Notice that the objects in the queue are considered to be tokens. This is a standard interpretation, and it will be discussed later. All the operators are assumed to be binary. (How would the pseudocode change if unary operators also are permitted?) To illustrate the intent of this algorithm, a simulation for the expression

$$A = 3*B-2 \quad \text{(postfix form, A3B*2-=)}$$

is shown in Figure 3.22 (B is assumed to have the value 2). Each "snapshot" shown in the scenario is taken at the top of the WHILE loop just before the DEQUE operation is performed. Notice that the stack "grows" from right to left. (What does the assignment operator do with its two operands?)

Applicable Data Structures

Two data structures have been used implicitly in the above algorithm.

1. The concept of a token was used to determine the type of the object DEQUEd from the queue. It is also useful to determine the specific operator to be applied to the operands and to determine whether operands are variables or constants.

2. The concept of a *symbol table* was used to associate a given variable with its corresponding value.

The token can be encoded as a 2-tuple: The first component indicates the kind or type of object (binary operator, variable, or constant), and the second component indicates the specific object within the given category. In the case of a variable, the

```
NAME: EVAL

INPUT PARAMETER: QUEUE, a queue containing the
    postfix expression to be evaluated.

OUTPUT PARAMETER: The value of the expression.

FUNCTION: This module evaluates a postfix
    expression held in the form of a queue.

DEFINITION: There is an internal stack
    (initially empty) available to this module.
    PUSH and POP insert and extract tokens
    from this stack.  DEQUE extracts tokens
    from QUEUE.  TOKEN, TOKEN1, TOKEN2 and
    TOKEN3 are 2-tuples containing a type
    and a value.

ALGORITHM:

    WHILE (QUEUE is not empty)
        DEQUE(TOKEN).

        CASE type of TOKEN OF

        operand:
            PUSH(TOKEN).

        operator:
            POP(TOKEN1).
            POP(TOKEN2).
            Apply operator to TOKEN1 and TOKEN2
                obtaining TOKEN3.
            PUSH(TOKEN3).

        ENDCASE

    ENDWHILE

    POP(TOKEN).
    Return value extracted from TOKEN.
```

FIGURE 3.21 *Pseudocode for postfix evaluator.*

second component might be a pointer to the symbol table; for a constant, it might constitute the actual value.

The symbol table can be thought of as an array of structures (as in PL/I) or a coupled pair of arrays (as in FORTRAN). The contents of a generic symbol table (after execution of the statements in Fig. 3.20) might look something like that shown in Figure 3.23.

Enhancements to the Postfix Evaluator

All the enhancements suggested in Project 5 can be adopted here. That project supplies the "front end" for this project, and any enhancements employed there would simply produce slight variations in the postfix expressions that are the input of this project. The only real variation to the basic postfix form presented above is produced by the inclusion of unary operators (and functions). Notice that if the

Token	Queue	Stack
undefined	A3B*2-=	$
A	3B*2-=	A$
3	B*2-=	3A$
B	*2-+	B3A$
*	2-=	6A$
2	-=	26A$
-	=	4A$
=	empty	4$

FIGURE 3.22 *Evaluation of* A3B*2−=.

concept of a token is employed, enhancements such as *5A, 5B, 5C,* and *5E* in no way affect the content or semantics of the postfix form.

The enhancements suggested here deal with alternative methods of evaluating the specific postfix form, once that form has been defined explicitly.

7A. Tree evaluation. An expression (in either infix or postfix form) can be thought of as a tree. For instance, the expression

$$R = (X**2 + Y**2)**.5$$

can be represented by the binary tree shown in Figure 3.24(*b*) (the generic node is shown in Figure 3.24(*a*)). Once the postfix form of an expression has been produced, it is easily transformed to its tree form. The algorithm is shown in Figure 3.25. Notice that the structure of the algorithm is very similar to the one in Figure 3.21.

When the tree form of the expression has been produced, a simple recursive algorithm (Fig. 3.26) can be used to evaluate it.

7B. Machine evaluation. In a compiler (such as PL/I), the purpose of translating to postfix is to produce a form that is translated more easily into *machine code*. It is possible to define a *stack machine* (see below) and to simulate its execution via software. In this enhancement, you are asked to design a software product to translate the postfix expression to the appropriate machine code and simulate the execution of this machine.

Variable	Value
X	3
Y	4
R	5

FIGURE 3.23 *Symbol table.*

(a)

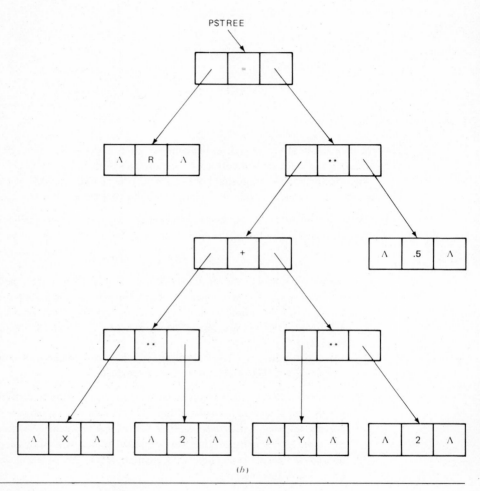

(b)

FIGURE 3.24 *Tree representation of*
$R = (X ** 2 + Y ** 2) ** .5$.

Machine Definition

This machine has a simple stack architecture. It has 64 words of (16-bit) storage and two registers: the SP and the PC. The PC points to the next instruction to be exe-

```
NAME: POSTFIX_TO_TREE

INPUT PARAMETER: QUEUE, a queue containing
    a postfix expression.

OUTPUT PARAMETER: P$TREE, a pointer to a tree.

FUNCTION: This module translates a postfix
    expression (held in the form of queue)
    to its tree form.

DEFINITIONS: There is an internal stack
    (initially empty) available to this module.
    PUSH and POP insert and extract pointers
    from this stack.  DEQUE extracts tokens
    from QUEUE.  TOKEN is extracted from QUEUE.
    P$TREE, P$LTREE, and P$RTREE are pointers
    to trees.

ALGORITHM:

    WHILE(QUEUE is not empty)
        DEQUE(TOKEN).
        Allocate new node, TREE (with pointer P$TREE).

        Put in TOKEN.

        CASE type of TOKEN OF

        operand:
            Make L_LINK and R_LINK of TREE null.


        operator:
            POP(P$RTREE); put in R_LINK of TREE.
            POP(P$LTREE); put in L_LINK of TREE.

        ENDCASE

        PUSH(P$TREE).

    ENDWHILE

    POP(P$TREE).
    Return P$TREE.
```

FIGURE 3.25 *Translation from postfix to tree form.*

cuted. Each time an instruction is fetched, one is added to the PC. The SP points to the stack, which is held in storage. It can point anywhere in storage; the stack moves in a positive direction, that is, the topmost stack element resides in a higher storage location than any other.

Whenever the machine is started, it is assumed that a program has already been placed in memory and that execution is to start at storage location zero. It is not a very interesting machine, but it is adequate for illustrative purposes. (It can easily be extended to include I/O and program control.)

The instruction format is shown in Figure 3.27, and the semantics of the operation codes is shown in Table 3.10. (In this table, the notation (SP) means *the contents of* SP.)

```
NAME: EVAL_TREE

INPUT PARAMETER: P$TREE, a pointer to the tree
        to be evaluated.

OUTPUT PARAMETER: VAL, the value associated with
        the tree pointed to by P$TREE.

FUNCTION: This module calculates the value associated
        with the tree pointed to be P$TREE.

ALGORITHM:

        IF P$TREE points to a leaf node (L_LINK
                and R_LINK are null)

        THEN    /* must be an operand  */
                Put in VAL the evaluation of the
                        TOKEN pointed to by P$TREE.

        ELSE    /* must be an operator  */
                Apply EVAL_TREE to L_LINK of TREE
                        (pointed to by P$TREE) obtaining VAL1.
                Apply EVAL_TREE to R_LINK of TREE
                        (pointed to by P$TREE) obtaining VAL2.
                Put in VAL the result obtained by applying
                        the operator (in TOKEN pointed to by
                        P$TREE) to VAL1 and VAL2.
        ENDIF

        Return VAL.
```

FIGURE 3.26   *Evaluation of tree form.*

8. A SYMBOLIC DIFFERENTIATOR

Functional Description

In this project an expression E and a variable V are read; E is to be symbolically differentiated with respect to V, and the result is to be printed.

This project can be considered as a "back end" or post processor to Project 5 and Project 7 (with a portion of Enhancement 7A). More specifically, it is fairly easy to differentiate an expression if it is held internally in tree form. Thus we can use the techniques of Project 5 to translate expression E to its postfix form; then we can use the techniques of Enhancement 7A (Fig. 3.25) to translate it to its tree form.

Applicable Algorithms

Once we have the expression in its tree form, symbolic differentiation can be performed by a relatively simple recursive algorithm. To be a little more specific, assume that the legal operands are variables and numeric constants; legal operators are: + and − (binary), + and − (unary), *, /, **, LN (logarithm base e), EXP (exponentiation base e), SIN, and COS. Table 3.11 presents the rules for differentiating with respect to these operands and operators. Notice that the last entry in the

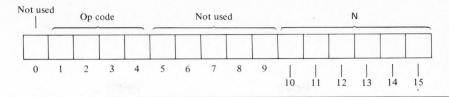

FIGURE 3.27 *Instruction format.*

table (the entry for a constant) corresponds to both numeric constants and variables which differ from the differentiation variable.

Table 3.11 presents differentiation rules for expressions in infix form; this, of course, must be interpreted for the expressions in tree form. This is fairly easy to visualize; a generic example for the first entry of Table 3.11 is shown in Figure 3.28. When a tree with a plus (+) as the root node is to be differentiated, a new tree with plus (+) as its root node is built, and the branches of this root node are the derivatives of the branches of the original tree. A more specific example for the expression 3+X is shown in Figure 3.29. Notice that the differentiation rules do not state anything about expression simplification. Thus the derivative of 3+X is 0+1. This is computationally correct but leaves something to be desired from our standpoint (see Enhancement 8*B*).

The pseudocode for differentiating an expression in tree form is straightforward but rather lengthy because of the number of operators involved. For this reason, it will not be given here. Suffice it to say that given a tree, the algorithm invokes itself recursively using the definitions shown in Table 3.11 to build a new tree, which is the derivative of the input tree. (As they say in mathematics books, it is intuitively obvious and left as an exercise to the reader. Right?)

TABLE 3.11 DIFFERENTIATION RULES

w	dw/dx
u+v	du/dx + dv/dx
u−v	du/dx − dv/dx
+u	du/dx
−u	−du/dx
u*v	u*dv/dx + v*du/dx
u/v	(v*du/dx − u*dv/dx)/v**2
u**v	u**v*(v/u*du/dx + (ln(u))*dv/dx)
ln(u)	1/u*du/dx
exp(u)	exp(u)*du/dx
sin(u)	cos(u)*du/dx
cos(u)	-sin(u)*du/dx
x	1
c(c a constant)	0

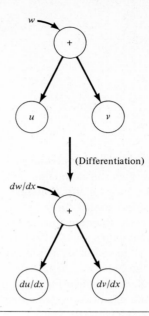

FIGURE 3.28 *Differentiation of addition tree.*

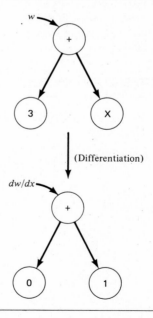

FIGURE 3.29 *Differentiation of 3 + X.*

Enhancements to the Symbolic Differentiator

8A. *Include more functions.* Notice that the operators (functions) included in the project thus far are self-contained; that is, taking the derivative of an expression that contains them does not produce an operator not already present. Any new operators that are introduced should have this same property. The following new functions might be included.

(1) All the remaining trigonometric functions.

(2) The hyperbolic functions.

(3) Square root or cube root.

(4) Integrals.

Notice that functions such as MOD and ABS, which do not have well-defined derivatives everywhere, should not be included.

8B. *Expression simplification.* Because derivatives will be printed, evaluated, or both, it is advantageous to produce their simplified forms. For instance, by the simple differentiation rules given so far, the expression 3*X has the derivative 3*1+X*0. This, of course, has value 3, and we would like to be able to produce the simplified tree for both display and computational purposes (Fig. 3.30).

Table 3.12 shows some simplifications that you may choose to incorporate. (Some of these transformations—for example, 9 and 10—may be used to produce intermediate canonical forms for recognition of similar expressions, and you may not choose to retain them in the final form.) In the table, *e, f,* and *g* represent arbitrary expressions, and *x* represents an arbitrary variable.

TABLE 3.12 SIMPLIFICATION RULES

1. e*1, 1*e −> e	11. x**n/x**m −> x**(n−m)
2. e*0, 0*e −> 0	12. e−e −> 0
3. e+0, 0+e −> e	13. e+(−e) −> 0
4. e−0 −> e	14. e/e −> 1 (e not 0)
5. 0−e −> −e	15. +−e −> −e
6. e**0 −> 1 (e not 0)	16. +e −> e
7. e**1 −> e	17. −−e −> e
8. x**n * x**m −> x**(n+m)	18. f*e + g*e −> (f+g)*e
9. g/e −> g*e**(−1)	19. constant arithmetic
10. x −> x**1	20. combining fractions

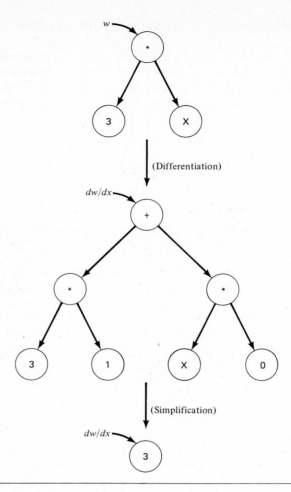

FIGURE 3.30 *Differentiation of* 3 * X.

8C. *Evaluation of derivatives.* Once we have the derivative of an expression in tree form, it can be evaluated, given specific values for the variables present. (See Enhancement 7A.)

9. A CHEMICAL-FORMULA EVALUATOR

We shall take the description of the chemical-formula evaluator presented in this chapter as the basis for this project. As described thus far, the type of molecule that can be described is somewhat restricted; it can have no branches and no cycles (except for the W group).

FIGURE 3.31 *Structural-formula of 2<Q>1.*

Enhancements to the Chemical-Formula Evaluator

9A. *Allow branches.* Let the symbols $<$ and $>$ represent the beginning and end of an auxiliary branch of a molecule. Thus the line-formula such as

$$2<Q>1$$

has the following meaning:

Take a chain of two carbon atoms. To the second of these atoms, attach two branches. The primary branch is a chain of one carbon atom (represented by the 1); the secondary branch is a hydroxyl group (represented by the Q).

Thus the above line-formula has the structural-formula shown in Figure 3.31. There can be branches within branches and multiple branches at a given atom. Thus the line-formula

$$2<1><1<2><2>2>1<2><2>2$$

has the structural-formula shown in Figure 3.32.

9B. *Extend printing model.* Once branches are introduced (as described in Enhancement 9A), many molecules, which cannot be printed by the simple model that produced the structural-formulas shown in Chapter 3 (see App. I), can now be described. The major reason is that hydrogen atoms (which are of secondary importance) get in the way of primary branches. To resolve this problem, extend the printing model, as exemplified by the structural-formula shown in Figure 3.32. (Is it possible to print all representable molecules with your new model?)

9C. *Table-driven functional groups.* Develop a notation capable of describing the structure of the six functional groups. Translate this notation to a tabular form so that processing of functional groups can be table-driven in the same way that element processing is table-driven.

9D. *User-defined functional groups.* Extend the notation developed in Enhancement 9C so that an arbitrary chemical group (for instance, a benzene ring) can be described. Allow the user to define his or her own functional groups *at execution time* and use these new groups in the line-formulas. This can be accomplished by

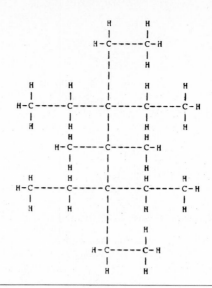

FIGURE 3.32 *Structural-formula of*
2<1> <1<2> <2>2>1<2> <2>2.

translating the extended notation to its tabular form and applying the table-driven technique suggested in Enhancement 9*C*.

9*E*. *Repetition*. Extend the line-formula notation so that substrings in the line-formula can be repeated more than once. Use parentheses to delimit the extent of the substring to be repeated, followed by a number indicating how many times it is to be repeated. Thus the line-formula

$$2O1O1O1O1O1O1O1O2$$

could also be written as

$$1(1O)7\ 2$$

There can also be repetitions inside repetitions. Observe that numbers are used in two different contexts: one to represent the number of carbon atoms in a chain and the other to represent a repetition factor. (Notice the requirement of the delimiting blank between 7 and 2.)

9*F*. *Macro facility*. Allow the user to define and name frequently used strings. Macro-names might be delimited by a period (.) on both ends so that they are easily distinguished. Thus the input

$$.X. = <2>$$

$$.Y. = 1.X..X.2$$

$$2<1><.Y.>.Y.$$

would be equivalent to

$$2<1><1<2><2>2>1<2><2>2$$

9G. Multirecord line-formulas. Molecules can be quite large, and their line-formulas may not fit in one 80-character record. Extend the input specification so that line-formulas can extend across record boundaries. Such an extension will require a special delimitor character, such as a semicolon (;), to indicate the end of a line-formula.

---

10. A TEXT FORMATTER

Background

A variety of documents must be revised many times and must be letter perfect in their final presentation. These include certain legal documents, progress reports, proposals, and scientific papers. Often these documents are very lengthy. It is advantageous to revise a typewritten document rather than a handwritten one. However, if each revision has to be retyped by a secretary, a significant amount of time (and money) is used, both for retyping and proofreading.

A computer is well suited for taking "raw" text and transforming it into a desired format. Once a language has been developed for describing formats, revision can be made easily by insertion, deletion, and replacement of text. Once revisions are made to specific regions of the text and verified to be correct, they need not be proofread again: The elimination of retyping removes the chance of introducing new errors.

This book was produced by use of such a formatter, called SCRIPT. Its production was greatly facilitated by the use of a text editor and this formatter.

Functional Description

What primitive operations must the text formatting language be able to express? A few fundamental operations will be discussed here, and more will be introduced in subsequent enhancements. Ultimately, a complete list reflects the requirements and outlook of its originator.

The language must be able to state how many characters there are on a line and how many lines there are per page. It must be able to state when a paragraph is to begin (so that the correct indentation can be performed), when a new page should be started, and when a new line should be started. Assuming that only uppercase letters can be submitted to the system, there must be a way of distinguishing between characters to be displayed in uppercase or lowercase.

We would like to be able to submit text in free format (any number of words per input line) and have the formatter produce output lines containing as many words as can be placed in the line (a function of the current line length). This is

---

known as *filling* the output line. We also would like to be able to direct the formatter to (right) justify the output lines so that the last character of each output line falls in the same column (the last column of the line). (For devices with fixed character size, this is accomplished by inserting extra blanks between words.)

Formatting Language

Formatting commands will be embedded in the text to be formatted. The following conventions will be used to be able to distinguish between command lines and text lines.

1. Each command will start at the beginning of a new line.

2. Each command will start with a right parenthesis:).

3. No text can reside on a command line.

A description of each formatting command follows.

1. The page length can be set by stating)PL=N, where N is an integer.

2. The line length can be set by stating)LL=N, where N is an integer.

3. A new paragraph is started by stating)PARA.

4. A new page is started by stating)PAGE.

5. A new line is started by stating)NL.

6. Right justification is turned on by stating)BJ.

7. Right justification is turned off by stating)EJ.

8. Filling of output lines is turned on by stating)BF.

9. Filling of output lines is turned off by stating)EF.

It is assumed that all input is uppercase. However, all letters will be printed in lowercase unless proceeded by a pound sign, #. In order to embed a pound sign in the text and to allow indiscriminant use of a right parenthesis, a special "escape character," /, will be utilized. Whenever this character is encountered in the text, it indicates that the next character is to be interpreted as itself, not as part of a command.

With these interpretations in force, the input shown in Figure 3.33 would produce the output shown in Figure 3.34.

```
) L L = 3 0
) B F
) N P
#THIS SHOWS THE USE OF SOME OF THE COMMANDS.
#NOTICE THE USE OF THE ), THE /#, AND THE //.
) B J
) N P
#FILLING IS ACCOMPLISHED BY PLACING A
/) #B#F
AT THE BEGINNING OF A LINE. #WHAT
OTHER FEATURES OF
SUCH A FORMATTER DO YOU THINK YOU
MIGHT WANT?
```

FIGURE 3.33 *Input to formatter.*

Algorithmic Primitives

What algorithmic primitives might be used in such a formatter? The following are some suggestions.

1. Get an input line.

2. Get a word from the input line.

3. Put a word in the output line.

4. Justify the current output line.

When placing a word in the output line, a special error flag should be returned if the word will not fit in the line. Line justification can be a little tricky. How should blanks be distributed throughout the line? From the left? From the right? The standard algorithm is to alternate distribution on successive output lines so that extra blanks are less conspicuous.

Enhancements to the Text Formatter

The following enhancements may be incorporated separately or in conjunction with one another. Some of them may be used internally for producing desired affects in the basic project described previously. Incorporation of some of the enhancements may require a change to the fundamental notation employed by the command language.

10*A*. *Nontrivial blank.* Often it is desirable to have a specific number of blanks between two words (not affected by justification). Define a special character (such as !) which is not interpreted as a blank upon input (obviously, blanks delimit words), but which is translated to a blank during output processing. (This can be used internally to produce the paragraphing affect.)

```
      This shows the use of
some of the commands. Notice
the use of the ), the #, and
the /.
      Filling  is  accomplished
by   placing   a  )BF  at  the
beginning  of  a  line.  What
other   features   of  such  a
formatter  do  you  think  you
might want?
```

FIGURE 3.34 *Output from formatter.*

10*B*. *Translation facilities*. In general, it is advantageous to be able to translate any specific input character to any other output character. Define command notation that allows the user to specify these character translations.

10*C*. *Command placement*. As described thus far, commands can appear only at the beginning of a line. Allow commands to be placed anywhere in a line (for instance, in the middle of text to be formatted).

10*D*. *Underlining*. It is useful to be able to underline text. Define a command notation that allows the user to specify the portion of the text to be underlined. (Should blanks be underlined? How about punctuation?)

10*E*. *Centering*. It may be important to be able to center text on a line (for instance, for headings). Define a command notation for centering text.

10*F*. *Indentation*. Often a portion of text should be indented from the right or left margins or both. Develop such a command notation.

10*G*. *Tabulation*. The user may wish to have a tabulation capability similar to that found on a typewriter (for instance, for formatting tables). Designate a special tab character (such as $) and develop a command notation for allowing the user to specify the positions of the tabs.

10*H*. *Conditional paging*. It is sometimes desirable to go to the next output page if there are not sufficient lines on the current page for a certain portion of the text. (This may be useful when printing the heading for a new section. It is not desirable to print the heading on one page and start the text of the section on the next.) Develop a command notation which continues output processing on the next page if a specific number of output lines will not reside on the current page.

10*I*. *Grouping*. It is sometimes important to print a certain portion of the output text entirely on one page (for instance, a table should not be split across a page boundary). However, the text must appear in the output in exactly the same sequence that it occurs in the input. Text in such a group should be output on the current page if there is room. Otherwise white space should be left on the current page and the text in the grouping should be output at the top of the next page. Develop a command notation that allows the user to define the extent of the group.

10*J*. *Figure grouping*. This enhancement is similar to the grouping enhancement in 10*I*. However, here the output need not be in exactly the same order as in the input. Thus if a figure grouping will not fit on the current page, it should be held until the next page. However, white space is not placed on the current page. Instead, the text following the figure grouping is output on the current page.

10*K*. *Page numbering*. The user may wish the formatter to number the output pages. Develop command notations that allow the user to turn page numbering on and off, set, increment, and decrement the page number, and designate the placement and format (decimal, Roman, words) of the page number.

10*L*. *Text holds*. Allow the user to define special character sequences (text holds) that are retained by the formatter and placed at the top or bottom of each page (as in most books).

10*M*. *Footnotes*. Develop a mechanism that allows the user to place footnotes in line (in the text), such that the formatter automatically moves them to the bottom of the page with appropriate reference notation.

10*N*. *Capitalization*. Often an entire word or sequence of words should be capitalized. However, forcing the user to place a pound sign in front of each character is very tedious. Develop a command notation that allows the user to turn on and turn off uniform capitalization.

10*O*. *Blank lines*. Develop a command notation that allows the user to insert a specified number of blank lines in the output text.

10*P*. *Overprinting*. The user may wish to overprint a portion of the text (possibly just a word or character) in order to highlight it. Develop a command notation that allows the user to designate the region to be overprinted and how many times it should be overprinted.

10*Q*. *Macros (without parameters)*. It is useful to allow the user to think of a collection of commands or text as a single concept or entity. This can be accomplished by providing the user with a macrofacility which allows him or her to collect together and name a given sequence of lines. Then, when the name appears in the text (within an appropriate context), the corresponding lines are simply substituted in place of the name. Develop a mechanism that allows the user to name and utilize such macros.

10*R*. *Macros (with parameters)*. This enhancement is similar to the one just described, but also allows the substitution of certain strings within the body of the macro. (This is similar to the use of parameters in a PL/I procedure.)

Structured
Programming

Contrary to most programmers' concepts, structured programming is not just a restriction on the language constructs that the implementer is allowed to use. Structured programming is a discipline encouraging a programmer to organize his or her thinking about the programming process and the problem-solving process in general. By restricting oneself to a few simple, easily understood control constructs, it is possible to produce clear, concise code that effectively conveys the content of the algorithm being implemented.

Clever, tricky code often has been used in the past to produce machine instructions that execute very efficiently. Such efficiency may be important in certain specialized applications (such as those meeting real-time requirements), but in general it is secondary to producing a clearly understandable presentation of the algorithm. Any code produced must be verifiable, analyzable, and modifiable. It is neither clever nor useful to produce code that, in the long run, must be discarded. If the programmer who replaces you on a project cannot understand the algorithmic content of your code (when asked to make a small modification, for instance), then your code will have to be discarded and replaced with his or her own. There is a tradeoff between saving a few seconds of execution time and the time required to analyze and modify virtually unreadable code. Using current hardware technology, a few more seconds of execution time almost universally is worth the personnel time saved in not having to wrestle with unduly convoluted software.

What about the GOTO? Is its use really such a cardinal sin? Yes and no! A GOTO should not be used indiscriminantly to transfer control to an arbitrary point in a program. However, a well-placed, well-understood, well-documented GOTO can sometimes help to simplify, reduce, and clarify the code. The statement that a

GOTO should never appear in "good" code constitutes an artificial measure of "good"; some good programs use the GOTO and some bad programs do not. It has been noticed, however, that the GOTO construct rarely appears in good programs. The use of strictly structured constructs will always eliminate the GOTO construct, although sometimes at the cost of brevity and clarity. One of the reasons for using structured programming is to produce clear, concise, readable, easily modifiable code. If this objective can be attained more readily by the use of a GOTO than by adhering to strictly structured constructs, then the GOTO may be more advantageous. Such situations are few and far between, and the GOTO should be used sparingly. In general, if you think you need to use the GOTO construct, there is probably a better way to do it. Rethink the problem before you implement by using a GOTO.

4.1 GENERAL PHILOSOPHY

Structured programming deals with the manner in which flow of control is implemented in a program. Simple solutions to problems are best, in practice. It has been found that clear, easily readable and modifiable code is produced by using a few well-understood constructs for flow of control. As long as these few constructs are sufficient to implement the algorithm at hand, there is no reason to expand beyond them if it means introducing confusion.

A set of constructs for flow of control will be presented in the next section. If programmers were to discipline themselves to use only this restricted set of constructs, then an accepted standard could be established. In fact, this set of constructs is widely accepted as the standard. They constitute a framework or shell into which algorithmic components can be embedded; they can be used as building blocks with which the desired algorithm can be developed. The adoption of these constructs can significantly help clarify the logical content of the process to be implemented.

4.2 STRUCTURED CONTROL CONSTRUCTS

The standard flowchart, pseudocode, PL/I implementation, FORTRAN implementation, and PASCAL implementation for six structured constructs for flow of control are shown in Figures 4.1-4.6. These implementation constructs correspond precisely to the pseudocode constructs. It is trivial to produce structured code from pseudocode; the mapping from the pseudocode constructs to the structured implementation constructs is obvious.

Restriction to these standard constructs still leaves a certain amount of latitude within the implementation. For instance, the CASE construct may be implemented in one of several ways. Small variations exist that will affect the code's efficiency;

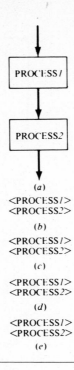

(a)

```
<PROCESS1>
<PROCESS2>
```

(b)

```
<PROCESS1>
<PROCESS2>
```

(c)

```
<PROCESS1>
<PROCESS2>
```

(d)

```
<PROCESS1>
<PROCESS2>
```

(e)

FIGURE 4.1 *Sequential (concatenation): (a) conventional flowchart; (b) Pseudocode; (c) PL/I implementation; (d)* FORTRAN *implementation; and (e)* PASCAL *implementation.*

this is an important consideration, but should be kept in perspective as it is secondary to clarity.

To illustrate the transformation of pseudocode to structured code, Figure 4.7 shows the structured PL/I code for the psuedocode shown in Figure 3.9. Note the close correspondence between the pseudocode and the implementation. This close correspondence can be obtained for a wide variety of high-level programming languages.

4.3 DECLARATIONS

All parameters and local variables used in a procedure should be declared. Some languages require such declarations and produce compile-time errors, which inhibit execution until such declaration requirements are satisfied. Although PL/I does not have such restrictions, it still is advisable to include these declarations. There are four major reasons for supplying them.

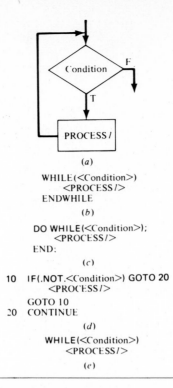

(a)

```
WHILE(<Condition>)
    <PROCESS I>
ENDWHILE
```
(b)

```
DO WHILE(<Condition>);
    <PROCESS I>
END:
```
(c)

```
10   IF(.NOT.<Condition>) GOTO 20
        <PROCESS I>
     GOTO 10
20   CONTINUE
```
(d)

```
WHILE(<Condition>)
    <PROCESS I>
```
(e)

FIGURE 4.2   *WHILE: (a) conventional flowchart; (b) pseudocode; (c) PL/I implementation; (d)* FORTRAN *implementation; and (e)* PASCAL *implementation.*

1. *Memorization of defaults is avoided.* If the attributes of all variables are declared explicitly, there is never any question about what these attributes are. Strange results sometimes will occur because the attributes of a variable have been specified only partially and unknown (and undesired) defaults have been used for those left unspecified. All attributes should always be included in the declaration.

2. *Undesired implicit information sharing is eliminated.* The scope-of-name rules of most block-structured languages allow information to be passed implicitly across procedure boundaries through "global" variables. Such information sharing is determined by the positions in which the variables are declared. Unanticipated (unwanted) information sharing can be eliminated by insuring that all logically local variables are declared.

3. *Mismatched (by type) procedure parameters are eliminated.* PL/I does no type data conversion across procedure boundaries unless the attributes of the parameters are explicitly presented in a declaration of the procedure entry point. (The procedure

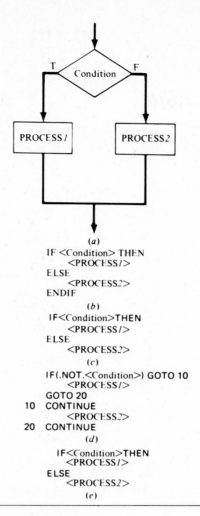

```
               T    Condition    F



        PROCESS1              PROCESS2
```

(a)

```
IF <Condition> THEN
        <PROCESS1>
ELSE
        <PROCESS2>
ENDIF
```

(b)

```
IF<Condition>THEN
        <PROCESS1>
ELSE
        <PROCESS2>
```

(c)

```
IF(.NOT.<Condition>) GOTO 10
        <PROCESS1>
GOTO 20
10 CONTINUE
        <PROCESS2>
20 CONTINUE
```

(d)

```
IF<Condition>THEN
        <PROCESS1>
ELSE
        <PROCESS2>
```

(e)

FIGURE 4.3 *IF-THEN-ELSE: (a) conventional flowchart;
(b) pseudocode; (c) PL/I implementation; (d)* FORTRAN
implementation; and (e) PASCAL *implementation.*

declaration is often completely absent.) Declaration of all parameters within a procedure can help to ensure that the parameters match the types of their corresponding arguments.

4. *The declarations supply a convenient mechanism for a dictionary of variables.* The logical content of each variable should be documented. A separate line can be used for declaring each variable, and the remaining blank space can be used for a brief comment that defines the intent of the variable.

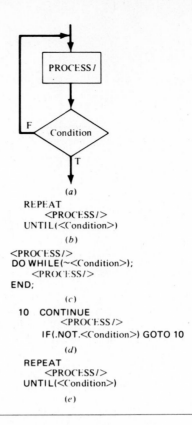

(a)

```
REPEAT
     <PROCESS I>
UNTIL(<Condition>)
```

(b)

```
<PROCESS I>
DO WHILE(~<Condition>);
     <PROCESS I>
END;
```

(c)

```
10   CONTINUE
          <PROCESS I>
     IF(.NOT.<Condition>) GOTO 10
```

(d)

```
REPEAT
     <PROCESS I>
UNTIL(<Condition>)
```

(e)

FIGURE 4.4 *REPEAT-UNTIL: (a) conventional flowchart; (b) pseudocode; (c) PL/I implementation; (d)* FORTRAN *implementation; and (e)* PASCAL *implementation.*

As an example of how undesired information sharing can occur, consider the skeletal code in Figure 4.8. The identifier J is declared neither in procedures B nor C, so it is global to both of them and thus represents the *same* variable. In the invocation of procedure B and within the first iteration of LOOP1, I should have the value 1. However, in the invocation of procedure C, the value of J is modified by LOOP2 and retains the value of 21 upon return to procedure B. For the remainder of the first iteration of LOOP1 (after the call to procedure C), J has the value 21. This is incremented to 22 at the bottom of LOOP1 and, since 22 is greater than 10, a second iteration of the loop is not performed.

This almost surely is not the logical intent of the code; it occurs because J was not correctly declared in the procedures. The solution is to declare J to be a local variable in both procedures B and C. In general, it is the programmer's responsibility to identify those variables that are local to a given procedure and declare them appropriately. Failure to do this properly will result in dubious and (predictably) unpredictable execution.

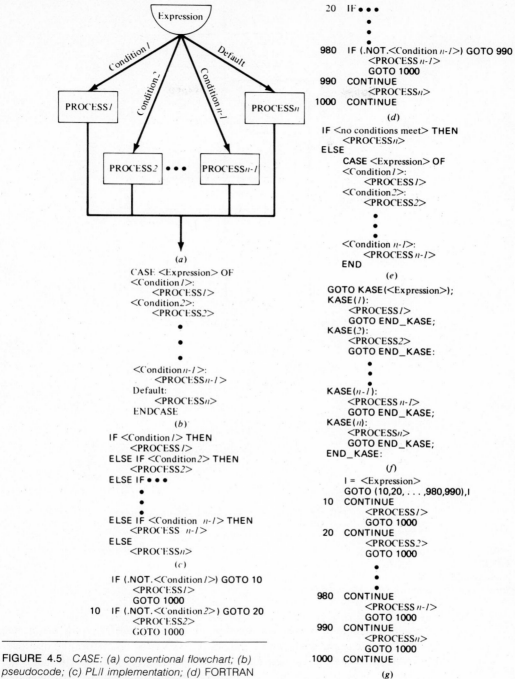

```
                                           20   IF • • •
                                                     •
                                                     •
                                                     •
                                          980   IF (.NOT.<Condition n-1>) GOTO 990
                                                     <PROCESS n-1>
                                                     GOTO 1000
                                          990   CONTINUE
                                                     <PROCESSn>
                                         1000   CONTINUE
                                                        (d)

                                         IF <no conditions meet> THEN
                                                <PROCESSn>
                                         ELSE
                                             CASE <Expression> OF
                                             <Condition 1>:
                                                    <PROCESS 1>
                                             <Condition 2>:
                                                    <PROCESS2>
                                                        •
                                                        •
                                                        •
                                             <Condition n-1>:
                                                    <PROCESS n-1>
                                             END
                                                        (e)

                                             GOTO KASE(<Expression>);
                                             KASE(1):
                                                    <PROCESS 1>
                                                    GOTO END_KASE;
                                             KASE(2):
                                                    <PROCESS2>
                                                    GOTO END_KASE:
                                                        •
                                                        •
                                                        •
                                             KASE(n-1):
                                                    <PROCESS n-1>
                                                    GOTO END_KASE;
                                             KASE(n):
                                                    <PROCESSn>
                                                    GOTO END_KASE;
                                             END_KASE:
                                                        (f)
```

(a)

```
CASE <Expression> OF
<Condition 1>:
       <PROCESS 1>
<Condition 2>:
       <PROCESS 2>
           •
           •
           •
<Condition n-1>:
       <PROCESS n-1>
Default:
       <PROCESSn>
ENDCASE
```

(b)

```
IF <Condition 1> THEN
       <PROCESS 1>
ELSE IF <Condition 2> THEN
       <PROCESS 2>
ELSE IF • • •
       •
       •
       •
ELSE IF <Condition n-1> THEN
       <PROCESS n-1>
ELSE
       <PROCESSn>
```

(c)

```
       IF (.NOT.<Condition 1>) GOTO 10
              <PROCESS 1>
              GOTO 1000
10     IF (.NOT.<Condition 2>) GOTO 20
              <PROCESS2>
              GOTO 1000
```

```
             I = <Expression>
             GOTO (10,20, . . . ,980,990),I
       10    CONTINUE
                    <PROCESS 1>
                    GOTO 1000
       20    CONTINUE
                    <PROCESS 2>
                    GOTO 1000
                        •
                        •
                        •
      980    CONTINUE
                    <PROCESS n-1>
                    GOTO 1000
      990    CONTINUE
                    <PROCESSn>
                    GOTO 1000
     1000    CONTINUE
                        (g)
```

FIGURE 4.5 *CASE: (a) conventional flowchart; (b) pseudocode; (c) PL/I implementation; (d) FORTRAN implementation; (e) PASCAL implementation; (f) alternative PL/I implementation (here KASE is a LABEL array); and (g) alternative FORTRAN implementation.*

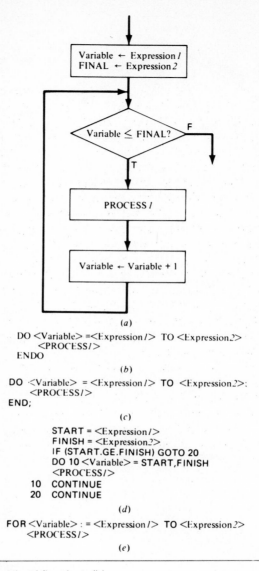

$$\text{Variable} \leftarrow \text{Expression } I$$
$$\text{FINAL} \leftarrow \text{Expression } 2$$

Variable $\leq$ FINAL?   F

T

PROCESS I

Variable $\leftarrow$ Variable + 1

(a)

```
DO <Variable> =<Expression/> TO <Expression 2>
     <PROCESS/>
ENDO
```

(b)

```
DO <Variable> = <Expression/> TO <Expression 2>:
     <PROCESS/>
END;
```

(c)

```
       START = <Expression/>
       FINISH = <Expression 2>
       IF (START.GE.FINISH) GOTO 20
       DO 10 <Variable> = START,FINISH
            <PROCESS/>
   10  CONTINUE
   20  CONTINUE
```

(d)

```
FOR <Variable> : = <Expression/> TO <Expression 2>
     <PROCESS/>
```

(e)

FIGURE 4.6 *DO loop; (a) conventional flowchart; (b) pseudocode; (c) PL/I implementation; (d)* FORTRAN *implementation; and (e)* PASCAL *implementation.*

As an example of how mismatched argument or parameter typing can occur, consider the code segment shown in Figure 4.9. Assuming no declaration of procedure SAMPLE is present (so that no automatic data conversion is performed), the bit configuration corresponding to the FIXED BINARY(31) value stored in A will be made available to SAMPLE by accessing the variable B. However, since B is not

```
/****************************************************************/
/*                                                              */
/*                      EXEC_SYM                                */
/*                                                              */
/*    THIS PROCEDURE INCREMENTALLY RECOGNIZES SEGMENTS          */
/*    OF THE MOLECULE AND "ATTACHES" IT TO THE                  */
/*    INTERNAL REPRESENTATION OF THE MOLECULE.                  */
/*        INPUT PARAMETER:                                      */
/*           TOKEN - TOKEN TO BE PRINTED                        */
/*        INPUT-OUTPUT PARAMETER:                               */
/*           MOL - THE MOLECULE                                 */
/*                                                              */
/****************************************************************/

       EXEC_SYM: PROC(TOKEN,MOL);

           DCL 1 TOKEN,
               2 TYPE FIXED BIN(15),
               2 VAL FIXED BIN(15);

           DCL 1 MOL,          /*  INTERNAL REPRESENTATION  */
               2 REP,
                   3 CONNECTION(*,*) FIXED BIN(15),
                   3 ATOM_CORR(*) FIXED BIN(15),
                   3 P$NEXT FIXED BIN(15),
               2 CONTEXT,
                   3 #BONDS FIXED BIN(15),
                   3 ATOM_PEND(*) FIXED BIN(15);

           DCL (
               I,           /*  DO LOOP PARAMETER  */
               P$ATOM       /*  POINTER TO AN ATOM  */
                            ) FIXED BIN(15),

               CASE(T$ATOM:T$NUM) LABEL INIT(ATOM,GROUP,NUMBER);

           GOTO CASE(TOKEN.TYPE);

           ATOM:
               P$ATOM = CREATE(MOL,TOKEN.VAL);
               CALL LINK(MOL,P$ATOM);
               CALL CHANGE_CONTEXT(CONTEXT,P$ATOM,$NULL);
               GOTO END_CASE;

           GROUP:
               CALL INSERT(MOL,TOKEN.VAL);
               GOTO END_CASE;

           NUMBER:
               DO I = 1 TO TOKEN.VAL;
                   P$ATOM = CREATE(MOL,A$C);
                   CALL LINK(MOL,P$ATOM);
                   CALL CHANGE_CONTEXT(CONTEXT,P$ATOM,$NULL);
               END;
               GOTO END_CASE;

           END_CASE:

       END EXEC_SYM;
```

FIGURE 4.7 *PL/I code for EXEC_SYM.*

```
A: PROCEDURE;
      /*   Declarations  */
      B: PROCEDURE;
            /*   Declarations which do not include J   */
                   o
                   o
                   o
      LOOP1:
            DO J = 1 TO 10;
                      o
                      o
                      o
                   CALL  C;
                      o
                      o
                      o
            END;
                   o
                   o
                   o
      END B;
      C: PROCEDURE;
            /*   Declarations which do not include J   */
                   o
                   o
                   o
      LOOP2:
            DO J = 1 TO 20;
                   o
                   o
                   o
            END;
                   o
                   o
                   o
      END C;
            o
            o
            o
      CALL B;
            o
            o
            o
   END A;
```

FIGURE 4.8 *Inadvertent (undesired) information sharing among procedures.*

declared, it has attributes of FLOAT DECIMAL(6) by default, and the machine language instructions that manipulate B will assume this internal data format. Because the internal bit configuration of any given number in FIXED BINARY(31) format is not the same as that of the same number held in FLOAT DECIMAL(6) format, the value passed across the procedure boundary will be incorrectly interpreted.

The solution is to declare B within SAMPLE so that its attributes are identical to those of its corresponding argument. Note that the "artificial" requirement that the programmer declare all parameters forces understanding of the intended attributes. It supplies a checkpoint for verifying understanding of how and why the data is flowing across the procedure boundary. In order to determine the attributes, the

```
DECLARE A FIXED BINARY(31);
    o
    o
    o
SAMPLE:PROCEDURE(B);
    /*  Declarations which do not include B  */
        o
        o
        o
END SAMPLE;
    o
    o
    o
CALL SAMPLE(A);
```

FIGURE 4.9 *Mismatched parameters and arguments.*

programmer must understand the logical meaning and intended use in the procedure.

The use of mnemonic names as identifiers, names that in this case sound like what they represent, is an undeniable aid to communicating the intent of the code. Names such as I, J, and K seldom portray the content of the corresponding variable. Boyfriend's or girlfriend's names can be used to give a segment of code an interesting flair, but again, little conceptual information about the code is transferred to the reader. Usually an abbreviation of a word (or words, with the use of the underscore, or break character _) clearly conveys the meaning. For instance, ATOM_TAB might be used to designate the atom table, and MOL_NUM might be used to designate the molecular number. In general, identifier names should not be extremely long because they may have to be typed many times (that is why abbreviations are used). However, enough characters should be used to ensure clarity.

One way of keeping identifier names short while still conveying a maximum amount of information is to develop an encoding scheme for a significant portion of the identifiers. There are many ways of doing this, and you can develop your own scheme. Whatever your scheme, it should be well documented at the beginning of your program and used consistently throughout. In fact, for transportability between programs, and for your own sanity, it is advisable to develop such a scheme early in your programming career and stick with it. The scheme used throughout the code presented in this text is described below.

Identifiers are broken into two fields delimited by a special character, the dollar sign $. The first field indicates the mode or type of the variable and the second indicates the logical entity with which the variable is associated. Thus identifiers have the form

<type>$<association>

Examples are EBAD_CHAR, PNEXT, T$ATOM, and A$CL. These four identifiers stand for error code for a bad character, pointer to the next atom, type code for an atom, and atomic code for a chlorine atom, respectively. The possible character strings used for <type> and <association> can easily be defined within the documentation for reference but should be picked on the basis of their mnemonic content. It should be clear that $ essentially encodes the phrase *corresponding to*. Some of the possible values of $<type>$ and $<association>$ are given below.

$<type>$	Meaning
E	Error
P	Pointer
F	Flag
T	Type
A	Atom
G	Group

$<association>$	Meaning
FORM	Formula
NEXT	Next atom
EOM	End of molecule
ERROR	Error

All identifiers may not fall within such a classification scheme, because their meanings may not contain the concept of *corresponding to*. However, when a variable does fall within the scheme, its identifier can easily be determined, and the meaning of the variable can be extracted quickly by the reader. Such a scheme also can readily be extended to include new types and associations. The actual scheme employed is probably of little importance. Its consistent use throughout the program and its clear documentation are essential, however.

4.4 FORMATTING GUIDELINES

The way in which a program is presented on the printed page can influence significantly the ease with which it is understood and modified. This section supplies some basic formatting guidelines to enhance readability and make the different components of the text independently accessible so that they are easily modified.

4.4.1 Indentation

Proper indentation to indicate the subordinate nature of one set of statements with respect to another set is the single most important formatting convention for clarifying the structure of the program statements. The human eye is amazing. At a glance, a well-trained eye can extract the block and control structure of an appropriately indented code segment with virtually no reference to the keywords that actually produce the structure.

The concept that indentation is a primary cue indicating control structure is so universally accepted that languages have been defined and implemented in which indentation is the sole mechanism used to indicate which statements are subordinate to others (that is, no keywords are present to indicate this). In some installations utilizing well-structured languages such as PL/I, PASCAL, and ALGOL, preprocessors have been developed to scan a program, determine the structure (by identifying keywords), and change the indentation of the text to reflect the program structure.

In general, a textual block of code should be indented whenever it is subordinate to statements around it. For instance, indentation should be used whenever a new program block (a PROCEDURE block or BEGIN block) is entered. Similarly, indentation should be used to indicate the inside of a DO loop or DO group. It also can indicate the subordinate nature of the THEN and ELSE clauses of an IF statement. Continuation lines of a statement too long to fit on one line also should be indented.

Generally, 3 to 6 spaces is considered acceptable indentation. A 1- or 2-space indentation is difficult for the eye to discern. More than 6 spaces are not necessary and, after only a few levels of indentation, a significant portion of an 80-character line is unavailable. Five spaces is probably the most universally accepted indentation unit.

If one or more lines of comments are to be incorporated within the body of a procedure, they should be indented at least two units from the surrounding code. In-line comments are a secondary source of information. They normally will be read only if the code itself is not clear enough to convey the intent. If such comments are not indented at all, their presence can distract the reader and destroy the continuity of the primary source of information, the code itself. If the comments are indented only one unit, they still may distract the reader because they can be confused with subordinate code.

4.4.2 White Space

In the same way that the horizontal visual cue of indentation can be used to indicate structure, a vertical visual cue of several blank lines can be used to set off major code segments. Two to four blank lines can be inserted between logically independent code segments in order to indicate their logical separation.

4.4.3 Line Independence

In general, it is advisable not to incorporate two or more concepts within the same physical line of code. This facilitates subsequent modification. For instance, a label associated with a block of code should reside on a line by itself and not be textually connected to the first line of the code segment. This reduces the editing changes if, for instance, a new first line of code is to be inserted or the entire code segment is to be replaced.

Also, each identifier in a declaration should reside on a separate line. This makes it easy to insert or delete identifiers without having to modify lines.

4.5 DOCUMENTATION

Comments embedded in the body of the code should be sparse and should not interfere visually with the code itself. The code itself, by use of structured constructs and mnemonic variable names, normally will be sufficient to convey the algorithmic content to the reader. However, a few well-placed comments can help to clarify the intent, and any subtle or intricate code should be well documented.

What type of comments might be included? A one- or two-line comment indicating the logical intent of each major block of code is appropriate. Conditions being tested—for instance, in an IF or DO-WHILE—can be supported by comments to indicate the "external" condition being considered. Assertions about assumptions being made or conditions that are true at a given point in the code also can be helpful in clarifying why special tests are omitted or superfluous.

It is better to have no comment at all than to have one that is wrong. Often, when code is modified, the documenting comments are ignored. This practice may leave remnant information that does not reflect the current content of the code. The programmer must be able to stand back and view the product as a total package.

4.6 VERIFICATION

Verification is the process of checking that the intended meaning is realized in the actual implementation. This process is performed at all levels of the development, including the original design, the algorithmic specification, and the actual coding of the final implementation.

Verification of the code is inherited, to a great extent, from the verification of the pseudocode that motivates it. By the time the coding process is begun, there should be no question that the algorithm to be implemented is correct. The only question is whether or not the implementation code reflects the algorithmic content presented in the pseudocode.

In translating the content of the pseudocode into actual structured code, there is never any question about the meaning or intent of the constructs to control flow. This is the major reason for insisting that the implementation constructs for flow of control correspond with those in the structured design. If no new constructs are introduced during the translation, the validity of the implementation constructs is inherited from that of the design constructs.

Processes in the pseudocode may be described somewhat amorphously because their presentation is language independent, and concrete data structures may not have been specified. This is the major area in which verification must be performed. It must be shown that the conceptual content of the pseudocode is retained by the translated implementation code. This requires detailed knowledge of the data types, data structures, and operators available in the implementation language. It also may depend on knowledge of the quirks of the specific language processor.

Verification and debugging are not the same process. Verification is a "desk confirmation" that the program, when actually run, will produce the desired results. Debugging involves the execution of the program against actual test data. Obviously, they have similar goals in that both are to "prove" that the program is correct. Verification is a conceptual affirmation; debugging is a pragmatic affirmation. However, neither process actually proves that the program is, in fact, correct.

It is virtually impossible to test any significant piece of code under every possible input that it might encounter. (This is why hand verification is of paramount importance.) Generally, when debugging a program, sample test data are selected from a set of different classes or categories of expected input. However, there may be untested values (often "on the boundary" between categories) for which the code will not produce the desired results. These are the situations that hand verification is intended to detect. Debugging can be relegated to resolving problems such as keypunching errors, undeclared, misdeclared, or uninitialized variables, and implementation quirks of the compiler rather than verifying the correctness of the algorithm.

The disciplined use of these structured implementation constructs aids the reader in verifying the correctness of the code even when higher-level external documentation is not available. If the translation from the pseudocode to the implementation code is performed carefully, then the content of the pseudocode should be evident in the code itself. Thus the inverse translation to recapture the pseudocode would be a fairly simple matter, because the form and content of the pseudocode and implementation code are virtually identical. This means that if code is exported to an external installation and the external documentation is omitted (which is often the case), the understanding and verification of the code still can readily be accomplished. Of course, this depends on the familiarity of the reader with the structured constructs being used. If the writer uses this standard of structured programming and the reader is also familiar with it, then proper information transfer is easily accomplished.

4.7 SUMMARY

Structured programming is a style of implementation in which the programmer restricts himself or herself to a specific, well-defined, well-understood set of constructs for flow of control. These constructs are inherited from those used in the pseudocode produced during the design phase. The major reason for restricting oneself to these constructs is to establish a conceptual bridge between the design and the implementation such that the correspondence between design constructs and implementation constructs becomes essentially transparent. In this way, verification of the correctness of the implementation code is, for the most part, inherited from the verification that the design is correct.

The code produced by the implementation phase must be readable, understandable, modifiable, and verifiable. The style of presenting the code can drastically affect how well these goals are met. The consistent use of indentation and white space can be used as a visual aid to indicate structure. Consistent, well-thought-out selection of mnemonic variables names can help the reader extract the meaning of the code. Correct, well-placed documentation is an indispensable aid in describing the intent of the code. The manner in which lines of code are constructed can significantly affect the modifiability of the code.

The practice of declaring all variables is extremely important. This is an aspect that is missing in the design phase and must be filled in during the implementation phase. A significant percentage of implementation errors can be directly traced to incorrect declaration of variables and missing declarations. A declaration error is difficult to identify as such. This is one aspect of code verification that is not inherited from the design phase, and extreme caution must be taken.

In general, it is the programmer's responsibility to produce code that has a significant number of desirable properties. The skill and techniques used in producing the code significantly affects the usefulness of the final product. It cannot be stressed too strongly that consistency and application of the concepts presented in this chapter are paramount to the production of quality code.

PROBLEMS

In each of the next six problems, the given sequence of language statements is rather poorly structured. Rewrite the code so that the same processing is specified in accordance with the structural guidelines explained in the chapter. Assume that all of the variables referred to in these problems have been declared properly and that values have been assigned to them (none of their contents are indeterminate).

```
1.       X = 1.0;
         Y = 1.0;
  CMA:   IF Z >= 22.4*S THEN GO TO ZGTS;
         IF Z <= 18.8*T THEN GO TO ZLTT;
  ZGTS:  X = X*Z;
         Y = Y*X;
         Z = Z+X*Y;
         GO TO CMA;
  ZLTT:  X = X-S;
         PUT DATA (X);
```

```
2.      IF X < Y THEN GO TO XLTY;
        IF X < Z THEN GO TO XLTZ;
CBA:    X = X+T;
CBB:    Y = Y+Z;
CBC:    PUT DATA (X,Y); GO TO RES;
XLTY:   IF X < T THEN GO TO XLTT; GO TO CBA;
XLTT:   X = X-1; GO TO CBB;
XLTZ:   X = X+1; GO TO CBC;
RES:    PUT DATA(Z);


3.      IF X < Y(1) THEN GO TO XLTY;
        IF X < Y(2) THEN GO TO XLTY2;
        IF X < Y(3) THEN GO TO XLTY3;
        IF X < Y(4) THEN GO TO XLTY4;
XLTY2:  X = 1.27*X;
LBA:    PUT DATA(X); GO TO RES;
XLTY:   X = X+4; IF X < Z THEN GO TO XLTZ;
        X = X+1.5; GO TO LBA;
XLTZ:   X = X+0.5*Z;
XLTY3:  X = X+0.7*Y(3); GO TO LBA;
XLTY4:  X = X+0.82*Y(4); GO TO LBA;
RES:    PUT DATA(Y);


4.      Y = 0;
        X = 0;
C1:     X = X+1;
C2:     Y = Y+LOG(X+0.05);
C3:     IF X < S THEN GO TO C1; X = X-LOG(S);
        IF X >= T THEN GO TO C2;
        X = X-0.18*T; IF X >= T THEN GO TO C3;
        PUT DATA (X,Y,S,T);


5.      I = 1;
        X = 1;
SA:     Z = Z+T(I)**X;
SB:     T(I) = T(I)+X;
SC:     S(I) = S(I)+T(I);
        IF S(I) > Z THEN GO TO SD; X = X+S(I);
        I = I+1; GO TO SA;
SD:     IF X > U THEN GO TO SE; X = X+1; GO TO SB;
SE:     IF I >= K THEN GO TO SF; I = I+1; GO TO SC;
SF:     PUT DATA(X,Z);


6.          IF LEVTAG = 2 THEN GO TO L740;
            IF LEVTAG > 2 THEN GO TO L750;
                        IF ADIFF <= 0 THEN GO TO L800;
    L725:   IF ADIFF >= QCEPS THEN GO TO L800;
    L730:   IF ADIFF <= CEPSF THEN GO TO L770;
            LEVTAG = 0;
            CEPS = ADIFF;
            EFACT = EFACT + CEPST*(X1-XZERO);
            XZERO = X1;
            GO TO L800;
    L740:   LEVTAG = 0;
            IF ADIFF <= 0 THEN GO TO L765; ELSE GO TO L725;
    L750:   LEVTAG = 0;
            IF ADIFF <= 0 THEN GO TO L775; ELSE GO TO L730;
      L765: CEPS = ADIFF1; GO TO L775;
```

```
L70:    LEVTAG = -1;
        FACERR = 1.0;
        CEPS = CEPSF;
L775:   EFACT = EFACT + CEPST*(X1-XZERO);
        XZERO = X1;
        QCEPS = 0.25*CEPS;
L800:
```

7. In order to encourage the use of efficient equipment, the Hadley's Mound Power and Light Company has set its industrial rates so that they are influenced by the type of motor equipment being used, as well as the amount of usage itself. The following schedule is in effect.

Motor Model	Rate
326W	$32.1 + 0.08*U$
14J3	$18.2 + 0.072*U**0.79$ (for $U < 30$)
	$17.9 + 0.068*U**0.68$ (for $U \geq 30$)
B3XY	$26.7 + 0.077*U**1.08$
C6	$38.08 + 0.113*U**1.72$

where U is some measure of usage favored by Hadley's Mound. In addition to the schedule given above, there are special considerations regarding Model C6. Unlike the other models, it can be equipped with one of several modifications, each of which has its own effect on the rate. (Assume that these modifications are mutually exclusive.)

(1) If the C6 has a racing option (never mind what a racing option is; suffice it to say that it is something left over from the Old Days and its owner neglected to have it removed), the rate is increased by $0.008*U**0.163$.

(2) If the C6 is equipped with an extra filter, the rate is discounted by 7 1/2 percent.

(3) If the C6 has a precipitator on it, the rate is decreased by $0.0116*U**0.087$.

Assume that, in some particular software design, it is reasonable to construct the process of determining rates as a single module.

a. Design this module and describe your design in terms of a complete pseudocode description. (What are the input and output parameters?)

b. Write the code corresponding to the pseudocode in (a). Be sure to include appropriate internal and external documentation. (What encodements should be used? Do the constants themselves reside in the code?)

8. Whiteknuckle Airlines is not very large. There is a possibility that you may not have heard of it. However, it exists, and it provides desperately needed service

for the cities of Acne, Beedville, Clay Pile, and Drudge Corners. The cost of flying between two given cities depends on the type (class) of ticket being purchased. Whiteknuckle offers a variety of plans, as summarized below.

(1) *First Class (F).* This is top-grade service. The plastic spoons actually are thrown away (under government supervision) after each flight.

(2) *Coach (Y).* This is standard service. Passengers correctly identifying the entree on meal flights do not have to eat it.

(3) *Night Coach (N).* This is the no-frills plan, available only after 11:00 P.M. Those passengers who remember to bring flashlights can read magazines, if they remember to bring magazines.

(4) *Excursion (E).* This is the rock-bottom economy plan, requiring its users to book at least 14 months in advance, pay for the tickets when they are booked, and give up the right to cancel within 6 months of the flight.

The following table summarizes the rate schedule. For convenience, we shall refer to the four plans as F, Y, N, and E (as defined above) and the four cities will be abbreviated A, B, C, and D. The rates given are for round trips. Whiteknuckle books only round trips that follow the same plan both ways; that is, a Whiteknuckle passenger cannot go from A to B on plan Y and then return on plan N.

Between	F	Y	N	E
A and B	$207	$193	$184	$179
A and C	—	$118	$104	$ 88
A and D	$241	$225	—	$211
B and C	$188	$179	$171	—
B and D	—	$ 89	—	—
C and D	$ 96	$ 91	$ 88	$ 86

The story is not complete. The schedule given above is qualified as follows.

(5) Between A and B, plan N is not available on Tuesdays.

(6) Between A and B, plan E carries a 5 percent discount if either leg of the flight (A to B or B to A) is taken on a Saturday.

(7) Between A and C, there is no plan N on Wednesdays or Sundays. (We have seen already that there is no plan F altogether between these cities).

(8) Between B and C, there is no plan N on Saturdays or Sundays. (There is no plan E for these cities at any time.)

(9) Between C and D, plan N applies only on Mondays. (That is, both legs of a plan-N trip must be taken on a Monday.)

(10) Between C and D, plan E is not available Monday, Tuesday, Thursday, or Saturday.

Assume that the designer of the overall data-processing software for Whiteknuckle has identified the need for a module that takes the appropriate reservation information for a given passenger and computes one item of information: the cost of the ticket between the two cities specified as its input. (What if there is no service for the specific reservation?)

a. Using the structure diagram notation (Chap. 2), describe the module in terms of its input and output requirements.

b. Develop a detailed pseudocode description of the module consistent with the structure diagram fragment in (a). Consider at least two alternative methods: table-driven and hard-coded. Which is better?

c. Write the code for the module described in the pseudocode in (b).

9. Imagine the surprise at Whiteknuckle's world headquarters when it was discovered that there were passengers who wanted to book more complex trips. Before this time when a passenger wanted to travel A to D to C to A, for example, he or she had to drive or take the bus. No more. Whiteknuckle is ready to provide such service. To do so, it had to adjust its rules for fare determination. When the dust settled, two adjustments were made.

(1) Each itinerary is considered as a collection of one-way trips. Fare for a one-way trip is half the round-trip amount.

(2) To encourage use of Whiteknuckle, generosity will enter into the picture: The rates charged for all the legs of an itinerary are taken from the most economical plan used in that itenerary. Thus, if a passenger books a four-flight itinerary (for instance) and only one of those four legs is booked under plan N, all four legs will be charged at plan-N rates, even though the actual scheduling may violate the plan's criteria. (Plan E is excluded from all of this because the entire trip has to be booked under that plan anyway.) If that particular plan is not available between two of the cities on the trip, the next higher available rate is used. Note that a two-leg round trip does not qualify for this adjustment. (For instance, the trip A-D-A is subject to the rules given in the previous problem; however, the trip A-C-D-A is eligible for the new rules.)

The airline's software designer would like to make use of the module designed earlier (in the previous problem). Specifically, since that module computes the round trip fare between two given cities for a given plan, it could (presumably) be integrated into a more comprehensive process that takes half of that computed amount and uses it as a leg of a more extensive itinerary. With that idea in mind, do these problems.

a. Prepare a structure diagram for a process that computes the total fare for a given itinerary. Be sure to include all input and output requirements. Note that the trip does not necessarily have to finish where it starts.

b. Develop a detailed pseudocode representation for each of the modules identified in (*a*).

c. Write the code for each of the modules developed in (*b*). Be sure to include appropriate documentation. How does the use of specific encodements help to simplify the code? What are the advantages or disadvantages (in this application) of table-driven design versus the hard-coded alternative?

10. Crankshaft Car Rental offers six kinds of automobiles for rent, each with its own rental plan.

(1) A Phantom rents for $25 per day plus 15 cents per mile, gas included.

(2) A LaFong rents for $22 per day plus 18 cents per mile, gas included.

(3) A Pineapple rents for $100 per week or any part thereof. There is no mileage charge and the customer pays for the gas. Mileage is guaranteed to be no worse than 22 miles per gallon.

(4) A Carbuncle rents for $24 per day. The first 50 miles are free. After that, it is 12 cents per mile. The customer pays for all the gas, and mileage is guaranteed not to be worse than 20 miles per gallon.

(5) A Fetlock rents for $89 per half week in increments of half weeks (3 days, 12 hours). There is no mileage charge and the customer pays for the gas, with mileage guaranteed to be no worse than 18 miles per gallon.

(6) An El Frumpo rents for $32 per day. The first 150 miles are free. After that, there is a charge of 15 cents per mile. The customer pays for all the gas, and mileage is guaranteed to be no worse than 15 miles per gallon. (The El Frumpo is a wonderful luxury vehicle).

a. Develop a pseudocode representation for a module named CRANK_MIN that determines the minimum amount of money required to rent a Crankshaft vehicle to drive a specified distance over a specified time period. Along with the dollar amount, CRANK_MIN should specify the corresponding type of auto. In this design, you may choose to delegate certain functions to subordinate modules. If you do so, include a structure diagram indicating all input/output requirements.

b. Write the code for the module(s) designed in (*a*). (Are table-driven techniques appropriate here?)

11. Using the Crankshaft rental information defined in Problem 10, design (and express in pseudocode) a module named CRANK_CHOICE for which the input includes a dollar amount in addition to the time and distance given before.

This time, the module is to determine whether or not it is possible to rent a Crankshaft auto for the specified amount *or less* and still fulfill the other requirements. Accordingly, CRANK_CHOICE is to indicate this and, if possible, the module is to enumerate the choices, with the least-expensive choice first. Code the module(s).

12. An algorithm that finds frequent use in a wide variety of applications is the *binary search*. This is a relatively simple and efficient process for searching a collection of items (such as a table) to determine whether or not a particular item (the input) is in that table. Success is usually indicated by delivering an output value indicating the position of the matching item in the table; failure is indicated by an output of zero or some other special signal.

   The major reason for the technique's efficiency lies in the fact that it is not necessary to examine every item in the table to establish success or failure. This is made possible by requiring that the items in the table be arranged (sorted) in ascending or descending order, thereby enabling entire portions of a table to be rejected on the basis of their respective bounds.

   Figure 4.10 shows a pseudocode representation for a basic binary search procedure. (The operational details are included). A look at the pseudocode should reveal that all is not well. The search will work properly for many cases, but not for *all* cases. Find the difficulties and correct the pseudocode. Then write the corresponding code for the corrected version.

13. A variation of the binary search algorithm (Prob. 12) involves a type of process in which an exact match, while desirable, is not crucial. If the value being sought is in the table, well and good; if not, it is useful to know the value of the nearest entries on either side of the input value, along with their respective locations.

   a. Develop a detailed pseudocode representation for a module whose input consists of a table name (TBLNAME), table size (TBLSIZE), search value (SRCHVAL), and tolerance level (EPSILON). The tolerance level is the largest absolute difference between a table entry and SRCHVAL that the user is willing to treat as a zero difference. If EPSILON is not specified, your module is to use a default value of 1.0E-4. Using this input, the module is to deliver the location and value (LOWINDX and LOWVAL, respectively) of the nearest table entry lower than SRCHVAL, and the location and value (HIGHINDX and HIGHVAL, respectively) of the nearest table entry greater than SRCHVAL. (*Note:* It is up to you to figure out how to report an ''exact'' match or a situation where SRCHVAL is less than the lowest table value or greater than the highest table value).

   b. Write the code corresponding to the result developed in (*a*).

   c. Generalize the design in (*a*) so that it will handle either numeric or character data. (*Note:* When a table's entries consist of arbitrary strings of characters, *lower than* means earlier in alphanumeric order. This order is linked to the

```
Define TBLSIZE, LMARGIN, RMARGIN, VALUE, TABLE, INDX.

Set LMARGIN to 0;
    RMARGIN to TBLSIZE + 1.

Set INDX to (LMARGIN + RMARGIN - 1)/2.

WHILE (INDX is not equal to LMARGIN)

       IF VALUE = TABLE INDX  THEN
            print INDX (search is successful).
            terminate.
       ELSE
            IF VALUE < TABLE INDX  THEN
                 Set RMARGIN to INDX.
            ELSE
                 Set LMARGIN to INDX.
            ENDIF
            Set INDX to (LMARGIN + RMARGIN - 1)/2.
       ENDIF

ENDWHILE

Set INDX to zero.
Print INDX (unsuccessful search).
```

FIGURE 4.10 *Binary search procedure for Problem 12.*

collating sequence built into the design of the particular processor (not language) you are using.)

14. Referring to Problems 2 and 3 from Chapter 2, prepare a pseudocode representation for a module that computes the variance and standard deviation. Input and output requirements for the module should be consistent with the structure diagram you developed from Figure 2.9. Use this as a basis for coding the resulting module.

15. Regardless of the type of internal processing that is performed, the displays described in Chapter 2, Problems 5, 6, 21, 22, 23, 24, 25, or 26 all need to be printed. Prepare a pseudocode description of a histogram printing module that will accept as many of these variations as possible. Write the corresponding code from your pseudocode.

16. Referring to Problem 7 in Chapter 2, we see that an essential component for that type of software is one that isolates an individual sentence from an arbitrarily long text in natural form. Consider the ways in which a sentence may start and end, and—based on those considerations—prepare a pseudocode representation for a module that isolates the next sentence in a text. You may assume that the text is available (as input) in 80-character increments with characters 72-80 being reserved for sequencing. Also available is the location of the next character to be examined relative to the beginning of the 80-character segment in which it resides. For convenience, you may impose a 256-character limit on the size of any one sentence.

Case Study—An Implementation

5

Now that we have some techniques for transforming a design into an actual program, we can turn our attention to the software design developed in Chapter 3. This chapter develops a specific implementation (of course, there are many) for that design. During this development, many implementation decisions will be made which have perfectly reasonable alternatives, some of which will be presented in Section 5.5.

All of the PL/I code presented in this chapter is executable and runs under PL/C-R7.6. The codes, data sets, and outputs all have been extracted directly from executing programs. This product was developed by employing incremental implementation, an indispensible technique for developing large software systems.

5.1 INCREMENTAL IMPLEMENTATION

Incremental implementation can be defined as the process of implementing a software product by the incorporation of a series of phases (either sequentially or in parallel), each phase producing a functionally self-contained segment of the system. In this section we shall discuss the need for incremental implementation, partitioning of the implementation phases, and methods for producing the corresponding implementations so that they can be combined to produce the desired software product.

5.1.1 Need for Incremental Implementation

A given software product may be extremely large, both in terms of the number of modules and the number of lines of code. Because of the complexity of programming languages, the complexity of large software systems, and the realization that people are inherently error prone, it is axiomatic that a large software product cannot be coded and debugged in a single phase. The inevitable problem of identifying and eliminating errors is just too complex for people to solve when there is a large amount of information (coding) to be scanned and many components (modules) involved in the processing being performed. We must use some vehicle or mechanism, such as incremental implementation, to reduce the complexity.

For instance, the software product treated in this chapter contains 28 procedures, approximately 1800 records (lines), and approximately 470 PL/I statements. Suppose that someone sits down and codes the entire program, and after eliminating keypunching errors, the program is run. If there are no compilation or execution errors, but the program produces the wrong answer (this assumption is not at all outlandish), where should the programmer start to look for the logic errors?

- Input module: Maybe the data were not read correctly.

- Processing of the data: This is the probable place of the error. However, this constitutes the bulk of the program.

- Output module: The correct answers may really be there but are being displayed incorrectly.

There is no way of selecting the component of the program to which the programmer should turn his or her initial attention. In most cases, there are many errors (10 to 15 errors is probably a conservative estimate for a product of the size mentioned before). These errors often interact with one another. Even if a specific error can be identified and "corrected," interaction with the remainder of the erroneous system makes it impossible to verify that the error was resolved adequately. (Novice programmers might infer that the above scenario is not commonplace and these problems will not riddle *their* programs. However, the seasoned programmer recognizes these problems as the rule, not the exception.) In short, large pieces of newly created code do not lend themselves to effective debugging. Therefore some technique—such as stubs and drivers and incremental implementation—must be employed to reduce the amount of newly written code that the programmer must juggle at any given time.

5.1.2 Selection of Components for Implementation in a Phase

The components to be included in a given implementation phase should constitute a portion of the system that is relatively functionally independent of the remainder of the system. Each component should be independently implemented and debugged to verify its correctness. The completion of an implementation phase occurs when these separate components are collected together, interfaced in roughly the manner that they will interact in the final product, and tested *as an integrated whole*. These tests must verify (at least empirically) that the desired results are obtained for specific test data. Completion of an implementation phase is a "checkpoint," at which it is established that a functionally complete segment of the final software product performs as desired.

Why are separate implementation phases useful? Why not just implement and debug each individual module of the final software product and interface them all together in a single implementation phase? There are several reasons for incorporating these intermediate checkpoints.

- The choice of internal data structures may have been inappropriate or may be inconsistent across modules.

- The method chosen for passing parameters may be inappropriate. For instance, problems encountered during an intermediate phase may indicate that it is preferable to pass a parameter explicitly through a parameter list instead of globally (or vice versa). It may be important to pass a parameter "by value" instead of "by address."

- The interfaces between modules may not be consistent. For instance, two arguments may be passed to a module invoked in one place, whereas three arguments may be passed to the same module, invoked in another place.

- An incorrect or incomplete functional definition may have been selected for incorporation into a module. When tested alone, it may perform the function it was implemented to perform, but this may not be sufficient to perform the ultimate task.

The point here is that the design gives only a rough outline of how to produce the implementation. It is during implementation that specific alternatives are selected. It must be verified that these implementation decisions are consistent with one another and that the integrated result performs in the prescribed manner. Often, the interaction between certain modules is so intimate or complex that it is not possible to verify *completely* the correctness of a module without interfacing it with others. (Such is often the case if indirect recursion is involved.) Again, the completion of an implementation phase is a checkpoint for verifying that the components implemented thus far perform as anticipated. If something is to be corrected, it should be identified *as soon as possible* to reduce the need for subsequent changes.

The software product produced in this chapter will be implemented in three phases. These are depicted by the structure diagrams shown in Figures 5.1-5.3 and will be discussed in detail in Sections 5.2, 5.3, and 5.4. Prior to that, we call attention to the flexibility derived from the top-down design.

Notice that the modules can be moved around in relation to one another. It is not necessary to configure them in the way that they will interface in the final software product. Such mobility allows modules to be moved easily from one context to another; it is an important aspect of incremental implementation. For instance, GET_FORM is related to SCAN_FORM in a different way in all three phases. This can be done only because the function of GET_FORM is completely

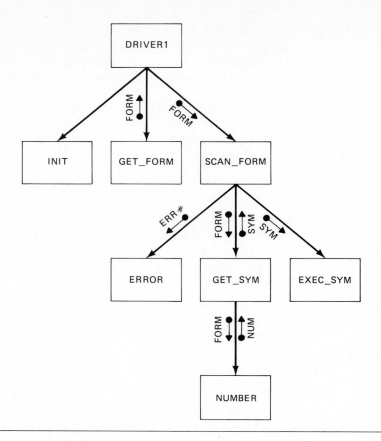

FIGURE 5.1 *Structure diagram for Phase 1.*

independent of that of SCAN_FORM. This functional independence is derived from the way in which we decomposed the original problem during the design phase. It should now be apparent why the design phase is so important, and that the philosophy employed during the design phase affects the ease with which incremental implementation can effectively be utilized.

The particular phases suggested here constitute, for the most part, a bottom-up implementation philosophy because modules at the *bottom* of the structure diagram are implemented in early phases and modules *farther up* in the structure diagram are implemented in later phases. A ''pipeline'' implementation philosophy is also used: Modules implemented in early phases are used in subsequent phases. Neither of these philosophies *need* be employed during an implementation. Once the design phase is complete, the implementer is free to implement in any order he or she desires (by selecting the particular modules to included in any given implementation phase). The choice of which modules to include in a given implementation phase can be affected by many factors, among which are the following.

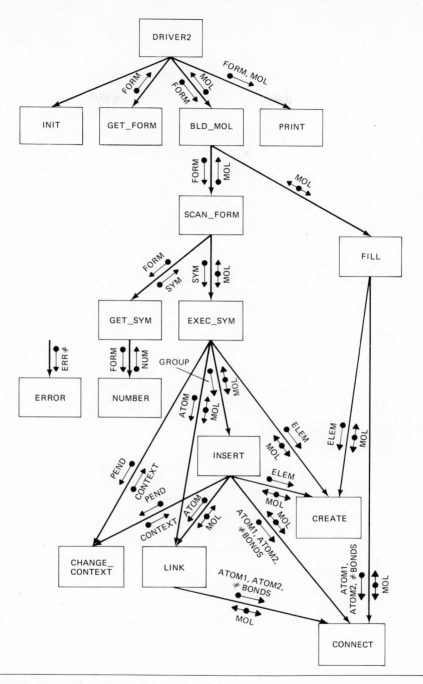

FIGURE 5.2 *Structure diagram for Phase 2.*

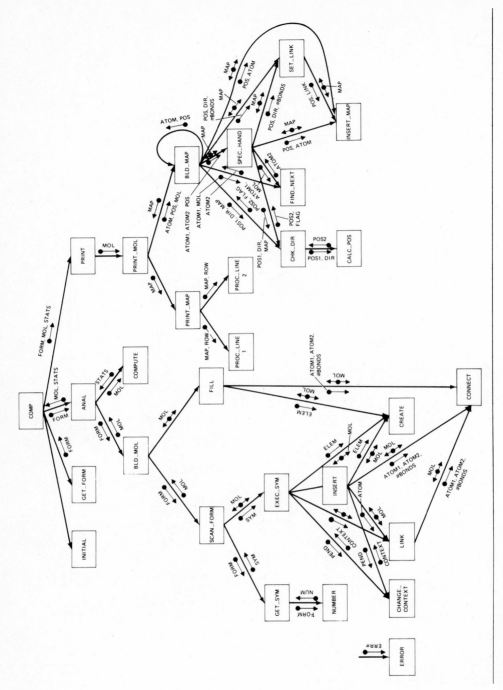

FIGURE 5.3 *Total decomposition of problem.*

- Functional completeness of the implementation phase.

- Personal preference of the implementer.

- Amount of the design completed at the time that implementation starts.

- External time requirements that certain subfunctions of the final product be available to the user.

5.1.3 Stubs and Drivers

The implementer can implement modules in any order he or she chooses. Let us assume that a specific module A has been selected to be implemented first. How can this be done if the module that invokes A and the modules that are invoked by A do not already exist? "Artificial" modules, known as stubs and drivers, can be written to simulate the actions of these temporarily absent modules. A module that simulates the invocation of A is called a *driver,* and a module that simulates a module invoked by A is called a *stub.*

Referring to Figure 5.3, assume that the implementer chooses to develop PRINT first. (This may be selected so that the end user can see exactly what statistics are to be calculated and the format in which they will be displayed. Thus the design can be changed early in the process if the statistics are not what the end user desires.) Obviously, the code for PRINT can be written exactly as it will appear in the final product, but how do we test PRINT to insure that it performs correctly? PRINT interfaces with two modules, COMP and PRINT_MOL. These two modules must be simulated by a driver and a stub, respectively. The stub for PRINT_MOL (it should have exactly the same name and interfaces as the final module) can be completely vacuous; whenever it is invoked, it simply returns, having printed and computed nothing. (Alternatively, it might print a message stating that it was invoked.) The driver somehow must obtain values for FORM and STATS and invoke PRINT with the appropriate protocol. (MOL may be left undefined since it is not used inside PRINT.) An appropriate method for obtaining these values might be to read them from cards. Alternatively, they might be calculated inside the driver by some trivial algorithm. Notice that the values in STATS need not be consistent with FORM, nor need they be consistent with themselves. All PRINT must do is print the data with which it is supplied. By using this technique, the complete version of PRINT that will reside in the final software product can be developed. No changes *at all* will have to be made as the surrounding context is incrementally supplied.

Returning to the more general situation, most modules can be developed independently of the remainder of the system by simulating the missing context via these drivers and stubs. Drivers are all very much alike; their standard function is to do the following.

- Obtain data necessary for the module to be invoked.

- Invoke the module with the correct protocol.

- Print any results returned by the module.

Stubs, on the other hand, have a variety of forms. A stub normally has one of three basic intents.

1. It is completely vacuous and performs no function at all. The stub for PRINT_MOL discussed earlier is such an example. This type of stub can always be used to simulate a module that does not change the internal state of the program. (What might a stub for PRINT look like?)

2. It simulates (partially or totally) the actions of the module for which it is a surrogate. An example (ERROR) will be given in Section 5.2.

3. It performs no simulation at all but is used to instrument some aspect of the system. Such a stub is also known as a *hook*. An example (EXEC_SYM) will be given in Section 5.2.

5.2 PHASE 1—EXTRACTING SYMBOLS

5.2.1 Functional Content

Phase 1 (Fig. 5.1) will implement that portion of the software product that reads a formula and sequentially extracts symbols (tokens) from it. It must be verified that the symbols on the card are legal (for instance, there are no illegal characters), but no assessment is to be made as to whether the formula, as a whole, represents a legal molecule. The internal representation is not to be built, nor are any statistics to be calculated or printed.

5.2.2 The Code

DRIVER1 must supply the necessary context in which the remaining modules will execute. Figure 5.4 presents a list of "constants" and structures that supply this needed context. The following identifier naming scheme will be used for certain categories of constants.

- Variables starting with T$ represent numeric encodements for types of tokens.

- Variables starting with A$ represent numeric encodements for specific atoms.

- Variables starting with G$ represent numeric encodements for specific groups.

- Variables starting with E$ are numeric encodements for error messages.

Figure 5.5 shows the computational content of DRIVER1. Notice that it is a completely coordinating procedure (Sec. 3.2.2.1).

The code for GET_FORM, SCAN_FORM, GET_SYM, and NUMBER are

```
DCL (           /* TYPES OF TOKENS */
      T$ERROR     INIT(0),  /* ERROR */
      T$ATOM INIT(1),        /* ATOM */
      T$GROUP INIT(2),       /* GROUP */
      T$NUM INIT(3),         /* NUMBER (OR CARBON CHAIN) */
      T$EOM INIT(4),         /* END OF MOLECULE */


           /* ATOMS */
      A$H INIT(1),     /* HYDROGEN */
      A$C INIT(2),     /* CARBON */
      A$N INIT(3),     /* NITROGEN */
      A$O INIT(4),     /* OXYGEN */
      A$F INIT(5),     /* FLUORINE */
      A$S INIT(6),     /* SULFUR */
      A$CL INIT(7),    /* CHLORINE */
      A$BR INIT(8),    /* BROMINE */
      A$I INIT(9),     /* IODINE */


           /* GROUPS */
      G$Q_OH INIT(1),     /* Q GROUP */
      G$V_C#O INIT(2),    /* V GROUP */
      G$W_O2 INIT(3),     /* W GROUP */
      G$M_NH INIT(4),     /* M GROUP */
      G$Z_NH2 INIT(5),    /* Z GROUP */
      G$U_DE INIT(6),     /* DOUBLE BOND */


           /* ERRORS */
      E$BAD_CHAR INIT(1),


           /* MISC. */
      #MOL INIT(1),        /* # OF POSSIBLE ATOMS IN MOL */
      #GROUPS INIT(6)      /* NUMBER OF GROUPS */
                 ) FIXED BIN(15),


      F$ERROR BIT(1),           /* ERROR FLAG */


      (           /* BOOLEAN */
      TRUE INIT('1'B),
      FALSE INIT('0'B)
                 ) BIT(1),


      ATOMS CHAR(A$I-A$H+1) VARYING,
      GROUPS CHAR(#GROUPS) INIT('QVWMZU');


DCL 1 FORM,      /* FORMULA */
      2 S_FORM CHAR(81) VARYING,
      2 T_FORM CHAR(81) VARYING,
      2 P$FORM FIXED BIN(15);


DCL 1 MOL,            /* INTERNAL REPRESENTATION */
      2 REP,
          3 CONNECTION(#MOL,#MOL) FIXED BIN(15),
          3 ATOM_CORR(#MOL) FIXED BIN(15),
          3 P$NEXT FIXED BIN(15),
      2 CONTEXT,
          3 #BONDS FIXED BIN(15),
          3 ATOM_PEND(2) FIXED BIN(15);
```

FIGURE 5.4 *Data context for Phase 1.*

```
ON ENDFILE(SYSIN) STOP;

CALL INIT;
DO WHILE(TRUE);                    /* UNTIL EOF */
    CALL GET_FORM(FORM);
    PUT SKIP(3) EDIT('FORMULA ANALYZED:',S_FORM)(A);
    CALL SCAN_FORM(FORM,MOL);
END;
```

FIGURE 5.5 *PL/I for* DRIVER1.

shown in Figures 5.6–5.9. These modules are relatively straightforward and will not be discussed further.

The code for INIT is shown in Figure 5.10. It contains a statement that initializes the value of the character "constant" ATOMS. In some sense, this version of INIT is a stub; it will be modified in a subsequent phase to extract the characters corresponding to the different atoms from the structure ATOM_TAB. In this way, the software product can be made somewhat self-adapting. Whenever

```
/***************************************************************/
/*                                                           */
/*                      GET_FORM                             */
/*                                                           */
/*    THIS PROCEDURE GETS THE NEXT CARD FROM THE CARD READER */
/*    AND TRANSLATES IT.                                     */
/*        OUTPUT PARAMETERS:                                 */
/*            IN FORM:                                       */
/*            S_FORM - SOURCE FORM                           */
/*            T_FORM - TRANSLATED FORM                       */
/*            P$FORM - POINTER TO THE FORM                   */
/*                                                           */
/***************************************************************/


    GET_FORM: PROC(FORM);

        DCL 1 FORM,
            2 S_FORM CHAR(*) VARYING,
            2 T_FORM CHAR(*) VARYING,
            2 P$FORM FIXED BIN(15);


        GET EDIT(S_FORM)(COL(1),A(80));
        S_FORM = S_FORM || ' ';
        T_FORM = TRANSLATE(S_FORM,
            'BAAAAAAAAAGGGGGGDDDDDDDDDDDIII',
            ' HCNOFSGEIQVWMZU0123456789ADB');
        P$FORM = 1;


    END GET_FORM;
```

FIGURE 5.6 *PL/I code for* GET_FORM.

```
/**************************************************************************/
/*                                                                      */
/*                         SCAN_FORM                                    */
/*                                                                      */
/*      THE PURPOSE OF THIS PROCEDURE IS TO COORDINATE                  */
/*      THE SCANNING OF THE TOTAL CHEMICAL FORMULA.                     */
/*      IT REPEATEDLY INVOKES GET_SYM AND EXEC_SYM UNTIL                */
/*      THE END OF THE FORMULA (T$EOM) IS REACHED. IF AN                */
/*      ERROR IS ENCOUNTERED, AN ERROR MESSAGE IS PRINTED.              */
/*                                                                      */
/*          INPUT-OUTPUT PARAMETERS:                                    */
/*              FORM - THE CHEMICAL FORMULA                             */
/*              MOL  - THE MOLECULE                                     */
/*                          NOT CURRENTLY USED                          */
/*                                                                      */
/**************************************************************************/

        SCAN_FORM: PROC(FORM,MOL);

            DCL 1 FORM,
                2 S_FORM CHAR(*) VARYING,
                2 T_FORM CHAR(*) VARYING,
                2 P$FORM FIXED BIN(15);

            DCL 1 TOKEN,
                2 TYPE FIXED BIN(15),
                2 VAL FIXED BIN(15);

            DCL 1 MOL,            /*  INTERNAL REPRESENTATION  */
                2 REP,
                    3 CONNECTION(*,*) FIXED BIN(15),
                    3 ATOM_CORR(*) FIXED BIN(15),
                    3 P$NEXT FIXED BIN(15),
                2 CONTEXT,
                    3 #BONDS FIXED BIN(15),
                    3 ATOM_PEND(*) FIXED BIN(15);

            CALL GET_SYM(FORM,TOKEN);
            DO WHILE(TOKEN.TYPE ¬= T$EOM);
                IF TOKEN.TYPE = T$ERROR THEN
                    CALL ERROR(TOKEN.VAL);
                ELSE CALL EXEC_SYM(TOKEN,MOL);

                CALL GET_SYM(FORM,TOKEN);
            END;

        END SCAN_FORM;
```

FIGURE 5.7 *PL/I code for* SCAN FORM.

another atom is to be recognized by the system, it only need be added to ATOM_TAB and the remainder of the system will adapt accordingly.

The code for ERROR is shown in Figure 5.11. It is a stub that simply prints the error number passed to it. In a subsequent phase, this procedure will be modified to print a more meaningful error message. However, during the development of the product, the error number is sufficient for the programmer to determine which error

```
/******************************************************************/
/*                                                              */
/*                      GET_SYM                                 */
/*                                                              */
/*   THIS PROCEDURE EXTRACTS A TOKEN FROM THE FORMULA           */
/*   AND DETERMINES ITS INTERPRETATION.  TOKENS ARE             */
/*   CLASSIFIED INTO ONE OF 5 CATEGORIES:                       */
/*          1) ERROR                                            */
/*          2) ATOM                                             */
/*          3) GROUP                                            */
/*          4) NUMBER                                           */
/*          5) END OF MOLECULE                                  */
/*                                                              */
/*   NOTE THAT THE VALUES ASSIGNED TO TOKEN.VAL AND             */
/*   TOKEN.TYPE CORRESPOND TO SPECIFIC "CONSTANTS"              */
/*   DEFINED IN THE MAIN PROCEDURE.                             */
/*      INPUT-OUTPUT PARAMETER:                                 */
/*          FORM - THE FORMULA                                  */
/*      OUTPUT PARAMETERS:                                      */
/*          TOKEN - THE INTERPRETED FORMULA                     */
/*                                                              */
/******************************************************************/


        GET_SYM: PROC(FORM,TOKEN);

            DCL 1 FORM,      /* FORMULA */
                  2 S_FORM CHAR(*) VARYING,
                  2 T_FORM CHAR(*) VARYING,
                  2 P$FORM FIXED BIN(15);

            DCL 1 TOKEN,      /* TOKEN */
                  2 TYPE FIXED BIN(15),
                  2 VAL FIXED BIN(15);

            DCL CASE(T$ERROR:T$EOM) LABEL INIT(BAD,ATOM,GROUP,NUM,BLANK);

            TOKEN.TYPE = INDEX('AGDB',SUBSTR(T_FORM,P$FORM,1));

            GOTO CASE(TOKEN.TYPE);

            BAD:
                  TOKEN.VAL= E$BAD_CHAR;
                  P$FORM = P$FORM + 1;
                  GOTO END_CASE;

            ATOM:
                  TOKEN.VAL = INDEX(ATOMS,SUBSTR(S_FORM,P$FORM,1));
                  P$FORM = P$FORM + 1;
                  GOTO END_CASE;

            GROUP:
                  TOKEN.VAL = INDEX(GROUPS,SUBSTR(S_FORM,P$FORM,1));
                  P$FORM = P$FORM + 1;
                  GOTO END_CASE;

            NUM:
                  TOKEN.VAL = NUMBER(FORM);
                  GOTO END_CASE;

            BLANK:
                  GOTO END_CASE;

            END_CASE:

        END GET_SYM;
```

FIGURE 5.8 *PL/I code for* GET_SYM.

```
/*****************************************************************/
/*                                                             */
/*                        NUMBER                               */
/*                                                             */
/*  THIS PROCEDURE EXTRACTS A NUMBER FROM THE CARD.            */
/*        INPUT PARAMETERS:                                    */
/*           IN CARD:                                          */
/*              S_CARD - SOURCE CARD                           */
/*              T_CARD - TRANSLATED CARD                       */
/*              P$CARD - POINTER TO THE CARD                   */
/*        OUTPUT PARAMETERS:                                   */
/*              NUM    - THE NUMBER EXTRACTED                  */
/*                                                             */
/*****************************************************************/


          NUMBER: PROC(CARD) RETURNS(FIXED BIN(15));


               DCL NUM FIXED BIN(15);          /* VALUE TO BE RETURNED  */
               DCL 1 CARD,
                   2 S_CARD CHAR(*) VARYING,
                   2 T_CARD CHAR(*) VARYING,
                   2 P$CARD FIXED BIN(15);


               NUM = 0;
               DO WHILE(SUBSTR(T_CARD,P$CARD,1) = 'D');
                   NUM = 10*NUM + INDEX('0123456789',
                         SUBSTR(S_CARD,P$CARD,1)) - 1;
                   P$CARD = P$CARD + 1;
               END;
               RETURN(NUM);


          END NUMBER;
```

FIGURE 5.9 *PL/I code for* NUMBER.

```
/*****************************************************************/
/*                                                             */
/*                         INIT                                */
/*                                                             */
/*  THIS PROCEDURE INITIALIZES THE VARIABLE ATOMS.            */
/*                                                             */
/*                                                             */
/*****************************************************************/


          INIT:PROC;


               ATOMS = 'HCNOFSGEI';
               F$ERROR = FALSE;


          END INIT;
```

FIGURE 5.10 *PL/I stub for* INIT.

```
/************************************************************/
/*                                                        */
/*                        ERROR                           */
/*                                                        */
/*    THIS PROCEDURE PRINTS AN ERROR MESSAGE.             */
/*        INPUT PARAMETER:                                */
/*            ERR# - ERROR NUMBER                         */
/*                                                        */
/************************************************************/

        ERROR: PROC(ERR#);

            DCL ERR# FIXED BIN(15);        /* ERROR NUMBER */

            PUT SKIP(3) EDIT('***ERROR',ERR#)(A,F(3));

        END ERROR;
```

FIGURE 5.11 *PL/I stub for* ERROR.

has occurred. In this way, the programmer can delay until a more appropriate stage of the development deciding exactly what words to use. However, the code invoking ERROR will not have to be changed when the final error messages are introduced; the changes will be completely local to ERROR. Similarly, no recoding of ERROR need be performed to accommodate additional error encodements.

Figure 5.12 shows the code for EXEC_SYM. It is a stub that is neither vacuous nor representative of the functional intent of the code that will eventually reside here. Its purpose is to instrument the verification of Phase 1 by displaying the tokens extracted by GET_SYM. GET_SYM and SCAN_FORM are coded *exactly* as they will appear in the final product; there is no instrumentation in them at all (so none has to be removed later). This type of stub allows the implementer to extract sufficient information to verify the correctness of the remainder of the system without perturbing it at all.

5.2.3 The Execution

When the code segments we have developed are integrated in an appropriate manner and executed against the data shown in Figure 5.13, the output shown in Figure 5.14 is produced. The test data in Figure 5.13 are not sufficient to verify the correctness of the software; however, the inclusion of a complete set will not enhance the illustration.

5.3 PHASE 2—BUILDING THE MOLECULE

5.3.1 Functional Content

Phase 2 (Fig. 5.2) encompasses that portion of the system which builds the internal representation of the molecule. The consistency of the molecule (that no atoms are

```
/**************************************************************************/
/*                                                                      */
/*                          EXEC_SYM                                    */
/*                                                                      */
/*     THIS PROCEDURE IS WRITTEN AS A STUB. IT                          */
/*     SIMPLY PRINTS THE INTERPRETATION OF THE                          */
/*     INCOMING TOKEN.                                                  */
/*         INPUT PARAMETER:                                             */
/*             TOKEN - TOKEN TO BE PRINTED                              */
/*         INPUT-OUTPUT PARAMETER:                                      */
/*             MOL - THE MOLECULE                                       */
/*                   NOT CURRENTLY USED                                 */
/*                                                                      */
/**************************************************************************/


        EXEC_SYM: PROC(TOKEN,MOL);


            DCL 1 TOKEN,
                  2 TYPE FIXED BIN(15),
                  2 VAL FIXED BIN(15);


            DCL 1 MOL,                /*   INTERNAL REPRESENTATION  */
                  2 REP,
                      3 CONNECTION(*,*) FIXED BIN(15),
                      3 ATOM_CORR(*) FIXED BIN(15),
                      3 P$NEXT FIXED BIN(15),
                  2 CONTEXT,
                      3 #BONDS FIXED BIN(15),
                      3 ATOM_PEND(*) FIXED BIN(15);


            DCL   A_MESS(A$H:A$I) CHAR(15) VARYING INIT(
                          'HYDROGEN',
                          'CARBON',
                          'NITROGEN',
                          'OXYGEN',
                          'FLUORINE',
                          'SULFUR',
                          'CHLORINE',
                          'BROMINE',
                          'IODINE'
                                    ),


                  G_MESS(G$Q_OH:G$U_DB) CHAR(60) VARYING INIT(
                          'Q - HYDROXYL GROUP, OH',
                          'V - CARBONYL CONNECTIVE, C#O',
                          'W - NONLINEAR DIOXO, O2',
                          'M - IMINO, NH',
                          'Z - AMINO, NH2',
                          'U - DOUBLE BOND'
                                    );


            DCL CASE(T$ATOM:T$NUM) LABEL INIT(ATOM,GROUP,NUMBER);


            PUT SKIP LIST('EXEC_SYM INPUT:');


            GOTO CASE(TOKEN.TYPE);
```

FIGURE 5.12 *PL/I stub for* EXEC_SYM.

```
ATOM:
        PUT EDIT(A_MESS(TOKEN.VAL),' ATOM')(A);
        GOTO END_CASE;


GROUP:
        PUT EDIT(G_MESS(TOKEN.VAL))(A);
        GOTO END_CASE;


NUMBER:
        PUT EDIT('CHAIN OF ',TOKEN.VAL,' CARBON ATOM(S)')
           (A,F(3),A);
        GOTO END_CASE;


END_CASE:


END EXEC_SYM;
```

FIGURE 5.12 *(continued)*

"excessively bonded") is to be determined, but no statistics are to be calculated or printed. Although the structural-formula will not be printed, the connection matrix (Sec. 3.1.3.4) will be displayed to verify its correctness.

5.3.2 Modifications to Previous Code

The context in which the code must now operate has changed; this is shown in Figure 5.15. A few new error types and miscellaneous "constants" have been added. To allow the software to be somewhat self-adapting, three character "constants", TRANS_TYPE, TRANS_TO and TRANS_FROM, have been introduced. TRANS_TO and TRANS_FROM are initialized in INIT and are referenced in GET_FORM to categorize characters into their respective classes. (In this way, new atoms can be introduced to the system merely by adding new "constants" and new entries to ATOM_TAB.) A new structure, ATOM_TAB, has been added to describe the characteristics of the specific atoms recognized by the system.

The new forms of INIT and GET_FORM, which have been modified to allow the software to be more flexible, are shown in Figures 5.16 and 5.17. Notice that INIT also prints ATOM_TAB to verify what the system assumes about the properties of the elements.

```
1 V1
WN1U1O1U1NW
SU3
G1UU1Z
11NUCUN1
#?@WHAT?
```

FIGURE 5.13 *Test data for Phase 1.*

```
FORMULA ANALYZED:1V1
EXEC_SYM INPUT: CHAIN OF   1 CARBON ATOM(S)
EXEC_SYM INPUT: V - CARBONYL CONNECTIVE, C#O
EXEC_SYM INPUT: CHAIN OF   1 CARBON ATOM(S)


FORMULA ANALYZED:WN1U1O1U1NW
EXEC_SYM INPUT: W - NONLINEAR DIOXO, O2
EXEC_SYM INPUT: NITROGEN ATOM
EXEC_SYM INPUT: CHAIN OF   1 CARBON ATOM(S)
EXEC_SYM INPUT: U - DOUBLE BOND
EXEC_SYM INPUT: CHAIN OF   1 CARBON ATOM(S)
EXEC_SYM INPUT: OXYGEN ATOM
EXEC_SYM INPUT: CHAIN OF   1 CARBON ATOM(S)
EXEC_SYM INPUT: U - DOUBLE BOND
EXEC_SYM INPUT: CHAIN OF   1 CARBON ATOM(S)
EXEC_SYM INPUT: NITROGEN ATOM
EXEC_SYM INPUT: W - NONLINEAR DIOXO, O2


FORMULA ANALYZED:SU3
EXEC_SYM INPUT: SULFUR ATOM
EXEC_SYM INPUT: U - DOUBLE BOND
EXEC_SYM INPUT: CHAIN OF   3 CARBON ATOM(S)


FORMULA ANALYZED:G1UU1Z
EXEC_SYM INPUT: CHLORINE ATOM
EXEC_SYM INPUT: CHAIN OF   1 CARBON ATOM(S)
EXEC_SYM INPUT: U - DOUBLE BOND
EXEC_SYM INPUT: U - DOUBLE BOND
EXEC_SYM INPUT: CHAIN OF   1 CARBON ATOM(S)
EXEC_SYM INPUT: Z - AMINO, NH2


FORMULA ANALYZED:11NUCUN1
EXEC_SYM INPUT: CHAIN OF  11 CARBON ATOM(S)
EXEC_SYM INPUT: NITROGEN ATOM
EXEC_SYM INPUT: U - DOUBLE BOND
EXEC_SYM INPUT: CARBON ATOM
EXEC_SYM INPUT: U - DOUBLE BOND
EXEC_SYM INPUT: NITROGEN ATOM
EXEC_SYM INPUT: CHAIN OF   1 CARBON ATOM(S)


FORMULA ANALYZED:#?ƏWHAT?

***ERROR  1

***ERROR  1

***ERROR  1

EXEC_SYM INPUT: W - NONLINEAR DIOXO, O2
EXEC_SYM INPUT: HYDROGEN ATOM

***ERROR  1

***ERROR  1

***ERROR  1
```

FIGURE 5.14 *Verification output for Phase 1.*

PHASE 2—BUILDING THE MOLECULE

```
DCL (            /* TYPES OF TOKENS */
      T$ERROR   INIT(0),  /* ERROR */
      T$ATOM INIT(1),     /* ATOM */
      T$GROUP INIT(2),    /* GROUP */
      T$NUM INIT(3),      /* NUMBER (OR CARBON CHAIN) */
      T$EOM INIT(4),      /* END OF MOLECULE */


         /* ATOMS */
      A$H INIT(1),     /* HYDROGEN */
      A$C INIT(2),     /* CARBON */
      A$N INIT(3),     /* NITROGEN */
      A$O INIT(4),     /* OXYGEN */
      A$F INIT(5),     /* FLUORINE */
      A$S INIT(6),     /* SULFUR */
      A$CL INIT(7),    /* CHLORINE */
      A$BR INIT(8),    /* BROMINE */
      A$I INIT(9),     /* IODINE */


         /* GROUPS */
      G$Q_OH INIT(1),     /* Q GROUP */
      G$V_C#O INIT(2),    /* V GROUP */
      G$W_O2 INIT(3),     /* W GROUP */
      G$M_NH INIT(4),     /* M GROUP */
      G$Z_NH2 INIT(5),    /* Z GROUP */
      G$U_DB INIT(6),     /* DOUBLE BOND */


         /* ERRORS */
      E$BAD_CHAR INIT(1),
      E$BONDS INIT(2),
      E$ATOM_OVER INIT(3),


         /* MISC. */
      ONE INIT(1),
      TWO INIT(2),
      #MOL INIT(45),        /* # OF POSSIBLE ATOMS IN MOL */
      #GROUPS INIT(6),
      $NULL INIT(0)
            ) FIXED BIN(15),


      F$ERROR BIT(1),       /* ERROR FLAG */


      (            /* BOOLEAN */
      TRUE INIT('1'B),
      FALSE INIT('0'B)
            ) BIT(1),


      (    /* CHARACTER DEFINITION AND TRANSFORMATION */
      TRANS_TYPE INIT('AGDB'),
      TRANS_TO,
      TRANS_FROM
            ) CHAR(80) VARYING,


      ATOMS CHAR(A$I-A$H+1) VARYING,
      GROUPS CHAR(#GROUPS) INIT('QVWMZU');
```

FIGURE 5.15 *Data content for Phase 2.*

```
DCL 1 FORM,       /*  FORMULA  */
     2 S_FORM CHAR(81) VARYING,
     2 T_FORM CHAR(81) VARYING,
     2 P$FORM FIXED BIN(15);


DCL 1 MOL,           /*  INTERNAL REPRESENTATION  */
     2 REP,
          3 CONNECTION(#MOL,#MOL) FIXED BIN(15),
          3 ATOM_CORR(#MOL) FIXED BIN(15),
          3 P$NEXT FIXED BIN(15),
     2 CONTEXT,
          3 #BONDS FIXED BIN(15),
          3 ATOM_PEND(2) FIXED BIN(15);


DCL 1 ATOM_TAB(A$H:A$I),       /*  ATOM TABLE  */
     2 NAME CHAR(9) VARYING
          INIT('HYDROGEN',
               'CARBON',
               'NITROGEN',
               'OXYGEN',
               'FLUORINE',
               'SULFUR',
               'CHLORINE',
               'BROMINE',
               'IODINE'),
     2 SYMBOL CHAR(1) INIT('H','C','N','O','F',
                           'S','G','E','I'),
     2 BONDS FIXED BIN(15) INIT(1,4,3,2,1,2,1,1,1),
     2 ATOM_NUM FIXED BIN(15) INIT(1,6,7,8,9,16,17,35,53),
     2 ATOM_WT FLOAT BIN(21) INIT(1.00797,12.01115,14.0067,
                           15.9994,18.9984,32.064,
                           35.453,79.904,126.9044);
```

FIGURE 5.15 *(continued)*

The code for SCAN_FORM, GET_FORM, NUMBER, and ERROR remains exactly the same as in Phase 1. Even though new error types have been introduced, the stub for ERROR need not be modified.

5.3.3 New Code

The code for DRIVER2 is shown in Figure 5.18. The structure is very similar to that of DRIVER1 (Fig. 5.5) because their intents are similar.

EXEC_SYM is the workhorse that performs the job of building the molecule. The old stub is extracted and the intended code (Fig. 5.19) is inserted in its place. Notice that the new code and the previously utilized stub have the same basic structure (this is not an accident). Also note the similarity of the code to the corresponding pseudocode (Fig. 3.12).

As indicated in the structure diagram (Fig. 5.2), EXEC_SYM uses a number of supporting modules for performing its function. The codes for INSERT, CHANGE_CONTEXT, LINK, CREAT, and CONNECT are shown in Figures 5.20–5.24. Here again, the similarity between these procedures and their corresponding pseudocode is not accidental.

```
/*****************************************************************/
/*                                                             */
/*                         INIT                                */
/*                                                             */
/*    THIS PROCEDURE INITIALIZES THE VARIABLE                  */
/*    ATOMS FROM SYMBOLS IN ATOM_TAB.                          */
/*    IT ALSO DETERMINES THE VALUES OF TRANS_TO AND TRANS_FROM.*/
/*                                                             */
/*****************************************************************/

      INIT:PROC;

          DCL I FIXED BIN(15);        /*  DO LOOP PARAMETER  */
          DCL ILLEGAL CHAR(80) VARYING;


                  /*   PRINT OUT ATOM TABLE  */


          PUT SKIP EDIT('ATOMIC','ATOMIC') (COL(31),A,COL(41),A);
          PUT SKIP EDIT('ELEMENT','SYMBOL','BONDS','NUMBER','WEIGHT')
              (A(10));
          PUT SKIP;
          DO I = A$H TO A$I;
              PUT SKIP EDIT(ATOM_TAB(I))
                  (A,COL(13),A,COL(22),F(2),COL(32),F(3),
                      COL(38),F(10,5));
          END;


                  /*   INITIALIZE ATOMS FROM ATOM TABLE   */
          ATOMS = '';
          DO I = A$H TO A$I;
              ATOMS = ATOMS || ATOM_TAB(I).SYMBOL;
          END;


                  /*   DETERMINE TRANS_TO & TRANS_FROM   */


          TRANS_FROM = ' 0123456789' || ATOMS || GROUPS;
          TRANS_TO = 'BDDDDDDDDDD' || REPEAT('A',LENGTH(ATOMS)-1) ||
              REPEAT('G',LENGTH(GROUPS)-1);
          ILLEGAL = TRANS_TYPE || ' ';


                  /*   DETERMINE TRANS_FROM & TRANS_TO   */


          I = 1;
          DO WHILE(I < LENGTH(ILLEGAL));
              IF INDEX(TRANS_FROM,SUBSTR(ILLEGAL,I,1)) ¬= 0 THEN
                  ILLEGAL = SUBSTR(ILLEGAL,1,I-1) ||
                      SUBSTR(ILLEGAL,I+1);
              ELSE I = I + 1;
          END;
          ILLEGAL = SUBSTR(ILLEGAL,1,LENGTH(ILLEGAL)-1);
          IF LENGTH(ILLEGAL) > 0 THEN DO;
              TRANS_FROM = TRANS_FROM || ILLEGAL;
              TRANS_TO = TRANS_TO || REPEAT('I',LENGTH(ILLEGAL)-1);
          END;


      END INIT;
```

FIGURE 5.16 *PL/I code for* INIT.

```
/*************************************************************************/
/*                                                                     */
/*                            GET_FORM                                 */
/*                                                                     */
/*      THIS PROCEDURE GETS THE NEXT CARD FROM THE CARD READER         */
/*      AND TRANSLATES IT.                                             */
/*          OUTPUT PARAMETERS:                                         */
/*            IN FORM:                                                 */
/*              S_FORM - SOURCE FORM                                   */
/*              T_FORM - TRANSLATED FORM                               */
/*              P$FORM - POINTER TO THE FORM                           */
/*                                                                     */
/*************************************************************************/


        GET_FORM: PROC(FORM);

            DCL 1 FORM,
                2 S_FORM CHAR(*) VARYING,
                2 T_FORM CHAR(*) VARYING,
                2 P$FORM FIXED BIN(15);


            GET EDIT(S_FORM)(COL(1),A(80));
            S_FORM = S_FORM || ' ';
            T_FORM = TRANSLATE(S_FORM,
                TRANS_TO,
                TRANS_FROM);
            P$FORM = 1;


        END GET_FORM;
```

FIGURE 5.17 *Modified PL/I code for* GET_FORM.

BLD_MOL is a completely coordinating procedure that creates the "spine" of the molecule by invoking SCAN_FORM. It fills in the unused bonds by invoking FILL. The codes for BLD_MOL and FILL are shown in Figure 5.25 and 5.26, respectively.

PRINT (Fig. 5.27) is present only to verify the correctness of the connection matrix. It is a stub and will be discarded when no longer needed. This procedure represents more work than is normally invested in a stub. The stub prints a connection matrix of arbitrary size and incorporates certain internal variables, which allow

```
        ON ENDFILE(SYSIN) STOP;

        CALL INIT;
        DO WHILE(TRUE);             /*  UNTIL EOF  */
            F$ERROR = FALSE;
            CALL GET_FORM(FORM);
            CALL BLD_MOL(FORM,MOL);
            IF ¬F$ERROR THEN CALL PRINT(MOL,FORM);
        END;
```

FIGURE 5.18 *PL/I code for* DRIVER2.

```
/******************************************************************/
/*                                                              */
/*                      EXEC_SYM                                */
/*                                                              */
/*    THIS PROCEDURE INCREMENTALLY RECOGNIZES SEGMENTS          */
/*    OF THE MOLECULE AND "ATTACHES" IT TO THE                  */
/*    INTERNAL REPRESENTATION OF THE MOLECULE.                  */
/*        INPUT PARAMETER:                                      */
/*            TOKEN - TOKEN TO BE PRINTED                       */
/*        INPUT-OUTPUT PARAMETER:                               */
/*            MOL - THE MOLECULE                                */
/*                                                              */
/******************************************************************/


        EXEC_SYM: PROC(TOKEN,MOL);

            DCL 1 TOKEN,
                  2 TYPE FIXED BIN(15),
                  2 VAL FIXED BIN(15);


            DCL 1 MOL,              /*  INTERNAL REPRESENTATION  */
                  2 REP,
                    3 CONNECTION(*,*) FIXED BIN(15),
                    3 ATOM_CORR(*) FIXED BIN(15),
                    3 P$NEXT FIXED BIN(15),
                  2 CONTEXT,
                    3 #BONDS FIXED BIN(15),
                    3 ATOM_PEND(*) FIXED BIN(15);


            DCL (
                 I,         /*  DO LOOP PARAMETER  */
                 P$ATOM     /*  POINTER TO AN ATOM  */
                            ) FIXED BIN(15),


                 CASE(T$ATOM:T$NUM) LABEL INIT(ATOM,GROUP,NUMBER);


            GOTO CASE(TOKEN.TYPE);


        ATOM:
                 P$ATOM = CREATE(MOL,TOKEN.VAL);
                 CALL LINK(MOL,P$ATOM);
                 CALL CHANGE_CONTEXT(CONTEXT,P$ATOM,$NULL);
                 GOTO END_CASE;


        GROUP:
                 CALL INSERT(MOL,TOKEN.VAL);
                 GOTO END_CASE;


        NUMBER:
                 DO I = 1 TO TOKEN.VAL;
                     P$ATOM = CREATE(MOL,A$C);
                     CALL LINK(MOL,P$ATOM);
                     CALL CHANGE_CONTEXT(CONTEXT,P$ATOM,$NULL);
                 END;
                 GOTO END_CASE;


        END_CASE:


        END EXEC_SYM;
```

FIGURE 5.19 *PL/I code for* EXEC_SYM.

```
/*****************************************************************/
/*                                                             */
/*                        INSERT                               */
/*                                                             */
/*  THIS PROCEDURE INSERTS A GROUP INTO THE INTERNAL           */
/*  REPRESENTATION OF THE MOLECULE BEING FORMED.               */
/*      INPUT PARAMETER:                                       */
/*          GROUP - THE GROUP TO BE INSERTED                   */
/*      INPUT-OUTPUT PARAMETERS:                               */
/*          MOL -     THE MOLECULE                             */
/*          #BONDS - NUMBER OF BONDS                           */
/*                                                             */
/*****************************************************************/


        INSERT: PROC (MOL,GROUP) ;



            DCL 1 MOL,           /*  INTERNAL REPRESENTATION  */
                  2 REP,
                    3 CONNECTION(*,*) FIXED BIN(15),
                    3 ATOM_CORR(*) FIXED BIN(15),
                    3 P$NEXT FIXED BIN(15),
                  2 CONTEXT,
                    3 #BONDS FIXED BIN(15),
                    3 ATOM_PEND(*) FIXED BIN(15);



            DCL (
                GROUP,      /*  GROUP TO BE INSERTED  */
                P$N,        /*  POINTER TO A NITROGEN ATOM  */
                P$C,        /*  POINTER TO A CARBON ATOM  */
                P$H1,       /*  POINTER TO HYDROGEN ATOM 1  */
                P$H2,       /*  POINTER TO HYDROGEN ATOM 2  */
                P$O1,       /*  POINTER TO OXYGEN ATOM 1  */
                P$O2        /*  POINTER TO OXYGEN ATOM 2  */
                ) FIXED BIN(15),


            CASE(G$Q_OH:G$U_DB) LABEL INIT(Q,V,W,M,Z,U);


        GOTO CASE(GROUP);


        Q:
            P$O1 = CREATE(MOL,A$O);
            P$H1 = CREATE(MOL,A$H);
            CALL CONNECT(MOL,P$O1,P$H1,ONE);
            CALL LINK(MOL,P$O1);
            CALL CHANGE_CONTEXT(CONTEXT,P$O1,$NULL);
            GOTO END_CASE;


        V:
            P$O1 = CREATE(MOL,A$O);
            P$C = CREATE(MOL,A$C);
            CALL CONNECT(MOL,P$O1,P$C,TWO);
            CALL LINK(MOL,P$C);
            CALL CHANGE_CONTEXT(CONTEXT,P$C,$NULL);
            GOTO END_CASE;
```

FIGURE 5.20   *PL/I code for* INSERT.

```
W:
        P$O1 = CREATE(MOL,A$O);
        P$O2 = CREATE(MOL,A$O);
        CALL CONNECT(MOL,P$O1,P$O2,ONE);
        CALL LINK(MOL,P$O1);
        CALL LINK(MOL,P$O2);
        CALL CHANGE_CONTEXT(CONTEXT,P$O1,P$O2);
        GOTO END_CASE;

M:

        P$N = CREATE(MOL,A$N);
        P$H1 = CREATE(MOL,A$H);
        CALL CONNECT(MOL,P$N,P$H1,#BONDS);
        CALL LINK(MOL,P$N);
        CALL CHANGE_CONTEXT(CONTEXT,P$N,$NULL);
        GOTO END_CASE;

Z:

        P$N = CREATE(MOL,A$N);
        P$H1 = CREATE(MOL,A$H);
        P$H2 = CREATE(MOL,A$H);
        CALL CONNECT(MOL,P$N,P$H1,ONE);
        CALL CONNECT(MOL,P$N,P$H2,ONE);
        CALL LINK(MOL,P$N);
        CALL CHANGE_CONTEXT(CONTEXT,P$N,$NULL);
        GOTO END_CASE;

U:

        #BONDS = #BONDS + 1;
        GOTO END_CASE;

    END_CASE:

END INSERT;
```

FIGURE 5.20 *(continued)*

the stub to be fine-tuned. A global page number is printed, as well as a page number within the presentation of each separate connection matrix. Alternative formats and methods for printing the connection matrix could have been used, but it was felt that the clarity of the output produced by PRINT warranted the work put in. (It is difficult enough to verify the correctness of the connection matrix without having to read through unformatted output.)

5.3.4 The Execution

When these code segments are integrated in an appropriate manner and executed against the data shown in Figure 5.28, the output shown in Figure 5.29 is produced.

5.4 PHASE 3—THE FINAL PRODUCT

5.4.1 Functional Content

Phase 3 will implement the final software product in its entirety. The major things still to be done are to calculate and print the statistics and to print the structural-

```
/****************************************************************************/
/*                                                                        */
/*                        CHANGE_CONTEXT                                   */
/*                                                                        */
/*    THIS PROCEDURE RESETS THE CURRENTLY CONTEXT                          */
/*    IN THE MOLECULE.                                                     */
/*        INPUT PARAMETERS:                                                */
/*            P$A1 - POINTER TO FIRST ATOM                                 */
/*            P$A2 - POINTER TO SECOND ATOM                                */
/*        OUTPUT PARAMETER:                                                */
/*            CONTEXT - THE CONTEXT                                        */
/*                                                                        */
/****************************************************************************/

        CHANGE_CONTEXT: PROC (CONTEXT,P$A1,P$A2);


        DCL 1 CONTEXT,
              2 #BONDS FIXED BIN(15),
              2 ATOM_PEND(*) FIXED BIN(15);


        DCL (
              P$A1,        /* POINTER TO ATOM 1 */
              P$A2         /* POINTER TO ATOM 2 */
                          ) FIXED BIN(15);


        ATOM_PEND(1) = P$A1;
        ATOM_PEND(2) = P$A2;
        #BONDS = 1;


        END CHANGE_CONTEXT;
```

FIGURE 5.21 *PL/I code for* CHANGE_CONTEXT.

formula. All loose ends (such as refurbishing ERROR) must be resolved so that the product is ready to be handed over to the end user.

5.4.2 Modifications to Previous Code

Again, the context in which the code must now operate has been changed; this is shown in Figure 5.30. A few new error types have been added, and a new structure (STATS) representing the statistics has been introduced. Notice that a new type of connector atom has been added (both as a constant and as an entry in ATOM_TAB). This "internal" atom is introduced to facilitate printing the W group on the line printer.

Because of this incorporation of the connector atom, a small change must be made to the processing of the W group in INSERT (Fig. 5.31). Notice how minor the change is and how easy it was to make.

Because this phase produces the final software, ERROR must be modified to supply more acceptable error messages. Its final form is shown in Figure 5.32. Notice that the numeric encodement for E$ATOM_OVER has been changed between Phase 2 and Phase 3 without any change to the code. This is one of the

```
/*******************************************************************/
/*                                                                 */
/*                          LINK                                   */
/*                                                                 */
/*      THIS PROCEDURE LINKS AN ATOM (P$ATOM) TO THE              */
/*      CURRENTLY PENDING ATOM(S) OF THE MOLECULE                 */
/*      WITH #BONDS BONDS.                                         */
/*          INPUT PARAMETERS:                                      */
/*              P$ATOM - POINTER TO THE ATOM                      */
/*              #BONDS - NUMBER OF BONDS                          */
/*          INPUT-OUTPUT PARAMETER:                               */
/*              MOL - THE MOLECULE                                */
/*                                                                 */
/*******************************************************************/


        LINK: PROC(MOL,P$ATOM);

            DCL 1 MOL,            /*  INTERNAL REPRESENTATION  */
                2 REP,
                    3 CONNECTION(*,*) FIXED BIN(15),
                    3 ATOM_CORR(*) FIXED BIN(15),
                    3 P$NEXT FIXED BIN(15),
                2 CONTEXT,
                    3 #BONDS FIXED BIN(15),
                    3 ATOM_PEND(*) FIXED BIN(15);


            DCL (
                P$ATOM        /*  POINTER TO THE ATOM  */
                        ) FIXED BIN(15);


            CALL CONNECT(MOL,ATOM_PEND(1),P$ATOM,#BONDS);
            CALL CONNECT(MOL,ATOM_PEND(2),P$ATOM,#BONDS);


        END LINK;
```

FIGURE 5.22 *PL/I code for* LINK.

advantages of employing ''constant'' variables. As it becomes advantageous to change these numeric encodements, it is not necessary to search all the code to find the places where they were used.

All the remaining procedures developed in Phase 2 are incorporated into Phase 3 without change.

5.4.3 New Code

The code for COMP is shown in Figure 5.33. Notice its similarity to that of DRIVER2 (Fig. 5.18). They are exactly the same except for the names and parameter lists.

ANAL (Fig. 5.34) is a coordinating procedure that builds the internal representation of the molecule by invoking BLD_MOL and computes the statistics by invoking COMPUTE (Fig. 5.35).

```
/***************************************************************************/
/*                                                                       */
/*                            C R E A T E                                */
/*                                                                       */
/*     THIS PROCEDURE CREATES AN ATOM IN THE NEXT                        */
/*     AVAILABLE ENTRY OF THE CONNECTION MATRIX.                         */
/*         INPUT PARAMETER:                                              */
/*             ATOM - TYPE OF ATOM TO BE CREATED                        */
/*     INPUT-OUTPUT PARAMETER:                                          */
/*             MOL - THE MOLECULE                                        */
/*     OUTPUT PARAMETER:                                                */
/*             POS - POSITION OF ATOM IN CONNECTION MATRIX              */
/*                                                                       */
/***************************************************************************/

       CREATE: PROC(MOL,ATOM)  RETURNS(FIXED BIN(15));

           DCL 1 MOL,            /*  INTERNAL REPRESENTATION  */
                 2 REP,
                     3 CONNECTION(*,*) FIXED BIN(15),
                     3 ATOM_CORR(*) FIXED BIN(15),
                     3 P$NEXT FIXED BIN(15),
                 2 CONTEXT,
                     3 #BONDS FIXED BIN(15),
                     3 ATOM_PEND(*) FIXED BIN(15);

           DCL (
                 ATOM,      /*  ATOM TYPE  */
                 POS        /*  POSITION OF ALLOCATED ATOM  */
                            )  FIXED BIN(15);

           IF P$NEXT > #MOL THEN DO;
               CALL ERROR(E$ATOM_OVER);
               F$ERROR = TRUE;
               POS = $NULL;
           END;
           ELSE DO;
               POS = P$NEXT;
               P$NEXT = P$NEXT + 1;
               ATOM_CORR(POS) = ATOM;
           END;

           RETURN(POS);

       END CREATE;
```

FIGURE 5.23 *PL/I code for* CREATE.

PRINT (Fig. 5.36) is fairly straightforward: It prints the statistics and invokes PRINT_MOL to print the structural-formula.

A description here of PRINT_MOL and the procedures that support it will not help illustrate the concept of incremental implementation, so the procedures will not be discussed here. However, they do illustrate recursion and some interesting encodement techniques. They are described in the appendix to allow the interested reader to see how this problem was handled.

```
/*******************************************************************/
/*                                                                 */
/*                      CONNECT                                    */
/*                                                                 */
/*    THIS PROCEDURE CONNECTS TWO ATOMS OF THE MOLECULE           */
/*    WITH #BONDS BONDS (IF THEY ARE BOTH NON-NULL                */
/*    ATOMS).                                                      */
/*       INPUT PARAMETERS:                                        */
/*            P$ATOM1 - POINTER TO FIRST ATOM                     */
/*            P$ATOM2 - POINTER TO SECOND ATOM                    */
/*            ##BONDS - NUMBER OF BONDS                           */
/*       INPUT-OUTPUT PARAMETER:                                  */
/*            MOL - THE MOLECULE                                  */
/*                                                                */
/*******************************************************************/


        CONNECT: PROC(MOL,P$ATOM1,P$ATOM2,##BONDS);


            DCL 1 MOL,            /*  INTERNAL REPRESENTATION  */
                  2 REP,
                    3 CONNECTION(*,*) FIXED BIN(15),
                    3 ATOM_CORR(*) FIXED BIN(15),
                    3 P$NEXT FIXED BIN(15),
                  2 CONTEXT,
                    3 #BONDS FIXED BIN(15),
                    3 ATOM_PEND(*) FIXED BIN(15);


            DCL (
                  P$ATOM1,       /*  POINTER TO ATOM 1  */
                  P$ATOM2,       /*  POINTER TO ATOM 2  */
                  ##BONDS        /*  NUMBER OF BONDS  */
                            ) FIXED BIN(15);


            IF P$ATOM1 ¬= $NULL & P$ATOM2 ¬= $NULL THEN DO;
                CONNECTION(P$ATOM1,P$ATOM2) = ##BONDS;
                CONNECTION(P$ATOM2,P$ATOM1) = ##BONDS;
            END;


        END CONNECT;
```

FIGURE 5.24 *PL/I code for* CONNECT.

5.4.4 The Execution

When the code segments developed earlier (plus those presented in the appendix) are integrated in an appropriate manner and executed against the data shown in Figure 5.28, the output shown in Figure 5.37 is produced. In this figure, the printing of ATOM_TAB has been suppressed.

5.5 ALTERNATIVES

The code presented in the previous three sections reflects the selection of specific alternatives from a very large set. What types of alternatives were there? Which

```
/*******************************************************************/
/*                                                                 */
/*                          BLD_MOL                                */
/*                                                                 */
/*      THIS PROCEDURE BUILDS THE INTERNAL REPRESENTATION          */
/*      OF THE MOLECULE.                                           */
/*          INPUT-OUTPUT PARAMETERS:                               */
/*              FORM - THE FORMULA                                 */
/*          OUTPUT PARAMETERS:                                     */
/*              MOL - THE MOLECULE                                 */
/*                                                                 */
/*******************************************************************/


        BLD_MOL: PROC(FORM,MOL);

            DCL 1 FORM,
                  2 S_FORM CHAR(*) VARYING,
                  2 T_FORM CHAR(*) VARYING,
                  2 P$FORM FIXED BIN(15);


            DCL 1 MOL,            /* INTERNAL REPRESENTATION  */
                  2 REP,
                      3 CONNECTION(*,*) FIXED BIN(15),
                      3 ATOM_CORR(*) FIXED BIN(15),
                      3 P$NEXT FIXED BIN(15),
                  2 CONTEXT,
                      3 #BONDS FIXED BIN(15),
                      3 ATOM_PEND(*) FIXED BIN(15);


            MOL = 0;
            P$NEXT = 1;


            CALL SCAN_FORM(FORM,MOL);
            CALL FILL(MOL);

        END BLD_MOL;
```

FIGURE 5.25 *PL/I code for* BLD_MOL.

were selected? Can we go back and substitute another alternative in the software without a significant amount of work? This section addresses these kinds of questions in order to examine what might have been done, what changes might be performed, and how much work is involved.

5.5.1 Coding Techniques

The coding style (choice of implementation constructs, variable names, documentation, and indentation) presented in this chapter mirrors the personal preference of the authors. There is no reason why you should pick this style over any other. However, the novice programmer (with proper guidance) should select his or her own style and use it consistently.

In this implementation, the CASE construct has been implemented uniformly via an array of labels. The alternative is to use a nested IF-THEN-ELSE construct,

```
/*******************************************************************/
/*                                                                 */
/*                          FILL                                   */
/*                                                                 */
/*    THIS PROCEDURE FILLS IN UNUSED BONDS WITH                    */
/*    DEFAULT HYDROGEN ATOMS.                                      */
/*         INPUT-OUTPUT PARAMETER:                                 */
/*            MOL - THE MOLECULE                                   */
/*                                                                 */
/*******************************************************************/


          FILL: PROC(MOL);

               DCL 1 MOL,             /*  INTERNAL REPRESENTATION  */
                   2 REP,
                     3 CONNECTION(*,*) FIXED BIN(15),
                     3 ATOM_CORR(*) FIXED BIN(15),
                     3 P$NEXT FIXED BIN(15),
                   2 CONTEXT,
                     3 #BONDS FIXED BIN(15),
                     3 ATOM_PEND(*) FIXED BIN(15);


               DCL (
                   I,     /*  DO LOOP PARAMETER  */
                   P$H    /*  POINTER TO HYDROGEN  */
                        ) FIXED BIN(15);


               DO I = 1 TO P$NEXT - 1 WHILE(¬F$ERROR);
                  IF SUM(CONNECTION(I,*)) >
                          ATOM_TAB(ATOM_CORR(I)).BONDS THEN DO;
                     CALL ERROR(E$BONDS);
                     F$ERROR = TRUE;
                  END;
                  ELSE
                     DO WHILE(SUM(CONNECTION(I,*))
                         < ATOM_TAB(ATOM_CORR(I)).BONDS & ¬F$ERROR);
                        P$H = CREATE(MOL,A$H);
                        CALL CONNECT(MOL,I,P$H,ONE);
                     END;
               END;


          END FILL;
```

FIGURE 5.26 *PL/I code for* FILL.

which is *always* applicable for implementing the CASE. Obviously, the array of labels is preferred by the authors. (It is more efficient at execution, and the syntax seems to read more clearly. The fact that a GOTO is used to exit from the CASE is irrelevant. It is a very restricted, well-understood application of the GOTO, and it is needed only because PL/I does not have a CASE statement as a primitive.) The array of labels is not appropriate when, for example, encoding the selection criterion into a single numeric value is difficult.

Although the incorporation of the "constants" is very important and should not be excluded, the method of naming them here (by use of $) is unimportant. However, some method should be employed to show that an identifier does repre-

```
/*******************************************************************/
/*                                                               */
/*                         PRINT                                 */
/*                                                               */
/*    THIS PROCEDURE PRINTS THE CONTENTS OF THE                  */
/*    CONNECTION MATRIX.  IF THE PRINTED FORM                    */
/*    IS TOO WIDE TO FIT ON ONE PAGE, IT SPLITS                  */
/*    THE TABLE AND PRINTS IT ON MULTIPLE PAGES.                 */
/*        INPUT PARAMETERS:                                      */
/*                MOL - THE MOLECULE                             */
/*                FORM - THE FORMULA                             */
/*                                                               */
/*******************************************************************/


        PRINT: PROC(MOL,FORM);


           DCL 1 FORM,
                 2 S_FORM CHAR(*) VARYING,
                 2 T_FORM CHAR(*) VARYING,
                 2 P$FORM FIXED BIN(15);


           DCL 1 MOL,              /*   INTERNAL REPRESENTATION  */
                 2 REP,
                     3 CONNECTION(*,*) FIXED BIN(15),
                     3 ATOM_CORR(*) FIXED BIN(15),
                     3 P$NEXT FIXED BIN(15),
                 2 CONTEXT,
                     3 #BONDS FIXED BIN(15),
                     3 ATOM_PEND(*) FIXED BIN(15);


           DCL (
                TPAGE INIT(0) STATIC,      /*  TOTAL PAGES  */
                FPAGE INIT(0),        /*  PAGES WITHIN GIVEN FORMULA  */
                K,I,      /*  DO LOOP PARAMETERS  */
                J,      /*  COLUMN COUNTER  */
                WIDTH INIT(4),        /*   WIDTH OF ONE COLUMN  */
                LEAD INIT(5),         /*   AREA BEFORE COLUMNS START   */
                START INIT(1),        /*   FIRST COLUMN OF A SEGMENT   */
                LAST,                 /*   LAST COLUMN OF A SEGMENT   */
                #COL                  /*   # OF COLUMNS IN A SEGMENT   */
                         ) FIXED BIN(15);


           ON ENDPAGE(SYSPRINT) BEGIN;
                TPAGE = TPAGE + 1;
                FPAGE = FPAGE + 1;
                PUT PAGE;
                PUT EDIT('PAGE',TPAGE) (COL(50),A,F(4));
                PUT SKIP EDIT('PAGE',FPAGE,' OF FORMULA ',S_FORM)
                    (A,F(4),A);
                PUT SKIP(4);
           END;

           #COL = (60 - LEAD)/WIDTH;
           DO WHILE(START < P$NEXT);
                SIGNAL ENDPAGE(SYSPRINT);
                LAST = MIN(P$NEXT,START+#COL) - 1;
                J = 0;
```

FIGURE 5.27 *PL/I stub for* PRINT.

```
DO I = START TO LAST;
    PUT EDIT (SYMBOL(ATOM_CORR(I)))
        (COL(LEAD + (J+.5)*WIDTH),A);
    J = J + 1;

    END;
DO I = 1 TO P$NEXT - 1;
    PUT SKIP(1) EDIT(SYMBOL(ATOM_CORR(I))) (A);
    J = 1;
    DO K = START TO LAST;
        PUT EDIT(CONNECTION(I,K))
            (COL(LEAD + J*WIDTH - 1),F(1));
        J = J + 1;
    END;
END;
START = LAST + 1;
END;

END PRINT;
```

FIGURE 5.27 *(continued)*

sent a ''constant'' and the intent of that ''constant.'' The method by which they are embedded within the program also may vary. For instance, both PL/I and PL/C have a macro facility, and the ''constants'' can be introduced through that mechanism instead of defining them directly in the program. (The appeal of this technique depends on the language used.) Some languages, such as PASCAL and FORTRAN 77, have a built-in declaration construct for defining such constants.

5.5.2 Data Structures

5.5.2.1 Internal Representation of the Molecule   The major data structure used in this system is the connection matrix, which represents the structure of the molecule. The connection matrix was selected because it is easy to define, manipulate, and display. There is also a large arsenal of algorithms applicable to such a data structure for determining connected components, shortest path between two atoms, and so on.

However, there is a major disadvantage to the connection matrix. For large molecules, the matrix is relatively sparse, and a significant amount of storage is wasted in holding zero elements (storage requirements are $0(N**2)$, where N is the number of atoms). For small molecules, this effect is not noticed. For instance, in a molecule containing 10 atoms, only 100 (10**2) storage locations are required. However, in a molecule containing 1000 atoms (not unreasonable in the biological

```
1 V1
WN1U1Ɔ1U1NW
SU3
```

FIGURE 5.28 *Test data for Phase 2.*

ELEMENT	SYMBOL	BONDS	ATOMIC NUMBER	ATOMIC WEIGHT
HYDROGEN	H	1	1	1.00797
CARBON	C	4	6	12.01115
NITROGEN	N	3	7	14.00670
OXYGEN	O	2	8	15.99940
FLUORINE	F	1	9	18.99840
SULFUR	S	2	16	32.06400
CHLORINE	G	1	17	35.45300
BROMINE	E	1	35	79.90400
IODINE	I	1	53	126.90440

PAGE   1 OF FORMULA 1V1

	C	O	C	C	H	H	H	H	H	H
C	0	0	1	0	1	1	1	0	0	0
O	0	0	2	0	0	0	0	0	0	0
C	1	2	0	1	0	0	0	0	0	0
C	0	0	1	0	0	0	0	1	1	1
H	1	0	0	0	0	0	0	0	0	0
H	1	0	0	0	0	0	0	0	0	0
H	1	0	0	0	0	0	0	0	0	0
H	0	0	0	1	0	0	0	0	0	0
H	0	0	0	1	0	0	0	0	0	0
H	0	0	0	1	0	0	0	0	0	0

PAGE   1 OF FORMULA WN1U1O1U1NW

	O	O	N	C	C	O	C	C	N	O	O	H	H
O	0	1	1	0	0	0	0	0	0	0	0	0	0
O	1	0	1	0	0	0	0	0	0	0	0	0	0
N	1	1	0	1	0	0	0	0	0	0	0	0	0
C	0	0	1	0	2	0	0	0	0	0	0	1	0
C	0	0	0	2	0	1	0	0	0	0	0	0	1
O	0	0	0	0	1	0	1	0	0	0	0	0	0
C	0	0	0	0	0	1	0	2	0	0	0	0	0
C	0	0	0	0	0	0	2	0	1	0	0	0	0
N	0	0	0	0	0	0	0	1	0	1	1	0	0
O	0	0	0	0	0	0	0	0	1	0	1	0	0
O	0	0	0	0	0	0	0	0	1	1	0	0	0
H	0	0	0	1	0	0	0	0	0	0	0	0	0
H	0	0	0	0	1	0	0	0	0	0	0	0	0
H	0	0	0	0	0	0	1	0	0	0	0	0	0
H	0	0	0	0	0	0	0	1	0	0	0	0	0

PAGE   2 OF FORMULA WN1U1O1U1NW

	H	H
O	0	0
O	0	0
N	0	0
C	0	0
C	0	0
O	0	0
C	1	0
C	0	1
N	0	0
O	0	0
O	0	0
H	0	0
H	0	0
H	0	0
H	0	0

FIGURE 5.29 *Verification output for Phase 2.*

	S	C	C	C	H	H	H	H	H	H
S	0	2	0	0	0	0	0	0	0	0
C	2	0	1	0	1	0	0	0	0	0
C	0	1	0	1	0	1	1	0	0	0
C	0	0	1	0	0	0	0	1	1	1
H	0	1	0	0	0	0	0	0	0	0
H	0	0	1	0	0	0	0	0	0	0
H	0	0	1	0	0	0	0	0	0	0
H	0	0	0	1	0	0	0	0	0	0
H	0	0	0	1	0	0	0	0	0	0
H	0	0	0	1	0	0	0	0	0	0

FIGURE 5.29 (continued)

```
DCL (            /*  TYPES OF TOKENS  */
     T$ERROR   INIT(0),  /*    ERROR  */
     T$ATOM INIT(1),     /*    ATOM  */
     T$GROUP INIT(2),    /*    GROUP  */
     T$NUM INIT(3),      /*    NUMBER (OR CARBON CHAIN)  */
     T$EOM INIT(4),      /*    END OF MOLECULE  */

        /*   ATOMS  */
     A$H INIT(1),        /*    HYDROGEN  */
     A$C INIT(2),        /*    CARBON  */
     A$N INIT(3),        /*    NITROGEN  */
     A$O INIT(4),        /*    OXYGEN  */
     A$F INIT(5),        /*    FLUORINE  */
     A$S INIT(6),        /*    SULFUR  */
     A$CL INIT(7),       /*    CHLORINE  */
     A$BR INIT(8),       /*    BROMINE  */
     A$I INIT(9),        /*    IODINE  */
     A$CONN INIT(10),    /*    SPECIAL CONNECTOR ATOM  */

        /*   GROUPS  */
     G$Q_OH INIT(1),     /*    Q GROUP  */
     G$V_C$O INIT(2),    /*    V GROUP  */
     G$W_O2 INIT(3),     /*    W GROUP  */
     G$M_NH INIT(4),     /*    M GROUP  */
     G$Z_NH2 INIT(5),    /*    Z GROUP  */
     G$U_DB INIT(6),     /*    DOUBLE BOND  */

        /*   ERRORS  */
     E$BAD_CHAR INIT(1),
     E$BONDS INIT(2),
     E$CONN INIT(3),
     E$MAP_OVER INIT(4),
     E$NO_DIR INIT(5),
     E$ATOM_OVER INIT(6),

        /*   MISC.  */
     ONE INIT(1),
     TWO INIT(2),
     #GROUPS INIT(6),
     #MOL INIT(45),
     $NULL INIT(0)
        ) FIXED BIN(15),
```

FIGURE 5.30 Data context for Phase 3.

```
        F$ERROR BIT(1),        /*  ERROR FLAG  */


        (          /*  BOOLEAN  */
        TRUE INIT('1'B),
        FALSE INIT('0'B)
            ) BIT(1),


        (     /*  CHARACTER DEFINITION AND TRANSFORMATION  */
        TRANS_TYPE INIT('AGDB'),
        TRANS_TO,
        TRANS_FROM
            ) CHAR(80) VARYING,


        ATOMS CHAR(A$I-A$H+1) VARYING,
        GROUPS CHAR(#GROUPS) INIT('QVWMZU');


  DCL 1 FORM,    /*  FORMULA  */
      2 S_FORM CHAR(81) VARYING,
      2 T_FORM CHAR(81) VARYING,
      2 P$FORM FIXED BIN(15);


  DCL 1 MOL,          /*  INTERNAL REPRESENTATION  */
      2 REP,
          3 CONNECTION(#MOL,#MOL) FIXED BIN(15),
          3 ATOM_CORR(#MOL) FIXED BIN(15),
          3 P$NEXT FIXED BIN(15),
      2 CONTEXT,
          3 #BONDS FIXED BIN(15),
          3 ATOM_PEND(2) FIXED BIN(15);


  DCL 1 ATOM_TAB(A$H:A$CONN),      /*  ATOM TABLE  */
      2 NAME CHAR(9) VARYING
          INIT('HYDROGEN',
               'CARBON',
               'NITROGEN',
               'OXYGEN',
               'FLUORINE',
               'SULFUR',
               'CHLORINE',
               'BROMINE',
               'IODINE',
               'CONNECTOR'),
      2 SYMBOL CHAR(1) INIT('H','C','N','O','F',
                   'S','G','E','I','+'),
      2 BONDS FIXED BIN(15) INIT(1,4,3,2,1,2,1,1,1,2),
      2 ATOM_NUM FIXED BIN(15) INIT(1,6,7,8,9,16,17,35,53,0),
      2 ATOM_WT FLOAT BIN(21) INIT(1.00797,12.01115,14.0067,
                      15.9994,18.9984,32.064,
                      35.453,79.904,126.9044,0.0);


  DCL 1 STATS,     /*  STATISTICS  */
      2 NUM_ATOMS(A$H:A$CONN) FIXED BIN(15),
      2 PCNT_WT(A$H:A$CONN) FLOAT BIN(21),
      2 PCNT_NUM(A$H:A$CONN) FLOAT BIN(21),
      2 RAT_UNSAT FLOAT BIN(21),
      2 MOL_WT FLOAT BIN(21),
      2 MOL_NUM FLOAT BIN(21);
```

FIGURE 5.30 *(continued)*

```
/***********************************************************************/
/*                                                                     */
/*                          INSERT                                     */
/*                                                                     */
/*    THIS PROCEDURE INSERTS A GROUP INTO THE INTERNAL                 */
/*    REPRESENTATION OF THE MOLECULE BEING FORMED.                     */
/*         INPUT PARAMETER:                                            */
/*             GROUP - THE GROUP TO BE INSERTED                        */
/*         INPUT-OUTPUT PARAMETERS:                                    */
/*             MOL -   THE MOLECULE                                    */
/*                                                                     */
/***********************************************************************/


        INSERT: PROC(MOL,GROUP);


            DCL 1 MOL,              /* INTERNAL REPRESENTATION  */
                  2 REP,
                      3 CONNECTION(*,*) FIXED BIN(15),
                      3 ATOM_CORR(*) FIXED BIN(15),
                      3 P$NEXT FIXED BIN(15),
                  2 CONTEXT,
                      3 #BONDS FIXED BIN(15),
                      3 ATOM_PEND(*) FIXED BIN(15);


            DCL (
                  GROUP,      /* GROUP TO BE INSERTED  */
                  P$N,        /* POINTER TO A NITROGEN ATOM  */
                  P$C,        /* POINTER TO A CARBON ATOM  */
                  P$CONN,     /* POINTER TO CONNECTOR ATOM  */
                  P$H1,       /* POINTER TO HYDROGEN ATOM 1  */
                  P$H2,       /* POINTER TO HYDROGEN ATOM 2  */
                  P$O1,       /* POINTER TO OXYGEN ATOM 1  */
                  P$O2        /* POINTER TO OXYGEN ATOM 2  */
                      ) FIXED BIN(15),


                  CASE(G$Q_OH:G$U_DB) LABEL INIT(Q,V,W,M,Z,U);

            GOTO CASE(GROUP);


            Q:
                  P$O1 = CREATE(MOL,A$O);
                  P$H1 = CREATE(MOL,A$H);
                  CALL CONNECT(MOL,P$O1,P$H1,ONE);
                  CALL LINK(MOL,P$O1);
                  CALL CHANGE_CONTEXT(CONTEXT,P$O1,$NULL);
                  GOTO END_CASE;


            V:
                  P$O1 = CREATE(MOL,A$O);
                  P$C = CREATE(MOL,A$C);
                  CALL CONNECT(MOL,P$O1,P$C,TWO);
                  CALL LINK(MOL,P$C);
                  CALL CHANGE_CONTEXT(CONTEXT,P$C,$NULL);
                  GOTO END_CASE;
```

FIGURE 5.31 *Modified PL/I code for* INSERT.

```
W:
      P$O1 = CREATE(MOL,A$O);
      P$CONN = CREATE(MOL,A$CONN);
      P$O2 = CREATE(MOL,A$O);
      CALL CONNECT(MOL,P$O1,P$CONN,ONE);
      CALL CONNECT(MOL,P$CONN,P$O2,ONE);
      CALL LINK(MOL,P$O1);
      CALL LINK(MOL,P$O2);
      CALL CHANGE_CONTEXT(CONTEXT,P$O1,P$O2);
      GOTO END_CASE;


M:
      P$N = CREATE(MOL,A$N);
      P$H1 = CREATE(MOL,A$H);
      CALL CONNECT(MOL,P$N,P$H1,#BONDS);
      CALL LINK(MOL,P$N);
      CALL CHANGE_CONTEXT(CONTEXT,P$N,$NULL);
      GOTO END_CASE;


Z:
      P$N = CREATE(MOL,A$N);
      P$H1 = CREATE(MOL,A$H);
      P$H2 = CREATE(MOL,A$H);
      CALL CONNECT(MOL,P$N,P$H1,ONE);
      CALL CONNECT(MOL,P$N,P$H2,ONE);
      CALL LINK(MOL,P$N);
      CALL CHANGE_CONTEXT(CONTEXT,P$N,$NULL);
      GOTO END_CASE;


U:
      #BONDS = #BONDS + 1;
      GOTO END_CASE;


END_CASE:

END INSERT;
```

FIGURE 5.31 (continued)

world), 1,000,000 (1000**2) storage locations are required—a significant portion of most computers' storage resources.

An alternative (just one of many, of course) is to use some form of linked-list data structure for representing the molecule. Using the fundamental nodes shown in Figure 5.38, the generic representation of 1V1 might look something like the structure shown in Figure 5.39. Notice that this representation is more complicated and more difficult to understand for 1V1 than the connection matrix (Figs. 3.4 and 5.29). The corresponding code for manipulating such a set of data structures also is more complicated than that required for a connection matrix. However, the storage requirements for holding a large molecule are much less for a linked-list than for a connection-matrix representation.

In the linked-list representation, a molecule with N atoms and B bonds requires N atom nodes, B bond nodes, and $2*B$ link nodes. Assuming each field of

```
/***************************************************************/
/*                                                           */
/*                         ERROR                             */
/*                                                           */
/*   THIS PROCEDURE PRINTS AN ERROR MESSAGE.                 */
/*       INPUT PARAMETER:                                    */
/*           ERR# - ERROR NUMBER                             */
/*                                                           */
/***************************************************************/


        ERROR: PROC(ERR#);

            DCL ERR# FIXED BIN(15),        /* ERROR NUMBER */
                MESSAGE(E$BAD_CHAR:E$ATOM_OVER) CHAR(40) VARYING
                INIT(
                    'ILLEGAL CHARACTER ENCOUNTERED',
                    'TOO MANY BONDS FOR GIVEN ATOM',
                    'CANNOT PRINT H GROUP CORRECTLY',
                    'MOLECULE TOO LARGE TO PRINT ON ONE PAGE',
                    'NO POSITION IN WHICH TO PRINT ATOM',
                    'EXCEEDED CONNECTION MATRIX SIZE'
                        );

            PUT SKIP(3) EDIT('*** ',MESSAGE(ERR#),' ***')(A);

        END ERROR;
```

FIGURE 5.32 *Final PL/I code for* ERROR.

each node requires one storage location, a molecule with N atoms and B bonds requires $2*N + 7*B$ storage locations. Thus, returning to our example molecule of 1000 atoms and, for example, no more than 2000 bonds, such a molecule would require no more than 16,000 storage locations. This is a significant reduction from the 1,000,000 storage locations required for the corresponding connection matrix.

Let us assume that after the system developed in this chapter has been in use for a while, it is realized that the molecules to be analyzed are very large, the connection-matrix storage requirements are astronomical, and the system *must* be revised to incorporate some form of linked-list representation. What are the ramifications of changing the system? What modules would have to be changed? How

```
        ON ENDFILE(SYSIN) STOP;

        CALL INIT;
        DO WHILE(TRUE);              /* UNTIL EOF */
            F$ERROR = FALSE;
            CALL GET_FORM(FORM);
            CALL ANAL(FORM,MOL,STATS);
            IF ¬F$ERROR THEN CALL PRINT(STATS,FORM,MOL);
        END;
```

FIGURE 5.33 *PL/I code for* COMP.

```
/***********************************************************************/
/*                                                                   */
/*                            ANAL                                   */
/*                                                                   */
/*      THIS PROCEDURE ANALYZES THE CHEMICAL FORMULA.                */
/*                                                                   */
/*          INPUT PARAMETERS:                                        */
/*              (EXPLICIT)                                           */
/*              FORM - THE FORMULA                                   */
/*              (GLOBAL)                                             */
/*              F$ERROR - INDICATES AN ERROR                         */
/*          OUTPUT PARAMETERS:                                       */
/*              MOL - THE MOLECULE                                   */
/*              STATS - THE STATISTICS                               */
/*                                                                   */
/***********************************************************************/

        ANAL: PROC (FORM, MOL, STATS);

            DCL 1 FORM,
                2 S_FORM CHAR(*) VARYING,
                2 T_FORM CHAR(*) VARYING,
                2 P$FORM FIXED BIN(15);


            DCL 1 MOL,              /*   INTERNAL REPRESENTATION   */
                2 REP,
                    3 CONNECTION(*,*) FIXED BIN(15),
                    3 ATOM_CORR(*) FIXED BIN(15),
                    3 P$NEXT FIXED BIN(15),
                2 CONTEXT,
                    3 #BONDS FIXED BIN(15),
                    3 ATOM_PEND(*) FIXED BIN(15);


            DCL 1 STATS,
                2 NUM_ATOMS(*) FIXED BIN(15),
                2 PCNT_WT(*) FLOAT BIN(21),
                2 PCNT_NUM(*) FLOAT BIN(21),
                2 RAT_UNSAT FLOAT BIN(21),
                2 MOL_WT FLOAT BIN(21),
                2 MOL_NUM FLOAT BIN(21);


            CALL BLD_MOL(FORM, MOL);
            IF ¬F$ERROR THEN CALL COMPUTE(MOL, STATS);

        END ANAL;
```

FIGURE 5.34 *PL/I code for* ANAL.

much will they have to be changed? Which can be retained as is? (In the following analysis, the fact that declarations would have to be changed will be ignored. These questions address procedural code.) Only modules which directly access fields of MOL must be modified. These modules are CREATE, LINK, CONNECT, CHANGE_CONTEXT, COMPUTE, BLD_MAP, FIND_NEXT, and FILL. (With minor changes, this latter procedure can be made representation independent.) The combined code represented by this collection of modules is a small percentage of the entire product.

```
/*********************************************************************/
/*                                                                 */
/*                        COMPUTE                                  */
/*                                                                 */
/*      THIS PROCEDURE COMPUTES STATISTICS ABOUT                   */
/*      THE MOLECULE.                                              */
/*                                                                 */
/*          INPUT PARAMETERS:                                     */
/*              MOL - THE MOLECULE                               */
/*          OUTPUT PARAMETERS:                                   */
/*              STATS - THE STATISTICS                           */
/*                                                                 */
/*********************************************************************/


        COMPUTE: PROC(MOL,STATS);


            DCL 1 MOL,           /*  INTERNAL REPRESENTATION  */
                  2 REP,
                      3 CONNECTION(*,*) FIXED BIN(15),
                      3 ATOM_CORR(*) FIXED BIN(15),
                      3 P$NEXT FIXED BIN(15),
                  2 CONTEXT,
                      3 #BONDS FIXED BIN(15),
                      3 ATOM_PEND(*) FIXED BIN(15);

            DCL 1 STATS,
                  2 NUM_ATOMS(*) FIXED BIN(15),
                  2 PCNT_WT(*) FLOAT BIN(21),
                  2 PCNT_NUM(*) FLOAT BIN(21),
                  2 RAT_UNSAT FLOAT BIN(21),
                  2 MOL_WT FLOAT BIN(21),
                  2 MOL_NUM FLOAT BIN(21);

            DCL (
                  I,COL,ROW,  /*  DO LOOP PARAMETERS  */
                  ##BONDS,    /*  NUMBER OF BONDS  */
                  #UBONDS     /*  NUMBER OF UNSATURATED BONDS  */
                      ) FIXED BIN(15);

            NUM_ATOMS = 0;
            DO I = 1 TO P$NEXT - 1;
                NUM_ATOMS(ATOM_CORR(I)) = NUM_ATOMS(ATOM_CORR(I)) + 1;
            END;

            MOL_WT = SUM(NUM_ATOMS*ATOM_WT);
            MOL_NUM = SUM(NUM_ATOMS*ATOM_NUM);
            PCNT_WT = NUM_ATOMS*ATOM_WT/MOL_WT*100;
            PCNT_NUM = NUM_ATOMS*ATOM_NUM/MOL_NUM*100;

                /*  CALCULATE RATIO OF UNSATURATED TO TOTAL BONDS  */
                /*  ALL BONDS ARE COUNTED TWICE  */
            ##BONDS, #UBONDS = 0;
            DO ROW = 1 TO P$NEXT - 1;
                IF BONDS(ATOM_CORR(ROW)) > 1 THEN
                        DO COL = 1 TO P$NEXT - 1;
                            IF BONDS(ATOM_CORR(COL)) > 1 THEN DO;
                                IF CONNECTION(ROW,COL) > 0 THEN
                                    ##BONDS = ##BONDS + 1;
                                IF CONNECTION(ROW,COL) > 1 THEN
                                    #UBONDS = #UBONDS + 1;
                            END;
                        END;
            END;
                /*  CORRECT FOR CONNECTOR ATOMS  */
            ##BONDS = ##BONDS - 2*NUM_ATOMS(A$CONN);
            RAT_UNSAT = #UBONDS/MAX(##BONDS,1);


        END COMPUTE;
```

FIGURE 5.35 *PL/I code for* COMPUTE.

Thus, as a result of the way the software was designed, the conversion from one representation to another can be performed with relative ease. The major portion of the system has been functionally isolated from the representation used. This functional isolation is of paramount importance in any system which may require major revisions. Do not underestimate the probability of major system modifications. Users are very fickle, and their concepts, requirements, and expectations change over time.

5.5.2.2 *Tokens*   As the software currently stands, tokens are encoded as numeric 2-tuples. There are several alternatives. One is to encode tokens as character 2-tuples. Thus a hydrogen atom might be encoded as <A,H>, and a chain of three carbon atoms might be encoded as <C,3>. Such encodements are perfectly reasonable. However, numeric encodements have certain advantages. Most languages manipulate numeric data more easily than character data. Sequential numeric encodements also lend themselves to specific CASE selection, whereas character data may require some translation before CASE selection can be performed.

A second alternative is to encode the token into one scalar value (numeric in type, for example). Such an encodement might associate the end-of-molecule token with 1, the ten atoms with 2-11, and the six groups with 12-17. Ten error tokens (18-27) might be reserved for different types of error conditions, and values of 28 and beyond might indicate the number of carbon atoms in a chain. Such an encoding scheme is acceptable, but it lacks flexibility when new types of tokens or new entries within a token class (for example, adding a new atom) are introduced.

5.5.2.3 *Table-Driven Techniques*   Certain aspects of the software product development in this chapter are already table driven. More specifically, the attributes of the different elements are held in tabular form. It should be clear that the software can easily be modified to allow the *user* to define the elements (and their attributes) *at execution time*. This gives the user a great deal of flexibility. When working with a given class of molecules, the user can define the pertinent atoms and the system need not address superfluous data (extraneous elements).

Extending this idea a little farther, it is possible to encode the structure of functional groups in a tabular form also. Once this is accomplished and a notation for describing such structure is developed, it then becomes possible to allow the user to define functional groups at execution time. Then the techniques employed in INIT (Fig. 5.16) become very useful.

5.5.3 Parameter Passing

How do we decide whether to pass parameters globally or explicitly through a parameter list? The answer depends on the context in which the procedure is employed and, more directly, on the designer's anticipation of the way in which that context may change. For instance, in the major body of the product (everything exclusive of PRINT_MOL and its supporting procedures), only one parameter, F$ERROR, is passed globally. Since there is only one molecule being analyzed, why pass MOL through each parameter list to lower levels of the structure diagram?

```
/********************************************************************/
/*                                                                */
/*                        PRINT                                 */
/*                                                                */
/*    THIS PROCEDURE PRINTS THE STATISTICS AND                  */
/*    THE GRAPHICAL REPRESENTATION OF THE                       */
/*    MOLECULE.                                                  */
/*                                                                */
/*        INPUT PARAMETERS:                                      */
/*            STATS - THE STATISTICS                           */
/*            FORM - THE FORMULA                               */
/*            MOL - THE MOLECULE                               */
/*                                                                */
/********************************************************************/


        PRINT:PROC(STATS,FORM,MOL);

        DCL 1 FORM,
              2 S_FORM CHAR(*) VARYING,
              2 T_FORM CHAR(*) VARYING,
              2 P$FORM FIXED BIN(15);


        DCL 1 MOL,              /*   INTERNAL REPRESENTATION   */
              2 REP,
                  3 CONNECTION(*,*) FIXED BIN(15),
                  3 ATOM_CORR(*) FIXED BIN(15),
                  3 P$NEXT FIXED BIN(15),
              2 CONTEXT,
                  3 #BONDS FIXED BIN(15),
                  3 ATOM_PEND(*) FIXED BIN(15);


        DCL 1 STATS,
              2 NUM_ATOMS(*) FIXED BIN(15),
              2 PCNT_WT(*) FLOAT BIN(21),
              2 PCNT_NUM(*) FLOAT BIN(21),
              2 RAT_UNSAT FLOAT BIN(21),
              2 MOL_WT FLOAT BIN(21),
              2 MOL_NUM FLOAT BIN(21);


        DCL (
              I,J      /*  DC LOOP PARAMETERS  */
                  ) FIXED BIN(15);


        PUT PAGE EDIT('FORMULA BEING ANALYZED IS: ',S_FORM)(A);
                    /*   PRINT PERCENTAGE TABLE   */
        PUT SKIP(5) EDIT('ELEMENT PERCENTAGE TABLE')
              (COL(25),A);
        PUT SKIP(2) EDIT('ELEMENT','NUMBER OF ATOMS',
              '% WEIGHT','% NUMBER')
              (A,COL(20),A,COL(40),A,COL(60),A);
        PUT SKIP;
        DO I = A$H TO A$I;
              IF NUM_ATOMS(I) ¬= 0 THEN
                    PUT SKIP EDIT(NAME(I),NUM_ATOMS(I),PCNT_WT(I),
                        PCNT_NUM(I))
                        (A,COL(11),F(17),(2)F(20,3));
        END;
        PUT SKIP(2) EDIT('TOTAL',SUM(NUM_ATOMS),SUM(PCNT_WT),
              SUM(PCNT_NUM))(A,COL(11),F(17),(2)F(20,3));
```

FIGURE 5.36 *PL/I code for* PRINT.

```
            PUT SKIP(3) EDIT('MOLECULAR WEIGHT IS',MOL_WT)
                (A,F(10,3));
            PUT SKIP EDIT('MOLECULAR NUMBER IS',MOL_NUM)
                (A,F(10));


                    /* PRINT UNSATURATION RATIO */
            PUT SKIP(5) EDIT('RATIO OF UNSATURATED',
                ' TO TOTAL BONDS IS',RAT_UNSAT)
                (A,A,F(10,4));


                    /* PRINT RELATIVE ATOMS TABLE */
            PUT SKIP(5) EDIT('ELEMENT RATIO TABLE (B/A)')
                (COL(10),A);
            PUT SKIP(2) EDIT('A ->') (COL(4),A);
            DO I = A$H TO A$I;
                IF NUM_ATOMS(I) ¬= 0 THEN
                    PUT EDIT(SYMBOL(I)) (X(7),A);
            END;
            PUT EDIT('B','|','V') (SKIP,A);
            DO I = A$H TO A$I;
                IF NUM_ATOMS(I) ¬= 0 THEN DO;
                    PUT SKIP(3) EDIT(SYMBOL(I),' ') (A,COL(9),A);
                    DO J = A$H TO I;
                        IF NUM_ATOMS(J) ¬= 0 THEN
                            PUT EDIT(NUM_ATOMS(I)/NUM_ATOMS(J))
                                (F(8,2));
                    END;
                END;
            END;


            CALL PRINT_MOL(MOL);

        END PRINT;
```

FIGURE 5.36 *(continued)*

Why not just make it globally available to all procedures? The reason lies in the anticipation that the context in which these procedures operate will change.

Recall (Chap. 3) the original discussion that motivated the development of this product. It was stated that what is really needed is a database capable of representing, updating, and analyzing chemical molecules. The product developed here does a restricted analysis of *one* molecule at a time. This product eventually may be embedded in a larger system which analyzes *several* molecules and compares their structure to determine what substructures they have in common, for instance. In this wider context, there will be several molecules around, and components (procedures) of the product developed here may have to distinguish among different molecules. If these components are written to assume that only one molecule exists (MOL is passed globally), then some mechanism must be used to select the correct molecule to place in MOL. Coordination of this selection mechanism can be extremely tedious, may be inefficient during execution, and often is error prone. Thus MOL has explicitly been passed through the parameter lists so that it is easy to designate exactly which molecule is to be manipulated.

Why is F$ERROR passed globally? Whenever any major error occurs any-

```
FORMULA BEING ANALYZED IS: 1V1

                          ELEMENT PERCENTAGE TABLE
   ELEMENT            NUMBER OF ATOMS      % WEIGHT              % NUMBER

   HYDROGEN                  6             10.413                18.750
   CARBON                    3             62.040                56.250
   OXYGEN                    1             27.547                25.000
   TOTAL                    10            100.000               100.000

   MOLECULAR WEIGHT IS     58.081
   MOLECULAR NUMBER IS        32


   RATIO OF UNSATURATED TO TOTAL BONDS IS     0.3333

           ELEMENT RATIO TABLE (B/A)
      A ->      H        C        O
   B
   |
   V

   H        1.00

   C        0.50     1.00

   O        0.17     0.33     1.00



   GRAPHICAL REPRESENTATION OF MOLECULE

           H    O    H

           |   |2|   |

      H  - C -  C -  C -  H

           |         |

           H         H



FORMULA BEING ANALYZED IS: WN1U1O1O1U1NW

                          ELEMENT PERCENTAGE TABLE
   ELEMENT            NUMBER OF ATOMS      % WEIGHT              % NUMBER

   HYDROGEN                  4              2.519                 4.878
   CARBON                    4             30.012                29.268
   NITROGEN                  2             17.499                17.073
   OXYGEN                    5             49.971                48.780
   TOTAL                    17            100.000               100.000

   MOLECULAR WEIGHT IS    160.087
   MOLECULAR NUMBER IS        82


   RATIO OF UNSATURATED TO TOTAL BONDS IS     0.1667

           ELEMENT RATIO TABLE (B/A)
      A ->      H        C        N        O
```

FIGURE 5.37 *Verification output for Phase 3.*

CASE STUDY—AN IMPLEMENTATION

```
B
|
V

H        1.00

C        1.00     1.00

N        0.50     0.50     1.00

O        1.25     1.25     2.50     1.00
```

GRAPHICAL REPRESENTATION OF MOLECULE

```
  + - O    H    H         H    H    O - +

  |    |    |    |         |    |    |    |

  O - N - C - C - O - C - C - N - O
          2              2
```

FORMULA BEING ANALYZED IS: SU3

ELEMENT PERCENTAGE TABLE

ELEMENT	NUMBER OF ATOMS	% WEIGHT	% NUMBER
HYDROGEN	6	8.157	15.000
CARBON	3	48.598	45.000
SULFUR	1	43.245	40.000
TOTAL	10	100.000	100.000

```
MOLECULAR WEIGHT IS    74.145
MOLECULAR NUMBER IS       40
```

RATIO OF UNSATURATED TO TOTAL BONDS IS   0.3333

```
        ELEMENT RATIO TABLE (B/A)
  A ->      H      C      S
B
|
V

H        1.00

C        0.50     1.00

S        0.17     0.33     1.00
```

GRAPHICAL REPRESENTATION OF MOLECULE

```
        H    H    H

        |    |    |

  S - C - C - C - H
  2
        |    |

        H    H
```

FIGURE 5.37 (continued)

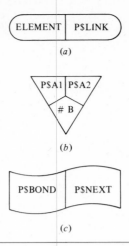

FIGURE 5.38 *Linked-list node definitions: (a) atom node;*
(b) bond node; and (c) link node.

where in the system, we would like all components to be aware of this fact so that they can take the appropriate action. Thus it seems reasonable to make this information (globally) available to everyone.

Another place where parameters are passed globally is within the supporting procedures of PRINT_MOL. Global parameter passing is used here because these procedures have a very *specific* support function and will not be useful outside of the context of PRINT_MOL. Because they are conceived of as functionally dependent on one another and no procedure will be extracted and used in some other context, there is no need to pass certain parameters explicitly through parameter lists.

5.5.4 Functional Content of Procedures

Once a procedure is embedded in a system with a specific functional intent, it is usually very difficult to change that functional intent without changing a significant amount of surrounding code.

More specifically, consider the procedure ERROR. This procedure does not have enough functional intent to convey needed information adequately to the user. For instance, if an illegal character is encountered, what character was it? Where was it in the line-formula? The user wants to know these things. (The system knows them. Why not tell the user? Why force the user to perform the same processing that the system has performed?) If it is determined that a given atom is "excessively bonded," which one was it? The error message does not tell the user.

The point here is that ERROR tells the user what the problem is but gives none of the (required) context. The original functional intent of ERROR was to state the error and not to give this context; that is, the original functional intent is not sufficient to meet the user's needs adequately.

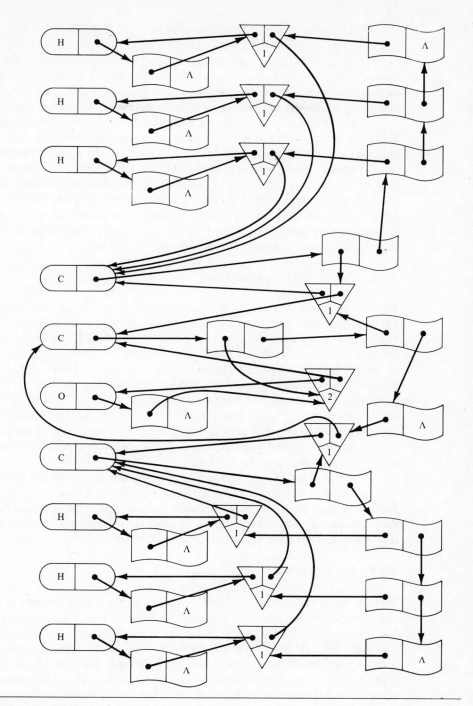

FIGURE 5.39 *Linked-list representation of 1V1.*

It is possible to modify the functional intent of ERROR so that this context is added. However, not only will the code for ERROR have to be changed, but every invocation of ERROR will have to be modified to incorporate the context into the parameter list. Thus it is important to determine explicitly the functional content of each module during the *design phase,* before implementation is started and before changes in functional content require additional work (in the form of code changes).

Another important concept that must be addressed during the design phase is functional isolation. For instance, in the design of this product (Fig. 5.3), the computation of the statistics is isolated from their display. These are two separate functions. The novice designer might have combined them. After all, since we are going to print the statistics anyway, why not print them while they are being calculated? We may not always want to print these statistics. When we embed this product in a larger system, we may want to compare statistics calculated for several molecules without printing them. If both functions have been embedded within the same procedure, it becomes impossible to achieve this separation.

5.5.5 Order of Implementation

There is no reason why the order of implementation employed here must be used. Let us assume that, for some reason, we choose to implement GET_SYM last. All implementation phases that require the invocation of GET_SYM can use a stub until the final code for GET_SYM is actually produced. Such a stub might take one of several forms. A very simple realization is shown in Figure 5.40. It can be written, keypunched, and tested in 5 minutes. The testing is to eliminate keypunching errors; it is so simple that there cannot be any logic errors. In the use of this stub, the developer must "preprocess" the line-formulas by hand and determine what data the procedure logically should return. These data are placed in the data stream so that the stub can read them. A sample data stream (corresponding to that shown in Fig. 5.28) is shown in Figure 5.41.

The use of this type of stub perturbs the input data stream and is error prone because the data stream must subsequently be modified. There are several alternatives. One is to place the additional data in a secondary file and read them from there. Another is to embed the additional data in a two-dimensional array within the stub itself and have the stub return values selected sequentially from the array.

5.5.6 Optimization

There is no doubt that the efficient execution of a software product is generally important. However, it is more important to obtain a product that is correct and can easily be modified. Once such a product is in hand, an optimization phase can be instituted. It should be realized that during this optimization phase, certain transformations may destroy some of the software's desirable properties (such as modifiability). If this is the case, then *both* copies of the product should be retained. Then, when major revisions are to be made, they can be performed on the unoptimized (modifiable) copy, and the optimization phase can be applied again.

```
GET_SYM: PROC(FORM,TOKEN);

        DCL 1 FORM,        /*  FORMULA  */
             2 S_FORM CHAR(*) VARYING,
             2 T_FORM CHAR(*) VARYING,
             2 P$FORM FIXED BIN(15);

        DCL 1 TOKEN,        /*  TOKEN  */
             2 TYPE FIXED BIN(15),
             2 VAL FIXED BIN(15);

        GET LIST(TOKEN);

    END GET_SYM;
```

FIGURE 5.40 *PL/I stub for* GET_SYM.

What techniques can be applied during the process of optimizing a software product? First of all, it is not productive to try to optimize all of the code. It is a well established fact that, in most cases, 90 percent of the execution time is spent in 10 percent of the code. Once this relatively small amount of code is identified, the developer can turn his or her attention to it and ignore the remaining code. Several existing compilers supply some help in determining frequently executed code. If such support is not available, the developer may have to instrument his or her own code to identify frequently executed code.

If an algorithm embedded in its own module is identified as inherently ineffi-

```
1 V1
3 1
2 2
3 1
4 0
WN1U1O1U1NW
2 3
1 3
3 1
3 6
3 1
1 4
3 1
3 6
3 1
1 3
2 3
4 0
SU3
1 6
2 6
3 3
4 0
```

FIGURE 5.41 *Test data when* GET_SYM *stub is used.*

cient and another functionally equivalent algorithm seems more suitable, it is an easy matter to extract one and insert the other. This is one of the advantages of the top-down design process.

If it is found that a specific language construct (or combination of constructs) is inherently inefficient, it may be necessary to select a different language construct or recode the code segment in assembly language.

It is not unusual for 40 to 50 percent of the execution time to be spent in procedure call overhead. This is especially true for procedures with very little computational content that are invoked frequently. Such procedures are prime candidates for elimination. Other candidates are procedures that are invoked at only one place in the code. Some of the procedures in our software product with these properties are BLD_MOL, ANAL, CHANGE_CONTEXT, LINK, CONNECT, CREATE, CALC_POS, SET_LINK, and FIND_NEXT. It usually is a relatively easy matter to eliminate procedure overhead by replacing each invocation of a procedure by the code that it represents.

Notice, however, that if such an optimization is performed, certain desirable properties of the software are lost. For instance, if the modules mentioned above are eliminated in this manner, flexibility is lost. We no longer have a module that can build the molecule. The ease with which we can perform the change of data structure discussed in Section 5.5.2.1 is lost. This is why the original, unoptimized version should also be retained. Be careful. Do not lose the flexible software resulting from a significant design and implementation effort by throwing it away during optimization.

5.6 SUMMARY

What are the properties of the overall implementation process employed in this chapter? Virtually no code was thrown away between implementation phases. (Drivers and stubs were discarded, but they are intended to be absent in the final version. Some stubs give insight into the structure of the final code.) Each implementation phase used code produced in an earlier phase, either in its original form or in an enhanced form. The enhancements always were extensions of the previous code. Nothing was found to be unnecessary or useless.

The software product, as it currently stands, is very flexible. Certain components can be extracted *as is* and incorporated into a larger system. Enhancements can easily be introduced to add more elements or groups. The software can be modified to allow the user to define his or her own elements or groups (or both). The internal underlying data structures can be changed with relative ease.

Why is such flexibility necessary? What if it is known that the underlying data structures will not change? What if it is known that no significant additions will be made? Why put all this work into producing flexible software? First of all, ''facts'' that are known to be ironclad one day can crumble to historic memorabilia the next. Factors external to the development effort often have a way of forcing modifications. (Congress may pass a new law that makes aspects of the current implementation obsolete.) Other people may be working on similar problems, and it may be decided to incorporate aspects of their software products into your own. If there is no other reason, flexible software should be produced so that newly detected errors can be resolved easily. For instance, the code produced in this chapter still has errors. (See procedure INSERT, case M, call to CONNECT, last argument.)

The flexibility of this software product is no accident. It is derived directly from the design and implementation philosophies that were employed. These techniques *work,* and they apply to all problems. Do a good, complete design and a clean, well-thought-out implementation and the reward will be a flexible piece of software. You will make your professors happy. You will make yourself happy. You will get a better job. The world will be your oyster. (Do not worry; you will like oysters!)

Modular Program Philosophy   6

In Chapter 4 some general implementation techniques were presented. In Chapter 5 these techniques were applied to develop software for a specific problem. However, more than just those techniques presented in Chapter 4 were used to develop the solution. The code was organized into a set of procedures (program modules), each of which could be invoked by a simple CALL statement. This method of organizing the code is often called the *modular program approach*. The modular program approach is well suited to the design methodology that has been developed. With this approach, each functionally complete algorithmic component is embodied within its own program module (such as a procedure, a subroutine or a function). The major candidates for such a modular implementation are the subproblems uncovered during the stepwise refinement process. In other words, each of the boxes present in the structure diagram will probably be implemented within a separate program module.

Some of the algorithmic components may be so simple that, for various reasons, they may be combined (or absorbed) with others to reside within a single program module. Some of them may still be very complex and further refinement may have to be performed, thus producing more program modules. It also may be found that certain utility routines not shown in the structure diagram can be appropriately implemented within separate program modules.

Although the implementer should not necessarily be locked into producing a modular program that corresponds exactly to the structure diagram, a reasonably close approximation usually is preferable. An implementation closely approximating the design probably was the designer's intent. If such an implementation is actually produced, the structure diagram and pseudocode can be used as program documentation.

6.1 ADVANTAGES OF MODULARIZATION

The modular implementation approach has many advantages. While implementing a given module, the implementer need concentrate only on the one functionally complete concept embodied within that module. There is no need to comprehend the total complexity of the system. The implementer need understand only the well-defined function of the module on which he or she is currently working, along with its (narrow, we hope) interface with the rest of the system. It can be viewed as a primitive operation (like addition) to be invoked whenever it is needed. For instance, a module such as the SQRT (square root) function is usually considered to be a primitive operation even though its implementation involves a separate program module.

Once the module is complete, it is not necessary to reconsider the specific algorithm embodied within it. As long as the module performs its required function, it can be invoked without any knowledge of its internal logic. For instance, we might have available three different square root modules, which use Newton's method, bisection, and false position, respectively. Although the performance characteristics of their execution will be different, they are functionally equivalent, and the user need not be familiar with the particular internal algorithm used. (Do you know how the square root is actually computed in FORTRAN or PL/I?)

If, for some reason, the specific algorithm implemented within a module has some undesirable side effects (such as taking too much time or storage), it may be possible to select another functionally equivalent algorithm, one that does not have the undesirable side effect, to replace it. Because the modules are invoked by name, the old (undesirable) module can be removed and a new module, with the same name, can be inserted in its place. Only the one module need be modified and nothing in the remainder of the system need be considered. Since the new module is functionally equivalent to the old one, the modification becomes virtually transparent to the remainder of the system. Only the undesirable side effect has been eliminated. For instance, if a square root module using the bisection method is used in the original implementation and it is found that this algorithm requires excessive time, it may be appropriate to replace it with a module that uses Newton's method.

Modules are invoked by name. Mnemonic names can be chosen to convey (or connote) the functional intent of the module. Code invoking these mnemonically named modules can then be read easily, and the functional content of the algorithm can be conveyed without including the details. Often a module will consist almost entirely of invocations of other modules (with appropriate control structures). The module then becomes essentially an outline of the method by which its internal algorithm is performed.

The primitive algorithmic building blocks of a specific system may be useful in building other systems. This is almost universally true; an algorithm whose implementation limits it to only *one* application is not a very useful algorithm. If the algorithms are implemented as modules (and designed to solve the general problem as opposed to a specific problem), then they can be "lifted" from one application and embedded within another. The ease with which this can be done depends on how well the control and data interfaces have been designed and implemented.

The solution to a problem is *recursive* if it is possible for a subcomponent to invoke itself directly or indirectly. When recursion is involved in the solution to a problem, a specific modular program structure may be forced upon the implementer in order to take advantage of the recursive capabilities of the implementation language. Within languages that allow recursion, there are algorithms for control and data linkage, implicitly embedded within the invocation of a module, that relieve the implementer from burdensome bookkeeping details.

In general, the modular approach to software implementation is extremely advantageous. It allows the implementer to compartmentalize his or her thinking and produce an implementation that corresponds closely to the design. Algorithms can be presented concisely so that the final product can easily be modified, updated, or redesigned. These modules then become potential building blocks that may be useful in developing other software products. Even in cases where a module is invoked only once, it usually is preferable to implement the module and invoke it in the one place it is needed instead of substituting the equivalent code. Any functionally complete algorithmic component is a prime candidate for implementation as a distinct module.

6.2   ORGANIZATION OF MODULAR PROGRAMS

In most current compilers, there are two basic ways of embedding modules within a program: as external modules and as internal modules. External modules are stand-alone modules that can be compiled separately from all the others; they are not (statically) embedded or nested within any other module. Internal modules are statically nested within some other module and must be compiled any time the containing module is compiled.

Different languages offer different combinations of these types of modules. For instance, FORTRAN allows only external modules, PL/I allows both internal and external modules, and ALGOL W allows only internal modules.

6.2.1   Advantages and Disadvantages of Internal Modules

The major purpose for including block structure in an implementation language is to supply the programmer with the ability to pass information (implicitly) across module boundaries without having to pass it (explicitly) through a formal argument list.

This can be accomplished by nesting modules within one another and applying scope-of-name rules, which are determined by the manner in which the variables are declared.

For instance, many of the modules implemented in Chapter 5 access the structure ATOM_TAB. For these procedures to work correctly, they must be embedded in a procedure that declares this structure (in this case, the main procedure). The advantage of passing this structure globally is that it need not be explicitly passed through the parameter list of procedures that do not access it in any way. This technique of globally passing information is most often used when many independent modules need to access common data, but the control structure does not lend itself to passing the data explicitly through a sequence of parameter lists. This has at least two advantages: First, it reduces the complexity of the implementation for the programmer. Second, it facilitates execution efficiency because parameter linkages need not be performed.

One of the advantages of internal modules is that implicit information passing can be accomplished easily. Another is that two different modules can have the same name, in the same way that two different variables may have the same name. Thus, within one region of the program, the invocation of a module named PUSH may access a different module than that invoked by the same name in a different region of the program (Fig. 6.1). This property (local scope-of-name convention) releases the implementer from the burden of having to know the names of all the modules present in the program. (Other programmers working on the same program may have chosen the same names.)

Unfortunately this scope-of-name convention can also be a disadvantage. For instance, if local variables with the same name (but in different modules) are incorrectly declared (not declared), then undesired information sharing can occur. In other words, two logically different variables can (due to programmer error) turn out to be the same variable within the program. For instance, in Figure 6.2, the identifier J refers to the same variable in both PROC1 and PROC2. Thus, if J is logically intended to be a local variable in PROC1, undesired information sharing results. Such errors are extremely difficult to debug.

Another disadvantage of internal modules is that any time a specific module is compiled, the modules internal to it also must be compiled. Thus, as a given module is modified and recompiled, all modules internal to it also must be recompiled even though they have not been modified. This may not be just a question of efficiency with respect to computer time. The newly modified set of modules may have characteristics (for example, too many identifiers) that violate some built-in limits implicit in the compiler implementation. Reaching such limits may force a reorganization of the modules involved.

A third disadvantage is that modules containing internal modules can have a very large textual scope. In other words, the number of lines of program from the opening line of the module to the closing line can be very large. Since the scope of the module may cross many page boundaries, it becomes difficult to read the module and determine its extent (the end of the module).

```
SAMPLE:PROCEDURE;
        o
        o
        o
    BEGIN;
        PUSH:PROCEDURE(A);
                    o
                    o
                    o
        END PUSH;
            o
            o
            o
        CALL PUSH(OBJECT);
            o
            o
            o
    END;        /*  OF BEGIN BLOCK  */
    PROBLEM1:PROCEDURE;
            o
            o
            o
        PUSH:PROCEDURE(A);
                    o
                    o
                    o
        END PUSH;
            o
            o
            o
        CALL PUSH(OBJ);
            o
            o
            o
    END PROBLEM1;
        o
        o
        o
END SAMPLE;
```

FIGURE 6.1 *Example of hidden procedure names.*

6.2.2 Advantages and Disadvantages of External Modules

The major advantage of external modules is that they can be compiled separately, their object code can be saved, and they can be linked together at execution time. This means that as a particular module is modified, only that one module need be recompiled. This consideration is strictly a matter of computer-time efficiency.

Another advantage is that erroneous implicit information sharing is not possible. This is because any variable not explicitly designated as a parameter (there may be several ways of doing this) is local to the module even if it is not declared. Thus the erroneous implicit information sharing that can occur with internal modules is eliminated by the use of external modules. For instance, consider the procedure structure shown in Figure 6.3. The variable corresponding to J in PROC1 will not be the same as that corresponding to the J declared in PROC2. (This is true even if J is not declared in PROC2.) For these two identifiers to correspond to the same

```
PROC1: PROCEDURE;
       /* Declarations that exclude J */
            o
            o
            o
       J = 3;
       CALL PROC2;
            o
            o
            o
END PROC1;

PROC2: PROCEDURE;
       /* Declarations that exclude J */
            o
            o
            o
       J = 5;
            o
            o
            o
END PROC2;
```

FIGURE 6.2 *Implicit data sharing.*

variable, they both must be declared with the EXTERNAL attribute. In other words, the programmer must state *explicitly* that the data are to be shared.

The inability to pass information implicitly to an external module is a restriction since this is one of the purposes of incorporating block structure within the implementation language. Within external modules, there are normally only two ways of sharing data with other modules. One is through the use of a formal parameter list. Another is through the use of "external" variables. (In PL/I, this is done by attaching the EXTERNAL attribute to the variables; in FORTRAN, a COMMON statement is used.) This second method is usually reserved for passing large amounts of data (thus the size of the parameter list can be reduced) or passing data to which the invoking module does not have access (and thus cannot place in its formal argument list).

Another restriction is that no two external modules can have the same name. Also, there may be a limit on the length of the names of external modules.

```
PROC1: PROCEDURE;
       DCL J FIXED BIN(15) EXTERNAL;
            o
            o
            o
END PROC1;
*PROCESS
PROC2: PROCEDURE;
       DCL J FIXED BIN(15);
            o
            o
            o
END PROC2;
```

FIGURE 6.3 *External procedures and variables.*

The choice of the type of module to implement depends on the context in which it will be used. If no information is to be passed to the module implicitly, then it is a candidate for implementation as an external module (unless there is already an external module with the same name). If information is to be passed implicitly, the module will be nested (at some level) within the module in which the implicitly passed variables are declared. In many cases the final decision of whether to implement a module as internal or external is made by the implementer. In languages that allow both types of modules, there is no reason to use either external modules or internal modules exclusively. A combination of the two is common, and the decision is made for each module (or set of modules) separately.

6.2.3 Factors Affecting Module Nesting

There are two major factors that affect module nesting, both of which involve scope-of-name conventions. The first deals with access to variables implicitly passed to the module. A module to which variables are implicitly passed must be nested within the module in which the variables are declared. If several variables declared in different modules are implicitly passed, the internal module must be nested within all of these modules. This observation is really more a restriction on the placement of the variable declarations than on the nesting of the module. In fact, the interplay between nesting of the modules and placement of variable declarations is somewhat of a "chicken-and-egg" problem. The two decisions must be considered jointly and are not independent of one another.

The second factor deals with the ability of invoking modules to access the module in question. This is normally straightforward, especially if the full program expansion of the structure diagram turns out to be a tree (that is, each node in the structure diagram has only one immediate ancestor). However, it can be more complicated if a module is invoked by more than one module.

Consider first the case in which the structure diagram is a tree. The preferred implementation is for each module to be nested within the module that corresponds to its immediate ancestor (one level up) in the structure diagram. This is a natural approach as it corresponds to the design documentation. Modules will have access to all modules they need to access and will be inaccessible to (or hidden from) modules that do not need to access them. Modules can be moved so that they are nested less deeply (and they will still be accessible to the modules that need them), but unless there is some good reason for doing this, it should be avoided.

If the structure diagram is not a tree (there is a module invoked by more than one module), then the above approach must be modified slightly. In general, a module should be nested within its "nearest" dominating ancestor. (A module P dominates module Q if every calling sequence ending in an invocation of Q includes an invocation of P.) For instance, consider the design structure of the stylized diagram in Figure 6.4. Module J cannot be nested within module F because it will not be accessible to module G. Similarly, it cannot be nested within module G. Module J should be nested within module B, its nearest dominating ancestor. Using similar logic, modules H and D should be nested within module A, and modules M and I should be nested within module C. The static nesting structure of the PL/I code corresponding to the structure diagram of Figure 6.4 is presented in Figure 6.5. If this rule is applied, each module will have access to the modules it needs. Again, modules can be moved so that they are nested less deeply than this rule suggests.

The actual nesting of the modules within the program depends on the implicit data-passing structure, the required accessability of the modules, and the personal preference of the implementer.

6.2.4 Subroutines Versus Functions

What criteria should be used in deciding whether to implement a module in the form of a function (a module which has an intrinsic data type and returns a value through the module name) or a subroutine (a module which does not return a value through the module name)?

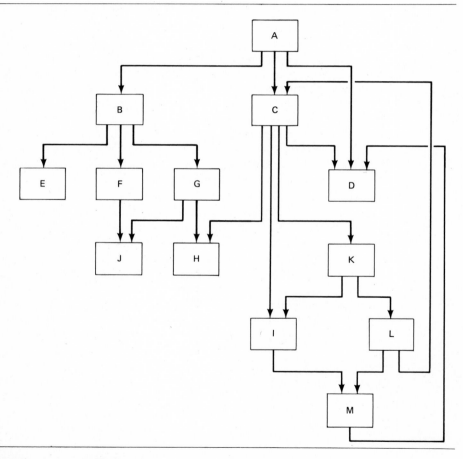

FIGURE 6.4 *Example structure diagram.*

```
A: PROCEDURE;
    B: PROCEDURE;
        E: PROCEDURE;
            o
            o
            o
        END E;
        F: PROCEDURE;
            o
            o
            o
        END F;
        G: PROCEDURE;
            o
            o
            o
        END G;
        J: PROCEDURE;
            o
            o
            o
        END J;
        o
        o
        o
    END B;
    C: PROCEDURE;
        K: PROCEDURE;
            L: PROCEDURE;
                o
                o
                o
            END L;
            o
            o
            o
        END K;
        I: PROCEDURE;
            o
            o
            o
        END I;
        M: PROCEDURE;
            o
            o
            o
        END M;
        o
        o
        o
    END C;
    H: PROCEDURE;
        o
        o
        o
    END H;
    D: PROCEDURE;
        o
        o
        o
    END D;
    o
    o
    o
END A;
```

FIGURE 6.5 *Static program structure.*

In general, the following guidelines can be used to decide if a module should be implemented as a function if:

1. one and only one value is to be returned to the invoking module, and

2. there is very little probability of an unexpected error occurring within the module, or any errors that do occur can be handled completely within the module itself.

A module should be implemented as a subroutine if:

1. there are zero or more than one values to be returned to the invoking module, or

2. there is a significant probability of an unexpected error occurring that the module itself cannot handle.

For instance, a module that determines the square root of a number is normally implemented in the form of a function because it has one input parameter (the value for which the square root is to be taken) and returns one and only one value (the square root). An error can occur within the module if the input value is negative. However, the probability of this occurring is considered to be small (because the programmer is assumed to know what he or she is doing) and the error can be resolved within the module by printing an error message and applying the algorithm to the negative of the input value.

A module that determines the inverse of a square matrix is normally implemented in the form of a subroutine because the value to be returned to the invoking module is not a single value; it is a square matrix of values. The array to be returned may not be calculable becaused the original input matrix may not be invertible. Thus an error may occur that cannot be handled entirely within the module.

Any module that can be implemented in the form of function can, of course, be implemented in the form of a subroutine. This can be done simply by adding one more argument to the argument list and passing the value that normally would be returned via the module name through the added argument. However, if the module meets the criteria of a functional implementation, a subroutine implementation is not preferable. One of the purposes of using a high-level language is the clarity and conciseness by which the implementer can present the algorithm. Functional notation is one of the features of most high-level languages that allows the implementer to convey an algorithm succinctly.

Consider the calculation of the value

$$(A**0.5 + B**0.5 + C**0.5)**0.5$$

using a square-root module. If a square-root function is used, this can be written very concisely in the form

```
ANSWER = SQRT(SQRT(A) + SQRT(B) + SQRT(C));
```

However, if we use a square-root subroutine, SQRT_SUB, in which the first argument is the value for which the square root is to be taken and the second argument is the returned square root, then the code might take the following form.:

```
CALL SQRT_SUB(A,SQRTA);
CALL SQRT_SUB(B,SQRTB);
CALL SQRT_SUB(C,SQRTC);
CALL SQRT_SUB(SQRTA + SQRTB + SQRTC,ANSWER);
```

The functional form of the code is much clearer and more concise; it does not require the explicit use of temporary variables and is probably more efficiently handled by the compiler (during both compilation and execution) than the subroutine form of the code.

6.3 DOCUMENTATION AND PRESENTATION

Each module should be documented within the program itself. External documentation is necessary and can be a significant aid in understanding the internal algorithm, interfacing, and use of a module. However, for various reasons, this external documentation may not be available when a given module is to be analyzed. A little documentation permanently embedded in the code itself can go a long way toward helping the reader understand the module. The following three forms of documentation have been found very useful in describing the overview of the module, and generally they are considered sufficient internal documentation.

- Top-level documentation.

- Variable dictionary.

- In-line comments.

6.3.1 Top-Level Documentation

The purpose of top-level documentation is to convey the overall content of the module. It precedes the procedure definition (comes before the PROCEDURE statement) and is preferably delimited by surrounding it with a box of asterisks. It should start at the top of a page.

This form of documentation should be an abstract of the logical content and the control and data interfaces of the module. In general, it should include the following.

- Statement of the function or purpose of the module.

- Name of the particular algorithm used (if it is well known and documented in the literature).

- Parameters, both explicit and implicit, along with a statement of their logical content.

- Names of all the other modules this module depends on.

If unusual or tricky code (such as an explicit GOTO that transfers control out of the module) is present within the module, it should be indicated here. In general, anything the reader should know before trying to understand the details of the implementation of the algorithm should be included.

6.3.2 Variable Dictionary

All formal parameters and local variables used within the module should be declared. This provides a perfect place for documenting the logical content of each variable.

A suggested format is to declare each variable on a separate line. Since variable names are usually relatively short and the variable name will reside on the leftmost portion of the line, a significant portion of the line is available for a comment. One-half to three-fourths of a line is often sufficient to convey the essence of the logical content of the variable.

Complicated data structures may require a more detailed description. A small block of comments can be placed just before the declaration of the data structure, and one-line comments can still be embedded within the structure itself.

6.3.3 In-line Comments

It often is helpful to include a few comments within the body of the module to describe the intent of the major code segments. Usually a one-line comment is enough to convey the required information. Comments need not be full sentences; they may be simple phrases. In-line comments might include these.

- Conditions true (or false) upon entering or exiting a loop.

- External conditions corresponding to program conditions being tested in an IF statement.

- Conditions true (or false) upon entering the THEN or ELSE clause of an IF statement.

- Assumptions about input data.

- Indication of which END statement corresponds to which DO statement (especially if they are reasonably far apart).

- Comment for each case of a CASE statement to indicate the specific case being processed.

In addition, any tricky or potentially confusing code should be *well* documented to indicate its functional intent.

In general, in-line comments should not be overdone. Only enough information should be included to convey the essence of the intent of the code. Comments should be formatted (indented) so that they do not interfere with reading the code itself. In general, the code should be written clearly enough that its intent is self-evident. In-line comments are *secondary* aids to the reader; they supply back-up information in the case that the reader cannot extract the intent from the code itself.

6.3.4 Order of Presentation

The content of all modules within a program should be presented in a consistent, standardized order so that the reader knows where to look for the information he or she wants to extract. The following order of presentation is preferred, although small variations are acceptable as long as the presentation remains consistent throughout the program.

- Top-level comment block.

- Procedure definition (the PROCEDURE statement).

- Declarations of parameters, local variables and internal modules (along with the variable dictionary).

- Definitions of internal modules nested within the module.

- The main code block for the module itself.

- The end of the module (the END statement).

White space (blank lines) should be used to delimit the different sections of the module from one another, and indentation can be used effectively to indicate block structure.

6.4 SUMMARY

The development of implementation modules that correspond to the conceptual modules identified in the design phase is a standard practice and has many pragmatic advantages. Verification of their correctness and the correctness of the total system is essentially inherited from the verification performed during the design phase. The structure of the implementation can be made to correspond to the structure diagram developed during the design phase, again facilitating verification. Because the implementation modules inherit functional independence from the design, they can be coded and tested separately (by use of drivers and stubs), thus reducing the complexity of the testing phase. Because of their functional independence and their encapsulation into self-contained computational units, the system can easily be reconfigured. These functions may be useful in other applications, and the modules can be extracted, as is, to supply building blocks for other systems.

In the development of modular systems, many implementation decisions must be made. These include the following.

- Implementation as an internal or external module.

- Nesting of internal modules.

- Method of data communication—global or parameter list.

- Implementation as a subroutine or function.

Criteria have been given for which options to select and their advantages and disadvantages.

Documentation and presentation styles have been presented. Although these styles are fairly standard, small variations are acceptable as long as consistency is maintained.

PROBLEMS

1. It was stated earlier (Sec. 6.2.4) that the square-root operation is suitable for implementation as a function. Suppose that we wanted to broaden its scope so that it would operate as follows: If the input value submitted to it were positive, it would operate as one would expect. If the input value were negative, it would return the square root of the absolute value.

   a. What additional considerations are implied in this redefinition of the operation's duties?

   b. Is a function still the appropriate structural choice for this new set of duties? If so, why? If not, why not?

2. For each of the following computational modules.

   a. Indicate whether it should be implemented as a function or subroutine. Give reasons to support your choice.

   b. List all input and output parameters.

   c. State which of the parameters listed in (b) should be passed explicitly and which should be set up globally. Describe your assumptions about the operating environment in which the module is to perform.

   (1) nth root of an arbitrary value A.

   (2) The inverse of an arbitrary matrix A.

   (3) The substring consisting of the fifth through ninth characters of an arbitrary character string A.

   (4) The logarithm to the base 2 of an arbitrary value A.

   (5) The logarithm to the base n of an arbitrary value A. (The two input parameters are n and A.)

   (6) The third largest element in an arbitrary array A.

(7) The nth largest element in an arbitrary array A.

(8) The position of an arbitrary entry E in an arbitrary table T.

(9) $A \mod B$.

How many of these "operations" have an intrinsic facility for indicating an error? For those that can indicate an error, how do they specify the error that has occurred? What implicit assumptions have you made about the parameters? For each operation in which you made such assumptions, indicate which assumptions can be dropped to generalize the module.

3. As a general supplier of software products, you have been contracted to prepare a module with a specific purpose of taking an arbitrary string of characters and centering that string on a line that eventually will be printed. The length and contents of this string are arbitrary, as is the length of the line in which this string is to appear. Assume that the contents of the rest of the line are unimportant.

   a. Indicate the design and implementation assumptions that you would consider reasonable in light of the fact that nothing is known about the context in which such an operation would be performed.

   b. Consistent with the assumptions made in (*a*), indicate exactly what the requirements would be to interface with this module. (Remember that you cannot assume that every invocation will be successful.)

4. In the design and implementation of self-contained modules, there are many ways of handling errors or other exceptional circumstances. A few are listed below.

   (1) Stop. For instance, an attempt to compute the square root of a negative number in a FORTRAN program often halts all processing.

   (2) Return an error code through an explicit error parameter. F$ERROR, used in the implementation in Chapter 5, encodes such information.

   (3) Return an indication of the error through a data parameter. For example, the PL/I built-in function INDEX returns the value zero if the desired string is not found.

   (4) Print an explicit error message, but give no other indication that an error occurred. For example, when PL/C encounters an uninitialized variable, it prints an error message and initializes the variable to a predefined value. However, the error is not reported to any other module; the program cannot take appropriate action.

   (5) Allow the user to specify conditional actions. The ON CONDITION facility in PL/I exemplifies this approach.

Describe the operating environments in which each of these approaches is appropriate and give their advantages for those environments. Give an example of a built-in function in PL/I (or another high-level language) for each of these approaches.

5. Suppose that the structural capabilities of a particular high-level language are rich enough to allow the organization of programs in which each module is external to all others. Alternatively, it is equally possible (in this language) to make all modules internal to the main procedure (and to other modules). Thus the choice of a particular organization becomes a matter of "taste."

   a. What criteria would you use for making such structural choices?

   b. What are the implications of choosing one organizational approach over the other?

   c. Based on your considerations in (a) and (b), how would you organize the modules described in Chapter 5 and the appendix? Give reasons for your answer.

6. Referring to Problem 5, assume that you chose to make all procedures (in Chap. 5 and the appendix) external to all others. Which parameters would you pass explicitly and which would you pass globally by use of the EXTERNAL attribute? (Include explicit lists of parameters in your answer.)

7. Analyze the method used for passing each parameter in the implementation of Chapter 5 and the appendix. (Note that three ways are employed: explicit transmission, global transmission, and transmission through function names; are there any others?) For each parameter, state why it should or should not have been passed in the way shown in the text. Give alternatives if you disagree. Be careful! Do not assume that the way presented in the text is the best way.

8. Is it always possible to select a module from a design and build a stub for it? Refer to the code given in the appendix.

   a. Build a stub for FIND_NEXT.

   b. Build a stub for SPEC_HAND.

   c. Build a stub for BLD_MAP.

9. Consider a structure diagram such as the one shown in Figure 3.13. Answer these questions for every module that is invoked by only one other module.

   a. Is it always possible to replace the invocation (in the invoking module) with the actual code?

   b. What are the implications of such replacement?

c. What are the implications when this type of replacement is done for a module that is invoked from several places?

d. Can this be done with recursive modules?

10. Write the pseudocode for a generic driver that is a model for *all* drivers. Find a specific application where your generic driver is not general enough. Try to generalize your generic driver to handle all situations. Can you do it?

11. Refer to Project 1 in Chapter 3. Here is a PL/I implementation for one possible way of computing $P(x)$, the value of an nth-order polynomial at some value x.

```
P: PROCEDURE (N,COEFF,X,POL);
/************************************************************/
/*  N:      THE DEGREE OF THE POLYNOMIAL                 */
/*  COEFF:  A VECTOR OF (N+1) COEFFICIENTS               */
/*  X:      THE VALUE AT WHICH THE POLYNOMIAL IS TO BE   */
/*          COMPUTED.                                    */
/************************************************************/
      DECLARE
         (COEFF(*), X) FLOAT BINARY,
          POL FLOAT BINARY (53),
         (N,I)             FIXED BINARY;
      POL = 0;
      DO I = N+1 TO 2 BY -1;
         POL = X * (POL+COEFF(I));
         END;
      POL = POL + COEFF(1);
      RETURN;
      END P;
```

Assume that this module is to be prepared for delivery to customers who will use it in completely arbitrary ways. Write a suitable driver to develop this module. Describe classes of input parameters that will cause it to malfunction.

12. In Enhancement 1C (of Chap. 3), you were asked to provide this software product with an input expression processor to make the integrator more flexible and, in some ways, more convenient to its users. If good structural design principles are followed, then the rest of the processing should be unaffected by the incorporation of this enhancement, regardless of the actual form such incorporation may take. Accordingly, detailed design decisions regarding the structure of the enhancement can be made separately.

a. Should the input expression processor be handled as one module or as several? Indicate the reasons for your choices. If your decision is for several modules, define the processing scope of each module as well as the interface among the various modules by means of a suitable structure diagram.

b. For each module defined in (*a*), design and code a suitable driver to be used for the development of that module.

    c. Design a skeleton for the overall input expression processor in which each of the modules defined in (*a*) is represented by a suitable stub.

13. Figure 3.18 presents the code for a pseudorandom generator suitable for certain types of computers. Specify the code for a suitable driver that can be used to exercise this module.

14. Refer to Project 3 in Chapter 3.

    a. Prepare a detailed structure diagram showing each specific module that you have defined for whatever version of the project you have selected to design. Indicate the information supplied as input to each module and the information delivered by that module as output. For each module, indicate how you have enforced the idea of functional isolation. Also, if applicable, explain why certain items of information are passed locally while others are set up as global items.

    b. Code a suitable driver for the project.

    c. Using the driver in (*b*) as a basis, build a framework for your project by representing each of the modules defined in (*a*) by a suitable stub.

15. After examining Problem 14, it is clear that the considerations voiced there apply to any of the projects specified initially at the end of Chapter 3. (In fact, Prob. 14 is intended to serve as a model for the project-related activities at this stage of the project's evolution.) Accordingly, apply the requirements of Problem 14 to the particular project (or projects) on which you are working.

16. The heart of the generalized frequency analyzer (Proj. 4, Chap. 3) is a process that updates a set of frequency counters to reflect the contributions of the most recent set of input data. Because it is to be functionally isolated, this process is (or should be) oblivious to the format of those input data. Moreover, it should be sufficiently general so that its operation will be unaffected by the number of variables to be counted, the number of categories in each variable, and even the way those categories happen to be encoded.

    With all of this in mind, design and code a software component that will perform the required updating activities. You may choose to implement your software as a single module or as a set of interacting modules.

    a. Explain why you chose to use one (or several) modules.

    b. Devise a suitable driver for developing this process in isolation.

17. Refer to Project 3, Chapter 3. Regardless of the particular design used, a basic data-file generator inevitably includes a component designed to construct the next record in the output file. One form this activity may take is a cyclic process in which the ''record builder'' is invoked for each variable in the

record. Using the value to be assigned to that variable (in the record being built), along with other (descriptive) information about the variable, the component installs the value (in proper form) in its proper position in the record.

   a. Does the record builder or the invoking component "know" when the record is complete? Give the reasons for your answer.

   b. Is the record builder a single module or a grouping of several modules under a single "supervisor"? Give reasons for your choice.

18. Refer to Enhancement 4*D* in Chapter 3. The crucial process involved in this enhancement is the actual substitution of a group encodement for a member of a set of encodements eligible for such replacement. Use the specifications given in the enhancement.

   a. Define the input and output requirements for a module designed to perform these substitutions.

   b. If you were to design such a module, would you process a single variable in an invocation or would your design handle a complete set of observations? Give reasons for your answer.

   c. Write the code for the module consistent with your decisions in (*a*) and (*b*).

   d. Write a suitable driver for the module produced in (*c*).

19. Refer to Project 5 in Chapter 3, especially Enhancement 5*I*. This enhancement indicates the possibility for identifying and correcting a variety of errors in infix expressions.

   a. Should the correction portion of this process be part of the same module that performs the error detection? Give the reasons for your reply.

   b. Regardless of your choice in (*a*), there is still a further choice of treating the error correction activity as a single module or as a group of interrelated modules operating under a supervisor. Describe the advantages and disadvantages of each approach.

20. Refer to Enhancement 6*H*, Chapter 3. The nucleus of this enhancement involves the computation of chi-square, along with an associated probability value.

   a. Should the value of chi-square (for a given two-way frequency table) and the accompanying probability be produced by a single module or should the probability computation be handled separately? Give reasons for your answer.

   b. Prepare a detailed structure diagram for a software component that produces a value of chi-square and the corresponding probability for a single table. Indicate the input and output requirements for the module (or modules) in your design.

c. Regardless of whether the probability is computed in a separate module or included in the same one that develops chi-square, there still is a choice of developing the probability by looking up values in a table or by direct computation. Discuss the advantages and disadvantages of each approach.

d. Implement a driver suitable for developing the software component designed in (*b*).

21. Refer to Project 10, Chapter 3. One of the most conspicuous services offered by a text formatter is that of line justification: the positioning of text on a line image so that it meets a particular set of line width requirements while still distributing text across the line's extent in a balanced manner.

a. Indicate the input and output requirements for a software component designed to perform such line justification.

b. Code a line justifier consistent with the characteristics identified in (*a*).

c. Write a driver suitable for developing the justifier in (*b*).

The following three problems develop computational algorithms for processing tables. Their use spans a wide range of applications, so that they represent powerful and useful techniques to know about. In addition, they will be helpful in solving Problem 25. Accordingly, we suggest that you read that problem before reading the material given below.

22. There are numerous *sorting algorithms* for ordering elements in an $N \times M$ table (array) into a specific sequence. The technique described here is called an *index sort*. Its intent is to reduce the amount of computational work involved in those situations in which entire rows are to be exchanged with each other.

In this technique, the data array is supplemented by an external array INDEX designed to "point to" the rows of the table. Initially, INDEX(I) = I (for $1 \leq I \leq N$). When the sorting procedure determines that two of the rows in the table are to be interchanged, the corresponding elements in INDEX, rather than the data values themselves, are interchanged.

This technique, embedded as a component in some (unspecified) sorting procedure, is shown as a flowchart in Figure 6.6.

a. Prepare a pseudocode representation of this algorithm, suitable for a table of arbitrary size. Include a list of input and output parameters, and state your assumptions regarding the ordering of the elements in the table.

b. Translate the pseudocode in (*a*) to program language statements. What have you assumed about the data types of the table entries?

c. Write a driver to test the module coded in (*b*).

d. Is it possible to change your pseudocode (and coding) so that the same algorithm can be used to sort a table either in descending or ascending

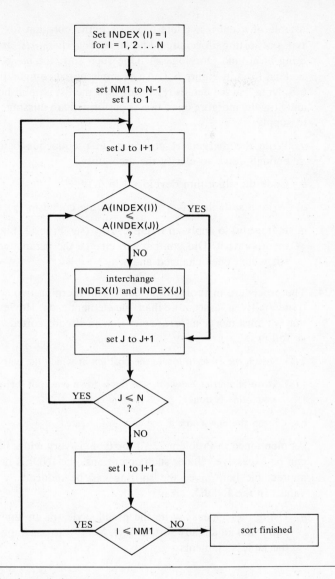

FIGURE 6.6 *Specification for an index sort.*

order? Introduce this modification. (The ease or difficulty of this task will tell you something about the quality of your design.)

23. The sorting algorithm in Figure 6.6 (often called a *linear*, or *jump-down*, sort) is one of many sorting algorithms. The level of its performance generally is expressed in terms of its *order*. This particular algorithm is of order $n**2$ (written $O(n**2)$), meaning that it takes roughly $C*n**2$ operations to process

a table of n entries. (Here C is a specific constant for the algorithm.) Other types of sorting procedures, known as *recursive sorts,* are more efficient, operating at around $O(n*\log_2 n)$. One such sort, the *merge-sort,* is presented in skeletal form in Figure 6.7. An example of the computation is shown in Figure 6.8. Note that the details regarding how the list is split, how the recursion ends, and how the merging operation is performed are missing. Those are left for you to supply.

   a. Write the merge-sort algorithm in pseudocode being careful to include enough detail to clarify the ambiguity.

   b. Code the algorithm developed in (*a*).

   c. Write a suitable driver for the module coded in (*b*).

   d. Is it useful to apply an INDEX array (see Prob. 22) in this algorithm? If so, incorporate it. Did you have to change the parameters to incorporate it? If so, which ones changed and why?

24. The procedure in Problem 23 dealt with merging two sorted lists that contain (potentially, at least) more than one element each. However, it is often the case that we must merge a *single* entry into an already sorted table. This can be done as follows.

   (1) Search the table to locate the position at which the entry is to be inserted.

   (2) Move all entries below this position down one spot (being careful of the order in which this is done).

   (3) Insert the new entry in the spot just vacated.

As mentioned in Problem 22, if the table is very wide, internal data movement can be excessive. Under such conditions, the INDEX array concept can be of appreciable help since the shifting can be reduced by transferring it to the values in the INDEX array.

   a. Using these ideas, write the pseudocode for an algorithm that inserts one entry into an already sorted table. State your assumptions about the order of the table's elements.

```
SORT(LIST1)
    Split LIST1 into two lists, LIST2 and LIST3.
        Sort LIST2, i.e., invoke SORT(LIST2).
            (Here, of course, is the recursion.)
        Sort LIST3, i.e., invoke SORT(LIST3).
        Merge LIST2 and LIST3 back into LIST1.
```

FIGURE 6.7 *Specification for a merge-sort.*

                MODULAR PROGRAM PHILOSOPHY

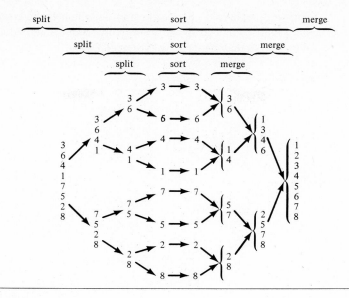

FIGURE 6.8 *Merge-sort example.*

b. Code the algorithm prepared in (*b*). (The more code you can lift from previous problems, the better.)

c. Write a driver for your module.

25. Upon return from an expedition up the Monanga River, a team of Washington University biologists found that they had inadvertently brought several specimens of the dreaded tsi-tsi beetle with them, hidden in their equipment. This discovery came too late, so that the creatures were introduced into the local ecology. Finding no tsi-tsi to eat, the beetles adapted quickly, selecting corn as their food.

    You can understand the biologists' concern. Hence, it is no surprise that they have undertaken the task of developing a pesticide to control the beetles. In this connection, they are asking you to prepare a program that will help them analyze and update their records. Here is the general problem: There are two separate subspecies—the hook-nose tsi-tsi and the pug-nose tsi-tsi, each of which responds differently to the pesticides being tested. Hence, separate analyses will have to be conducted for each subspecies. Each poison has a numeric code of four digits or less and is categorized as one of three types.

(1) Poisons that attack the central nervous system.

(2) Poisons that enter the circulatory system.

(3) Poisons that act on the respiratory system.

Data are prepared on punched cards, in which each card provides either summary information or update information about a particular poison. Both summary and update cards have the same format.

Card Columns	Entry
1	Card type (1 = update, 2 = summary)
7-10	Poison identification code
12	Poison type (1, 2, or 3, as explained above)
16-21	Date (*mmddyy*): For update cards, this is the completion date of the experiment; for summary cards, this is completion date of most recent experiment.
25-27	Number of hook-nose beetles to which the poison is administered.
28-30	Number of pug-nose beetles to which the poison is administered.
36-38	Number of hook-nose beetles dying.
39-41	Number of pug-nose beetles dying.

You are supplied with a data deck containing 15 summary cards followed by an unknown number of update cards.

(1) Read the entries from the first 15 data cards into arrays. Sort the table by poison code in ascending order using an index sort procedure. Print the sorted table, displaying poison code, poison type, date, number of beetles exposed, number of beetles dying, and percent of beetles dying. The latter three items should be subdivided into three sets of results: hook-nose, pug-nose, and total.

(2) Read and process each update card separately. The last update card will have a zero poison code and should not be processed. If the poison code on a given update card is not in the table, insert it at the appropriate position. If it is already there, perform an update as follows.

The new information from the update card following the date (starting in column 25) should be *added* to the corresponding table entries.

The date on the update card should replace the date in the table.

For each update card, print one line of information echoing what was read from the card. After all update cards have been processed, print the new (updated) table. You may assume that no more than 25 entries will exist in the table after all updates have been processed.

a. Develop a total design, including a structure diagram and pseudocode for all modules.

b. Code your algorithm. How much code were you able to lift from Problems 22-24?

c. What special editing should be performed on the input fields? Are all of the columns of the table independent of one another? Which ones are not? Are rows of the table independent of one another? Finally, describe the actions your design takes upon finding an error during the input editing process.

The Design of
Program Modules

7

In the previous chapter we discussed the role of the modular programming approach within the larger context of the structured design process. With this as background we are ready to examine the major issues underlying the design of the module itself. In order to do that effectively, it will be helpful to look at the idea of modularization in terms of its past usage.

The idea of modularization is not new. The concept of a subroutine emerged almost simultaneously with that of the program itself. However, there have been some important changes in basic attitudes regarding program modules that have a direct bearing on structured design and our view of it. Originally, the major benefit of a program module was perceived to be the replacement of redundant physical copies of code with a single one, accessible from an arbitrary number of points in a program. In this light the outcome was (and continues to be) a spectacular success.

With growing experience came the realization that this idea of arbitrary accessibility can be generalized so that a subroutine or other structural entity, once completed and validated, could be made available to any number of independent programs. The construction and use of separately compiled subprograms thus became an increasingly popular practice. For many computer installations there were visions of a type of operating environment in which extensive libraries of such modules would be available for all to use. Presumably, then, implementation of a new program would involve little more than a synthesis of existing modules tied together by means of a main program consisting of little more than calls to these various modules. As a result, modularization was seen by many people as a complete methodology, or an end in itself.

With this orientation the results of modularization were decidedly less spectacular. In fact, the effectiveness of this practice varied widely among computer installations that followed it. Surveys of such usage revealed a surprisingly high incidence of cases in which program modules were crafted as potential library components, only to end up being used in a single application. The resulting libraries were filled with many such subprograms (often hundreds) whose incorporation into additional applications was highly unlikely. To salt the wound a little more, many of these subprograms were accessed from only one place in their respective containing programs. Thus the programs suffered the storage and execution time penalties imposed by the additional overhead of subprogram invocation and return mechanisms, with none of the accompanying benefits.

While it may be tempting for such installations to downgrade or even condemn modularization for its unfulfilled promise, we must bear in mind the relatively limited perspective within which the technique was being advocated: In many instances the basic difficulty was that the physical process of breaking a program into subprograms was perceived as the crux of an overall methodology for implementing computer applications. Stated somewhat extremely, the contention was that a program is intrinsically better because of its modularity.

In dealing with a structured design methodology, we must adopt a broader attitude with regard to modularization. It is worth reemphasizing that modularization and structured design are not synonymous. Rather, the division of a program into functionally identifiable subprograms turns out to be a very effective and convenient way to help reduce apparent complexity (at the more abstract levels of the design) by subdividing a large (impossibly) complex problem into distinct logical pieces whose respective boundaries lie within our capacity. This means that the reduction of complexity, rather than potential usefulness in a general library, becomes the primary motivation in designing and constructing such modules. It is certainly not necessary to abandon the latter objective completely. However, we shall find that the actions we take to design a particular module to simplify its structure and its interconnections with other modules in a program will tend to increase the utility of that module in other contexts.

7.1 GUIDING CONCEPTS IN MODULAR DESIGN

Before we speak about those factors influencing the extent, form, and contents of a well-designed module, it will be helpful to state explicitly what we mean by *module*. We are dealing with a structural unit of implementation, that is, a program or subprogram whose organizational construction is self-contained. As indicated in Chapter 6, this unit may be embedded in another, larger unit, broken further into smaller units, or concatenated with another unit, the choice depending on a variety of factors. Transcending these decisions (the details of putting together the modules) is the notion that the module represents a cohesive unit of processing identified as such. Saying the same thing in terms of a program or subprogram, this means that the module has a name that identifies the entire extent of its processing. Accordingly, that name is available to other modules, serving as a means for referring to (invoking) the module. Similarly, because of its status as a single processing entity, the module can invoke other modules because those names are available to it.

In block-structured programming languages, there are likely to be organizational units that might be considered as modules under certain circumstances. For example, the BEGIN block or DO group in PL/I may plausibly exhibit the behavior of a processing unit: It can represent a single unified activity of arbitrary extent or complexity. However, in our context the overall purposes of structured design are better served if such a processing entity also fulfills the organizational requirements of a separate identity. Not only can it be invoked this way and, in turn, invoke other modules, but it can also be developed and tested separately when constructed as a distinct procedure. If a particular processing activity is sufficiently extensive or complex to be treated separately, it is beneficial to recognize it as a separate implementation unit and set it up as a procedure or subprogram.

A second notion worth reemphasizing is *design*. In trying to set up and use guidelines for the design of procedural modules, we must continue to bear in mind the implications of the design activity. Regardless of the context, design is basically a creative undertaking requiring a combination of talent and insight that cannot be replaced by laws, rules of practice, and household hints. Guidelines are, thus, meant to support ingenuity with the benefits of accumulated experience and observations so that known pitfalls and blind alleys can be avoided when possible. Guidelines are not meant to (nor can they) produce a ''perfect'' design process that can be learned like typing. Nor can they avoid the necessary use of iteration in arriving at a satisfactory design. Under the best of conditions, there will be situations in which design decisions are made whose implications do not become completely clear until we try to implement some particular component motivated by that design. For example, we may find that a particular algorithm selected for building a table performs poorly because it is unexpectedly sensitive to the distribution of values going into that table. In such circumstances it is perfectly reasonable to repeat the algorithmic design or selection activity, followed by validation of the new candidate. This can be done in an orderly fashion. Thus, in our example, discovery that a table builder is inefficient brings us back to the previous stage in which we designed the table builder. It does not (and should not) bring us back to an even earlier stage where we decided that there should be a table builder of some kind.

7.1.1 Design Objectives

Obviously, each module will have a set of functional objectives that have to be met if that module is to play its proper role in the overall application. Consistent with the structured approach, such objectives will have been defined when the overall implementation was partitioned into modules. The design objectives in that context were to define each module such that its functional scope could conveniently be grasped and comprehended. At this point, therefore, we build on the notion that we already know what the module is supposed to do, and we are ready to focus on how it can be organized and constructed effectively for this purpose.

The traditional design objective of good performance (speed of execution and conservation of main storage) is still a factor, but certainly not the primary one. In light of our earlier discussion regarding software problems, this goal must share our attention with others, each of which is likely to be at least as important.

1. *Reliability*. The objective is to deliver a module free of operating errors so that it can be integrated into the application without concern about whether it does what it is supposed to do. As a precursor, the design should be such that the module approaches its first test with a minimum of errors. Instead of coding carefully and counting on elaborate testing to find and remove the errors, the idea is to *design* carefully so that many of these errors are not introduced in the first place when the module actually is coded.

2. *Maintainability*. While the delivery of an error-free module is a reasonable design objective, it is unrealistic to assume that it will always be met. Accordingly, we should aim for error-free products but the design should make it as easy as possible to locate and correct errors when and if they occur. In many instances this means that a well designed module is equipped with code whose primary purpose it is to detect and react to errors. We shall have more to say about this later.

3. *Generality*. Frequently a module intended for a specific use within an implementation can easily be expanded at the design stage to broaden its applicability. In addition to making this module potentially useful in other implementations, this type of attention during design often anticipates correctly some area of growth in the application itself. It is a good practice to look for opportunities to generalize when the module is being designed.

4. *Simplicity*. This is another aspect of the campaign to reduce apparent complexity. Complementing the restriction of a module's functional scope is the idea of explicitly hiding those aspects of the module's operational and structural characteristics that do not contribute to one's understanding. Thus it is desirable to make the module as easy as possible to use by maximizing its structural independence.

Fulfillment of these design objectives is interlinked with the size of the modules identified during the design. In the next section, we shall discuss some of the basic ideas regarding module size and the factors that may affect it.

7.1.2 The Size of a Module

As a rule of thumb, modules should be restricted to roughly *one page,* including documentation. This manageable size makes modules easier to read and comprehend; it is not necessary to flip back and forth across page boundaries in order to extract the pertinent concepts. For various reasons (such as lengthy documentation or use of a large CASE component), a module may be longer than a page. This is acceptable as long as it does not affect the code's clarity; but any module longer than two pages should be analyzed carefully to see whether it should be decomposed into multiple modules.

The physical extent of a module cannot be used by itself as an absolute criterion for proper length. Although 50 statements often is specified as being a reasonable limit, it should be emphasized that this yardstick must be qualified carefully as each situation dictates. The need to encompass a functional component with clear boundaries and limited complexity is the overriding one. Experience has indicated that an independent functional component, once defined and recorded, often turns out to be about 50 lines. Furthermore, since that corresponds to a block of code that fits comfortably on a single page of most printout devices, it is comfortable to read and easy to grasp.

Thus, for most situations, the length of the module really is a consequence rather than a predefined explicit objective. There will be times when a group of closely related activities requires more extensive code to express the intent, yet there is no particular difficulty in comprehending the overall meaning. For example, suppose a data-processing application performed a variety of tasks to prepare components for an output record. At some point, all this processing has been completed and it is appropriate to gather up the components and position them to create a final record image. Although the series of assignments required to do this may be quite extensive, this affects neither the complexity of the overall process nor our ability to understand and cope with it. Consequently, we should not want to break up these multiple assignments just because the extent of the resulting module happens to come out ''too long.''

Conversely, it is equally plausible to find a situation where each of two rather intricate decision structures may be represented by a dozen lines of high-level language code. The fact that each decision structure is a functional entity argues for its expression as a distinct module. There is no good reason to combine the two processes into a single module just because both will fit on one page.

Under some conditions we may identify a functionally distinct activity whose overall complexity is well within our grasp and whose expression as a module results in code that is easy to follow and comfortably brief. However, the number of pieces of data directly affected by that single module in nontrivial ways requires an inordinate amount of testing to make sure that the full spectrum of combinations has been checked. Practicality, then, will force further subdivision into two or more modules, each of which can be implemented and tested independently. Then, with a few additional tests, it will be possible to evaluate the operation of the modules working together.

For instance, suppose that a module had 6 interdependent yes-or-no decisions, so that each had to be tested 2 ways in order to provide a complete evaluation. Therefore, a total of 2**6 or 64 tests would be required for this purpose. On the other hand, assume that a procedural division could be made so that the functional intent of the module were restated in terms of 2 modules, each of which handled 3 of the interdependent decisions. Interaction between the modules, moreover, is assumed to require 2 data items. Then, evaluation of each module would require 2**3 or 8 tests (still assuming 2 tests per decision). In addition, 4 tests would be required to check the interaction, so that a total of 20 tests would replace the 64 required for exhaustive evaluation of a single module. These savings, of course, would be more or less dramatic depending on the complexity of the module and the number of tests required for a complete (or satisfactory) evaluation.

7.1.3 Connections Between Modules

As with the size of a module, there are no exact rules that prescribe a "correct" way to connect modules with one another. That is, we cannot give a formula or recipe that defines the most desirable combination of control mechanisms and data transfers for establishing the relationships between a module and other modules that invoke it or are invoked by it. This does not alter the fact that, in a given situation, certain types of interconnections will be more desirable than others. The factors motivating such choices often will include a considerable amount of judgement, so that each of several approaches might be equally defensible. However, we can still impose some discipline by relating back to the basic intents of modularization, that is, the reduction of apparent complexity by identifying and developing functionally independent units of processing. Let us take a little closer look at what it means to implement a functionally independent module in a collection of such modules.

> Other parts of the system are (or should be) unaffected by the inner workings of such a module. Thus it is possible to develop and perfect the module in isolation.
>
> Conversely, the module itself should be unaffected by the workings of others in the system. Accordingly, operation of other system components (individually or in concert) could be tested effectively in the module's absence by use of a stub.
>
> Following from the above two implications but worth noting explicitly is the notion that any change in a module's surroundings should not force a corresponding change within the module.

Thus, when it comes to discussing connections between modules, there is strong motivation to restrict such connections to a bare minimum. In general, this is helped by combining two organizational concepts.

1. If a piece of information is processed by one particular module, it is a good practice to localize that information, along with its structure, within that module. The other modules need not know how the information is organized or exactly how it is processed. In fact, such knowledge is unnecessary clutter. For example, if module B builds a complex data record and module C processes a particular component that it supplies to module B, there usually is no reason for C to know that its output will occupy a given position in a record organized in a certain way.

2. If certain information inevitably must be shared by several modules, that information (and its description) should be defined centrally. In many instances the definition may even be restricted to a separate module. Such global information (or COMMON areas in FORTRAN) is then available to all modules needing it without intricate and complicated interfaces. At the same time, any necessary changes in the nature or organization of such data are handled in one central place instead of being distributed through several modules.

Another important consideration that helps identify potentially worrisome connections between modules is the purpose of the transfer of information from one module to another. When a module is given arguments on which to operate, it generally is possible to assign these arguments to one of two broad categories: Arguments may be data in the sense that the invoked module performs certain predetermined activities using the supplied values. Alternatively, an argument may be intended specifically as a signal generated externally to control the behavior of the invoked module. This latter type of interconnection usually is undesirable because it implies the type of close functional interdependence that we are trying to avoid.

One additional point is worth noting: When setting up modular boundaries and determining the nature of the interfaces between the modules, it is often a helpful exercise to imagine (and even to list) the types of organizational, physical, and procedural changes that might occur throughout the life of a program. Once these have been identified and associated with the modules directly affected by such changes, it can be determined to what extent these alterations affect other modules. Ideally, such effects should be highly localized, involving single modules. For example, suppose an application receives personnel records from an input file on magnetic tape and processes those records for payroll purposes. Suppose further that conditions necessitate a change in which the file is moved to a magnetic disk. As a result, the format (but not the content or meaning) of the information is changed. Since only the format changed, this should have no effect on the internal calculations (for instance, gross pay from hours worked and wage rate, or net pay from gross pay and deduction rules). Therefore, with reasonably defined modules equipped with simple interfaces, it would be perfectly reasonable to expect to replace only the input module without touching any of the others.

7.2 ADDITIONAL DESIGN CONSIDERATIONS

There are some additional design considerations that can contribute to the development of a clear, reliable, easily used module. These are concerned more with the internal contents of a module than they are with the overall scope and interconnections. Specifically, two issues should be discussed: The importance of evaluation and its effect on a module's construction and the detection of operational errors.

7.2.1 Internal Error Detection

Whenever we improve the extent to which a software component is tested, we strike directly at the heart of a major problem that always plagues haphazard implementation; that is, we avoid excessive maintenance by presenting a product that is closer to perfection in the first place. A particularly effective strategy in this regard is to design functionally isolated program modules with the explicit objective of making them easy to test. This means that the designer is alert for opportunities to equip a module with features specifically intended to aid in debugging. The techniques for doing this are neither exotic nor intricate. Rather, they rely on a thorough scrutiny of a module to pinpoint potentially sensitive areas.

The basic idea is to make the work of the module as visible as possible during the testing phase. Accordingly, the initial version of a module includes code that displays interim values of variables affected by that module. A particularly helpful idea is to identify those places within a module where its variables undergo changes, and then to surround those places with output statements that provide "before" and "after" information about those variables. These temporary aids can be removed once some testing has established that the values thus displayed are correct. In some high-level languages, the inclusion of such support is automated. For example, PL/I provides the CHECK condition whereby a single specification can earmark selected variables for automatic display every time their values are changed. To illustrate, if we augmented the ordinary PROCEDURE statement

DESCR:PROCEDURE;

by including a CHECK option; that is,

(CHECK(X,Y,N)):DESCR:PROCEDURE;

the variables X,Y, and N will be displayed automatically, along with their respective names, every time they undergo a change throughout the entire extent of the procedure DESCR. Once this supporting mechanism no longer is required, it can be turned off simply by removing the CHECK prefix. A much more versatile mechanism may be implemented by means of the ON CHECK statement in PL/I. With this facility, it is possible to specify any type of desired diagnostic action. To illustrate, the statement

ON CHECK(X,Y,N) action;

indicates that the activity (which may be a single statement or an entire block) indicated by *action* will be performed anytime X,Y, or N undergo any change. This type of statement may be installed anywhere in a module and will apply to all subsequent code until the statement is rescinded or the module concludes.

Even if a particular high-level language does not contain very convenient facilities for automating such diagnostic support, it is a good idea to include it as part of the overall design. This coding can be made more conspicuous for easier subsequent removal by flagging it in some way. For example, it could be uniquely indented or surrounded by "comments," consisting of symbols reserved for that explicit purpose.

Complaints against such practices are usually lodged in terms of excess baggage, unnecessary use of storage, and extra computer time. In the light of the enormous costs incurred by having to mend inadequately tested and prematurely released programs or modules, the yawn and the shrug are reasonable responses to such objections.

7.2.2 Designing for Operational Error Detection

The previous section dealt with a general approach whose adoption makes it easier to find and eliminate coding errors within a module. When this is done, however, it does not follow automatically that the module will work all the time. Since a particular module is likely to depend on other parts of the software for its data, the validity of such information is beyond the module's control. Thus it is quite plausible for a malfunction to occur in a module "known to be correct."

This is not a new development, by any means. However, the imposition of increasingly complex software requirements has intensified the need to provide each module with its own internal protection. Ultimately, it is more expensive to design a module with the assumption that its input values will be "right." Use of such a ground rule is equally naive whether the input is "real input" (input from outside the processor) or data generated internally. Unsporting as it may seem, the intrinsic design must include mechanisms for detecting and handling incorrect input. Otherwise, when such input is encountered (this surely will happen, sooner or later), a disproportionate amount of work will be required to recognize and deal with the situation. During system testing, when the interactions between modules are being evaluated, these detectors can be of considerable help in tracking down program errors that slipped through the module tests. During actual use of the software, they provide valuable safeguards against the most insidious kinds of errors—those that allow the program to complete its processing with wrong results.

There are no precise rules that characterize the exact protection a module should include. If we insist that a module should have "reasonable" protection, the meaning of *reasonable* must depend to a large extent on the individual circumstances. For example, when the users of a software product think the consequences of an operating error are severe, it is not unusual to find modules dominated by protective tests. The statements that do the "useful" processing, for instance, those that actually prepare the payroll, compute the stress distribution, or generate the optimum product mix, may comprise 20 percent or less of the code.

In the absence of exact definitions, however, it is possible to identify some common situations whose detection often saves trouble. With this as a basis, you can begin to acquire a combination of skill, awareness, and judgment that will help dictate the appropriate protection for a given module design.

1. If a module is responsible for initial input processing, it should include tests for inconsistencies in the data. A common difficulty is the occurrence of nonnumeric data (such as letters) in what is supposed to be a number. PL/I provides a convenient way to handle this. By including a statement of the form

   ON CONDITION action;

   it is possible to intercept such occurrences. Of course, the nature of the specified action depends on the particular process being implemented. FORTRAN 77 includes an internal file feature that allows input to be read and tested, after which it can be reread in accordance with the test results.

2. A variety of other mishaps relate more directly to each specific application: A meaningless value may be submitted for a numerical variable. For instance, a value of 331 might be submitted for a variable representing body temperature in degrees Fahrenheit. Explicit checks for proper range can avoid potentially disastrous misuse of an otherwise innocent module. The effectiveness of such precautions applies to argument values passed by an invoking module as well as to raw input. (Some more recent languages, such as PASCAL, include features that enable the programmer to specify allowable ranges as part of variable definitions so that range tests are built into the processing automatically.)

3. Another type of misinformation includes values that are inconsistent with a particular process. For example, module M1 may supply a value of zero to module M2, which then uses it as a factor in a multiplication that supplies an argument to the logarithm function.

The general point, then, is to recognize that we cannot assume a module will be immersed in guaranteed surroundings. Because of this, the internal protection of that module must be part of its design. Operational errors will occur, sooner or later, and for certain applications it may be possible to intervene with remedial or evasive action of some kind that will allow the processing to continue. (For example, what does the standard square-root routine do when it is supplied with a negative argument?) If this cannot be done, then at the very least, the difficulty can be pinpointed and rectified with a minimum amount of wrecking and rebuilding.

7.3 A SIMPLE ILLUSTRATIVE EXAMPLE

To see how some of these concepts can be put to work, let's consider a relatively straightforward application of limited complexity. The objective is to produce and print bowling scores for some number of games played by a single bowler. Input for each game is submitted on a separate punched card containing the bowler's two-digit identification number, followed by a series of numbers representing the number of pins knocked down by each successive ball. Input is in list-directed format, and the value for the last ball of each game is followed by additional values of 99, which fill out the input. (In one of the problems at the end of the chapter you are asked to modify the software so that this is unnecessary). Thus each game has the maximum possible number of input values (21, as the rules explain later). There is no information about the frame number of a particular ball. The game-related input is preceded by a single card, also in list-directed format, containing the bowler's name and identification number. A sample set of input is shown below.

```
'A.M.F. Brunswick' 26
26 10,10,9,1,9,0,8,2,9,0,10,7,2,9,1,9,0,99,99,99,99
26 9,0,9,0,9,0,9,0,9,0,9,0,9,0,9,0,9,0,9,1,9
26 9,1,9,1,9,1,9,1,9,1,9,1,9,1,9,1,10,10,10
```

After an initial line of output containing the bowler's name, each game is to produce two lines of output: an echo of the input data, followed by a frame-by-frame score. Output for the final game is followed by a summary containing the score for each game, total pins credited, and the average. An example is given below with the echo omitted:

```
29 49 68 77 96 105 124 133 152 161
 9 18 27 36 45  54  63  72  81 100
19 38 57 76 95 114 133 152 172 202

SCORES:  161   100   202
TOTAL:   463   AVERAGE:   154.3
```

We shall work our way through this application by breaking it into smaller subproblems and examining how they can be organized with relation to one another. This example is small and simple enough so that reduction of complexity is not a severe problem. However, the approach is indicative of the method's applicability to any problem.

7.3.1 Initial Breakdown

Division of this application into major functional components is rather straightforward. We can specify these divisions by starting with an overview of the basic procedural activities.

After reading the initial input card, a loop is performed in which each successive game is read in, scored, printed, and the overall summary is updated. When all the individual games have been processed, the cyclic operations are terminated and the summary itself is printed. This level of abstraction is represented by the structure diagram in Figure 7.1.

A closer look at the requirements indicates some fairly clear-cut distinctions between events related only to individual games and those pertinent to the overall summary: The most apparent one is the process for determining the score of an individual game. The data and processing required to determine this score center only around the events during the game itself and have nothing to do with other factors, such as the number of games already played or yet to be played. Thus it would appear to make sense to separate the preparation of single-game game scores from any processing related to the summary. In this light, then, we can see that the overall initialization process would pertain only to those factors concerning the summary. Any initialization required for an individual game would be submerged within the processing dealing with that game. This separation between individual game and overall summary prompts the organization shown in Figure 7.2.

To help emphasize the independence of the functional duties in modules B, C, D, and E, Figure 7.2 lists the pertinent data used by each module. We shall go through these briefly.

Module B. Because this module sets up items whose values will be developed strictly for the summary, our concern here is limited to the overall pin counter,

```
Set up initial conditions.
REPEAT
        Process each game.
UNTIL no more games.
Print summary.
Stop.
```

FIGURE 7.1 *Basic structure of the bowling program.*

game counter, repository for individual scores, and identifying information.

Module C. What we do here affects the summary but is not affected by it. Accordingly, we develop (and ultimately deliver) a game score dealing only with the pins credited. The processes for computing and displaying the individual game performance have no interest in such things as the game number or total pins for all the games.

Module D. Once an individual game score is available, we can move beyond its bounds to the overall score, where we are interested in such things as game number and total pins, but we do not care about how the score was obtained.

Module E. After all of the game scores have been computed, the final requirements can be fulfilled by displaying the overall statistics.

With the basic requirements thus established, we can see that module C is tied to the overall application (via A, the control module) through an individual game score and the bowler's identification number; the latter is included only for verification purposes. This suggests an organization in which modules B, D, and E conveniently share their data by being placed within the control module, module A. Module C, on the other hand, is constructed separately. The redrawn structure diagram in Figure 7.3 reflects this view.

Now we can focus our attention on the game processor itself. For convenience, we shall specify the rules of the game, restating them so that transition to an appropriate algorithm is sufficiently direct not to be of concern here. (This will allow us to concentrate on the modular design considerations themselves):

1. There are 10 pins on the alley at the beginning of each frame.

2. Each game consists of 10 frames. All pins knocked down during a given frame are restored to standing position prior to the beginning of the next frame.

3. At least one ball is thrown in each frame. A second ball is to be thrown only if the first ball did not succeed in knocking down all 10 pins.

4. Scoring is as follows.

   a. Each frame is credited with the number of pins knocked down during that frame regardless of the number of balls (1 or 2) thrown during that frame.

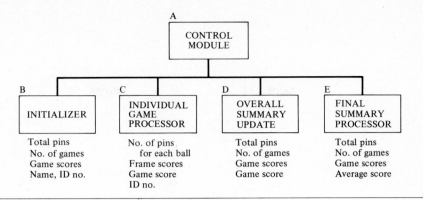

FIGURE 7.2   *Decomposition of the bowling program.*

     b. If all the pins are knocked down with the first ball in a frame, the 10 pins thus credited to that frame are augmented by the number of pins knocked down with the next 2 pins. Those balls belong to other frames and will be credited there as well.

     c. If the first ball thrown in a frame does not knock down all the pins but the second ball disposes of those remaining, the 10 pins thus credited to that frame are augmented by the number of pins knocked down with the next ball. Those pins will be credited to their proper frame as well.

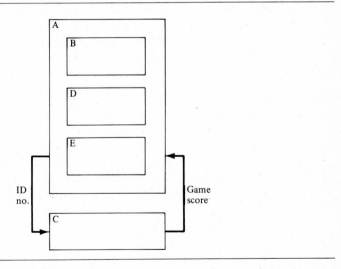

FIGURE 7.3   *Interrelation of bowling program components.*

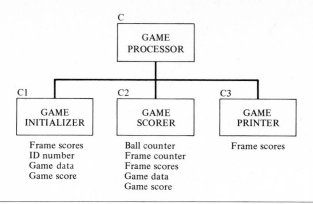

C

GAME
PROCESSOR

C1
GAME
INITIALIZER

Frame scores
ID number
Game data
Game score

C2
GAME
SCORER

Ball counter
Frame counter
Frame scores
Game data
Game score

C3
GAME
PRINTER

Frame scores

FIGURE 7.4 *Decomposition of individual game processor.*

d. If all 10 pins are knocked down in the last (tenth) frame either by 1 or 2 balls, the appropriate number of additional balls will be thrown and credited to that frame.

e. The game's score is the sum of the pins credited to each of the frames. Traditionally, the score in each frame is reported as the cumulative score up to that point in the game. Accordingly, with that method of recording, the score shown in the tenth frame is identical to the overall game score.

By juxtaposing these scoring rules with the application's requirements, we can identify a reasonable set of procedural components within the game processor (Fig. 7.4). We see that the major game-dependent ingredients used in support of the input data include a counter to keep track of the ball currently being processed, another counter to maintain correspondence between the ball number and the frame (or frames) to which it is to be credited, and a vector of some kind for retaining the frame-by-frame cumulative scores, which eventually will be printed. Note that after the initializer sets the stage and the processor computes the score, the module reporting the score has no interest in anything but the collection of individual frame scores. Accordingly, a somewhat more developed organizational picture of the application might be the one shown in Figure 7.5. A more direct sense of the procedural flow is given in Figure 7.6.

There is no intent here to imply that each of these modules maps directly to an individual subprogram. For some cases (module C3, for example) this may be true. In other instances, further examination may indicate that the advantages of functional independence and simplified interfaces may be served better by further decomposition. For instance, the scoring rules given above make it possible to compute the score in exactly the same way in any frame. Consequently, it may be appropriate to isolate the individual frame score (which is totally oblivious to the frame number and the vector of frame scores). By doing this, the game scorer becomes a loop, which cycles exactly 10 times, updating the overall score between

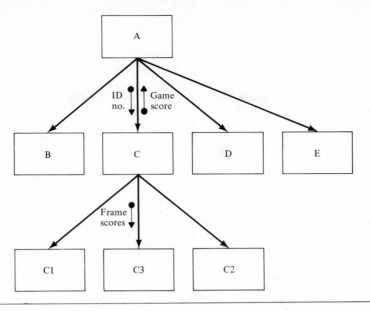

FIGURE 7.5 *Structural relations within the game processor.*

each use of the frame scorer. The advantage to that type of separation is that the actual frame-by-frame scoring, driven by the intrinsic rules of the game, would be completely insensitive to any changes in the data structure to maintain the scoring. This is nothing more than an extension of the same kind of reasoning that motivated the separation of the game scorer (module C2) from the game initializer (module C1). In that arrangement, the score-generating process is impervious to the appearance and form of the input data. Thus any future changes in such input characteristics have no effect on the scoring process. Saying it another way, the module performing the input (whether an integral part of C1 or a separate implementation within C1) has no effect on (exercises no control over) the operation of the game scorer.

```
Initializer  (  B  ).  REPEAT
     Game initialization (  C1  ).
     Game score preparation (  C2  ).
     Game score output (  C3  ).
     Summary update (  D  ).   UNTIL no  more games.
     Print summary (  E  ).
Stop.
```

FIGURE 7.6 *Developed structure of the bowling program.*

```
BOWL: PROCEDURE OPTIONS(MAIN);
/**********************************************************************/
/*        THIS PROGRAM COMPUTES INDIVIDUAL BOWLING SCORES FOR ANY     */
/*        NUMBER OF GAMES. EACH GAME IS ON A CARD SHOWING:            */
/*             GAME NO.                             COLS   4-5         */
/*             PINS DOWNED BY 1ST BALL             COLS   7-8         */
/*             PINS DOWNED BY 2ND BALL             COLS  10-11        */
/*             PINS DOWNED BY 3RD BALL             COLS  13-14        */
/*                          .                                          */
/*                          .                                          */
/*                          .                                          */
/*             PINS DOWNED BY 21ST BALL            COLS  64-65        */
/*                                                                     */
/*        SINCE A GAME MAY NOT REQUIRE THE MAXIMUM NUMBER OF 21 BALLS  */
/*        (E.G., A PERFECT GAME NEEDS ONLY 12), VALUES OF 99 WILL BE   */
/*        USED TO FILL OUT 21 ENTRIES FOR EACH GAME. TO KEEP IT        */
/*        SIMPLE WE SHALL ASSUME ONLY ACCURATE INPUT.                  */
/*        THE MAIN PROCEDURE INVOKES THREE PROCEDURES:                 */
/*             PREAD: GETS THE INPUT FOR ONE GAME                      */
/*             PGAME: COMPUTES A GAME SCORE                            */
/*             PPRT: PRINTS THE GAME SCORE                             */
/*        THE FOLLOWING VARIABLES ARE USED BY THE MAIN PROCEDURE:      */
/*        IDNO: -- THE PLAYER'S I.D. NUMBER                            */
/*        NAME: -- THE PLAYER'S NAME                                   */
/*        PINS: -- AN ARRAY CONTAINING THE 21 INPUT ENTRIES           */
/*        SCORE: -- THE 10 FRAME SCORES (SCORE(10) & GAME SCORE)       */
/*        FLAG: -- A BIT STRING USED TO OVERSEE AN ENDLESS LOOP        */
/*        NFRM: -- AN INTEGER USED AS A LOOP INDEX                     */
/**********************************************************************/
```

FIGURE 7.7 *Overall description of the bowling program.*

A game processor based on these considerations may be coded as shown in Figures 7.7–7.11.

7.4 SUMMARY

We have examined the factors influencing the size, organization, and contents of a module as well as its relations to other modules in a software product. The major objective driving all the other considerations is the need to identify a module that is functionally independent and sufficiently restricted in its duties so that its operation and behavior can easily and completely be grasped by one person. Once that criterion is met (and this is a matter of considered judgment), these additional guidelines can help to simplify the development, evaluation, and verification of that module.

Many functionally independent modules whose scope is conveniently grasped turn out to be about a page long.

To support and enhance functional independence, each module should have access only to the information it must use in order to function properly. All other (extraneous) information should be explicitly suppressed.

```
/******************************************************************/
/*                            PREAD                              */
/*  THIS PROCEDURE READS AN INPUT CARD CONTAINING DATA FOR A SINGLE*/
/*  BOWLING GAME. ONCE THE DATA ARE READ, THE PROCEDURE ECHOES THE */
/*  INPUT ON THE PRINTER.                                        */
/*    THE 21 (X(1),F(2)) SAVES WRITING X(1),F(2) 21 TIMES        */
/******************************************************************/
     PREAD: PROCEDURE(GAME,BALL);
            DECLARE
            (GAME,
            BALL(21)) FIXED BINARY (15);
            GET EDIT (GAME,BALL)(COLUMN(1),F(2),21 (X(1),F(2)));
            PUT SKIP(2) EDIT('GAME NO. ',GAME,BALL)
                      (X(5),A(9),X(2),F(2),X(5), 21 (F(2),X(2)));
            RETURN;
     END PREAD;
```

FIGURE 7.8 PREAD *procedure for the bowling program.*

PROBLEMS

1. Modify the code for Problem 3 of Chapter 6 so that improper attempts to use the module will be caught and reported. Demonstrate your instrumentation by operating this module with a suitable driver.

2. Refer to Problem 11 in Chapter 6. Modify the code given in this problem so that users of this polynomial evaluator will obtain a more detailed picture of the module's behavior. For each modification that you include, indicate the following.

   a. The kind of information the instrumentation provides.

   b. How that information helps the user understand the module's behavior.

3. In Problem 12 of Chapter 6, you were asked to consider the design of an input expression evaluator for use with polynomials.

   a. List the kinds of input that would make it impossible for such a processor to function properly.

   b. Describe the kind of instrumentation that you would use to detect and report each of the difficulties listed in (*a*).

   c. Prepare a pseudocode representation of the input expression processor with your instrumentation installed.

4. Here we are at Figure 3.18 again. That this is a *pseudorandom* number generator means that its output is not random; it merely imitates randomness. Conse-

```
/**********************************************************************/
/*                          PGAME                                   */
/*       THIS PROCEDURE USES BLNO, A COUNTER TO KEEP TRACK OF WHICH   */
/*       BALL WE ARE WORKING ON. SINCE IT IS NOT NEEDED ANYWHERE      */
/*       ELSE, IT IS SET UP AND USED AS A LOCAL VARIABLE: IT DOES     */
/*       NOT APPEAR IN THE PARAMETER LIST AND IS UNKNOWN EVERYWHERE   */
/*       IN THE PROGRAM.                                             */
/**********************************************************************/
    PGAME: PROCEDURE (ROLL,SC);
           DECLARE
           (ROLL(21),
            SC(10),
            BLNO) FIXED BINARY (15);
            SC = 0;   BLNO = 1;
      FRLP: DO NFRM = 1 TO 10;
            IF ROLL(BLNO)=10 THEN DO;
                                     SC(NFRM)=10+ROLL(BLNO+1)
                                            +ROLL(BLNO+2);
                                  BLNO=BLNO+1;
                                  END;
            ELSE IF ROLL(BLNO)+ROLL(BLNO+1)=10
                 THEN DO;
                        SC(NFRM)=10+ROLL(BLNO+2);
                        BLNO=BLNO+2;
                        END;
                 ELSE DO;
                        SC(NFRM)=ROLL(BLNO)+ROLL(BLNO+1);
                        BLNO=BLNO+2;
                        END;
            IF NFRM > 1 THEN SC(NFRM)=SC(NFRM)+SC(NFRM-1);
            END FRLP;
         RETURN;
    END PGAME;
```

FIGURE 7.9 Game scorer for the bowling program.

quently, it may be important to certain users if they could discern the generator's properties.

a. Describe the instrumentation that you would attach to the module so that its behavior can be observed.

b. Install (code) the instrumentation that you described in (a).

5. Refer to Problem 16, Chapter 6. The process discussed in this problem (a module for updating a set of frequency counters) may be subject to various kinds of improper input that jeopardize the action of the module.

a. List the potential difficulties that you anticipate and indicate how each one may endanger the proper functioning of the updating process.

b. Describe the instrumentation that can be used to detect the difficulties.

c. Modify the code prepared for Problem 16, Chapter 6, so that it now includes the instrumentation identified in (b).

```
/**************************************************************************/
/*                              PPRT                                      */
/*   THIS PROCEDURE PRINTS THE FRAME-BY-FRAME SCORE FOR A SINGLE           */
/*   BOWLING GAME. THE SCORE CORRESPONDING TO EACH FRAME SHOWS THE         */
/*   TOTAL NUMBER OF PINS ACCUMULATED THUS FAR IN THE GAME.                */
/**************************************************************************/
       PPRT: PROCEDURE (NGM,NPN);
             DECLARE
             (NGM,
              NPN(10)) FIXED BINARY (15);
             PUT SKIP EDIT('SCORE FOR GAME ',NGM,' : ',NPN)
                 (X(5),A(15),F(2),A(3), 10(F(3),X(2)));
             RETURN;
       END PPRT;
```

FIGURE 7.10 *Game printing procedure for the bowling program.*

6. In Problem 17 of Chapter 6, you were asked to consider the design of a component to build a record in a generated data file. Use the design you defined for that problem.

   a. Identify the aspects that you consider particularly vulnerable, and indicate the input conditions that could lead to malfunctions in your software.

   b. Indicate how your design would be instrumented to detect the difficulties described in (*a*).

7. Problem 18 of Chapter 6 asked for the input/output requirements for a module designed to produce group encodements to encompass a specified collection of original encodements.

   a. What specific difficulties can you identify with regard to the information to be supplied to this component?

   b. Show the instrumentation that you would provide to make the software sensitive to the problems described in (*a*). Indicate how the software would make use of this instrumentation.

8. Consider the software component addressed in Problem 19 of Chapter 6.

   a. In addition to its intended duties (detecting and correcting errors in infix expressions), the design also may (erroneously) "detect" (and try to "correct") nonexistent errors in legitimate infix expressions. Indicate how your design ensures against this.

   b. Is an empty (null) expression considered legal or illegal in your design? What does your design do in such an instance?

9. Refer to Problem 21, Chapter 6.

```
/**********************************************************************/
/*                         THE MAIN PROCEDURE                       */
/**********************************************************************/
         DECLARE
          (IDNO,
           PINS(21),
           SCORE(10)) FIXED BINARY,
           NAME CHARACTER(25),
           FLAG BIT(1);
         FLAG = '1'B;
         PUT PAGE;
         GET LIST (NAME,IDNO);
         PUT SKIP (2) LIST (NAME,IDNO);
            CALL PREAD (IDNO,PINS);
         ON ENDFILE (SYSIN) BEGIN;
                          PUT SKIP(3) LIST('--END OF RUN--');
                          STOP;
                          END;

  BGLP:  DO WHILE (FLAG);         /*  AN ENDLESS LOOP BROKEN BY ENDFILE  */
            CALL PGAME (PINS,SCORE);
            CALL PPRT(IDNO,SCORE);
            CALL PREAD(IDNO,PINS);
            END BGLP;

  END BOWL;
```

FIGURE 7.11   *Main procedure for the bowling program.*

a. Using the input and output requirements identified in (*a*) of Problem 21, Chapter 6, describe the problems that a text-line justifier should be prepared to recognize and handle.

b. Devise and code suitable instrumentation consistent with your answer in (*a*).

c. Modify the module in Problem 21, Chapter 6, to accommodate the instrumentation devised in (*b*).

d. Suppose that the line justifier were to be expanded so that it would increase the (average) amount of text on a line by hyphenating the last word. Show the extent to which the module (in its present form) would be affected by this change.

e. Referring to (*d*) above, how would you determine the procedural rules that would comprise a suitable algorithm for a component that does ''reasonable'' hyphenation?

f. How would you determine whether it is worthwhile to introduce hyphenation into a software component that does text-line justification?

10. Prepare suitable instrumentation for the software component designed in Problem 23, Chapter 6. Describe the kinds of problems your instrumentation is

intended to anticipate and indicate the ways in which your instrumentation is effective.

11. Prepare suitable instrumentation for the software product designed in Problem 24, Chapter 6. Relate each type of instrumentation to the specific problem or group of problems that it is designed to handle.

12. Instrument the software designed for Problem 25, Chapter 6.

13. Eliminate the need for 99s in the example in Sec. 7.3.

An Overview of the Module Implementation Process

8

The rapidly accumulating evidence of a software crisis leaves little doubt that a substantial factor in this crisis stems from a generally inadequate effort to make sure that "working" software actually does work. In fact, many people insist that insufficient development is the major cause of software deficiencies (such as redundancy, ambiguity, incomplete definition, and inconsistencies among system components) that keep plaguing users. Regardless of how we rank the contribution of the development process to the overall software effort, it is impossible to think of a systematic approach to the production of effective, reliable software without treating this process as an explicit part of the overall sequence. Specifically, the events that occur between the time the code is written and the time the resulting application is declared to be operational must be treated with the same discipline that characterizes all the preceding steps.

The discussion in this chapter emphasizes an approach to the development process and discusses a number of techniques that help impose a degree of discipline on that process. Some of these techniques, oriented around the individual processsing module, are aimed at producing a module that is easier to test.

8.1 GENERAL CHARACTERISTICS OF SYSTEMATIC DEVELOPMENT

A well-organized method for developing software carries no specific motivation of its own. Rather, it should be viewed as an integral part of the overall design and implementation process in that we are dealing with the same objective: Regardless of the application's requirements, the programming language used, or the characteristics of the implementation approach, a systematic development process seeks to help reduce apparent complexity. Earlier, we explored the decomposition of a problem into functionally independent subproblems, each of which should be easier to encompass. Having done this, it is important to be able to perfect each resulting module so that we take full advantage of its isolation. When we deliver a particular module for use in a larger and more complex environment, it should be a fully tested, working product independent of its eventual surroundings. Similarly, when we deliver a multimodular system, we should be able to certify that the product is a system in which all the modules work together, not just a collection of modules.

8.1.1 Recognition of the Importance of Testing

Until investigators began to gather statistics on the production and maintenance of software, relatively few people were aware of the sensitivity of software costs to the care taken during its development. As a result, many installations treated the coding and testing of processing modules as relatively distinct endeavors: A block of code was written and then it was tested, with the tests defined as afterthoughts.

This approach has undergone basic changes in the light of mounting evidence that much (if not most) of the overall cost of a software project traces back to the detection and repair of flaws that were not supposed to be there. Now, increasingly, the development process has become more systematic, built on the idea that testing software is no different in concept from testing any manufactured product; and tests are defined and organized early in the product's history (even at design time). The person developing the module knows the kind of tests to be performed *before* the product is ready for them. Moreover, the module itself is constructed in anticipation of the fact that it will be tested extensively. Features are included that specifically assume that the module will contain errors and that, even after those errors are found and eliminated, there will be conditions in which the module can function improperly. Should this occur (and the most meticulous design, implementation, and testing cannot guarantee against it), the software will have the capability (already built in) of providing valuable help in tracking down and removing these difficulties. (This issue was addressed initially in Sec. 7.2.1, and we shall continue to expand on it here.)

Another important aspect of the development process is to recognize that effective testing takes time and effort, the extent of which must be anticipated and taken into account. Observations made on a wide variety of successful software projects indicate that testing accounted for about half of the overall effort, with roughly an even split between component and system evaluation.[1] Although this testing is considerable, it represents reality and, therefore, should exert an appropriate influence on the project's schedule. Moreover, this level of effort is surprisingly

[1]*Some of these findings are discussed in F. P. Brooks's excellent collection of essays,* The Mythical Man-Month, *Addison-Wesley Publishing Company, Reading, Mass., 1975.*

modest compared to that required to do the poking, patching, and bandaging when a supposedly working but inadequately tested software product breaks down during its use in production. In short, emphasis on planned testing during development changes the attitude toward error detection from fire fighting to fire prevention.

8.1.2 Exploitation of Functional Isolation

The commitment to perform systematic evaluation as part of the development process makes it easier to take additional advantage of a system's modularity. Recall that we discussed modularization as a practice that enhances the drive for reduced complexity: If done properly, the conceptual scope of each module corresponds to a subproblem whose total extent is within our intellectual grasp. Part of the ensuing benefits of modularization come from the fact that the module can be completely developed and perfected by itself, without the availability of other system components. Furthermore, if the module's processing duties are truly isolated, this means that we can perfect it without even having to be aware of how it will be integrated into a larger package. An important facet of effective software development is to organize and schedule component testing so that the incorporation of a module into some larger body of software can be deferred until that module is considered to be correct. Then, when the module is introduced into its surroundings, subsequent testing is not cluttered with difficulties within the module; instead, the evaluation can be concentrated where it belongs—on the behavior of the module in the system.

8.1.3 Defensive Programming

When we combine the concepts discussed in the previous two sections, it is obvious that the best situation is one in which a module is designed and implemented so that it works properly: Avoid worrying about error removal simply by not having any to remove. This is not as farfetched as it may sound. Use of the structured techniques and documentation aids explored in the previous chapters can help to achieve this ideal in a surprising number of instances and bring it close in others.

However, we must be realistic. Present understanding of software design and implementation leaves us far short of the ability to produce error-free products all the time. Nor can we guarantee the accuracy of these products even after testing. (For many modules or systems, we are willing to accept the definition of an error-free product as one that has not failed *thus far* when used under its design conditions; we are considerably less comfortable when such a product is to be defined as one which will *never* fail when used under its design conditions). Next to newly implemented software without errors the best software is software that is alert to errors and invulnerable to their effects.

Such protection does not occur by accident. It must be part of the production effort. At the implementation stage we can think of this fortification as ''defensive programming''—an attitude built on the expectation that things will go wrong for two basic reasons: Improper implementation due to oversight, and improper use of the module in a larger software product. These difficulties can be lessened by using more cautious coding practices that seek to provide a maximum amount of explicit information about a module's behavior as it proceeds through its activities. Exactly how this is done depends primarily on the properties of the implementation language and the application's requirements. However, discussion of some examples will provide a helpful basis from which individual approaches can be extended.

8.1.3.1 Safe coding practices

A particularly shaky coding practice stems from the assumption that the right things will happen because we want them to happen. For example, a particular variable may not be initialized because the implementer is sure that this variable unavoidably will receive an assigned value somewhere during the processing. Such assurance may even be valid at the time the product is defined and may remain valid for some time during the product's useful life. Moreover, users may insist that it will remain that way forever. Nevertheless, the only way to guarantee that a particular variable always will have a meaningful value assigned to it is to put it there explicitly, prior to the body of the processing. This is no less pertinent for those languages whose compilers, in a burst of maternalism, initialize variables to default values. The compiler can provide only a value; it still is up to the designer to provide a meaningful (or reasonable) value. The two are not always the same.

A similar precaution, viewed in a somewhat different context, relates to the construction of selection (case) processes. When one of two alternatives is to be chosen, there is a temptation to assume that failure to choose the first one automatically implies selection of the second. Yet there may be situations in which neither alternative is actually wanted, as illustrated by the following PL/I fragment.

```
IF CHOICE = 'A' THEN CALL SLCT$A;
               ELSE CALL SLCT$B;
```

A more defensive approach would include an explicit test for B:

```
IF CHOICE = 'A' THEN CALL SLCT$A;
               ELSE IF CHOICE = 'B' THEN CALL SLCT$B;
                                    ELSE CALL BADCHC;
```

This caution is also necessary in more elaborate selection. For example, suppose a value SPGRV is to be matched against the nearest entry (on the high side) in a 20-entry table called SGTBL (sorted in ascending order). When the appropriate table entry (for instance, SGTBL(i)) is found, the corresponding entry in a table named REFR (REFR(i)) is to be assigned to a variable named REFRAC using a 21-element table (with the extra element providing a maximal upper bound). The PL/I code sequence

```
DO I=1 TO 20;
  IF SPGRV >  SGTBL(I)
   & SPGRV <= SGTBL(I+1) THEN REFRAC = REFR(I);
END;
```

opens the door to possible errors because it implies that the search of the table SGTBL will always be successful. A more cautious approach would exercise more control over the value of REFRAC.

```
REFRAC = 0;
DO I=1 TO 20 WHILE (REFRAC=0);
   IF SPGRV >  SGTBL(I)
      & SPGRV <= SGTBL(I+1) THEN REFRAC=REFR(I);
END;
IF REFRAC = 0 THEN CALL REFRERR;
```

In addition to guaranteeing a known value in REFRAC, the revised coding also may be somewhat more efficient in that it avoids going through any unnecessary tests once a match has been found.

Frequently, a procedurally correct module runs into computational difficulties. Attempts to divide by zero or to take the logarithm of a negative number are frequently quoted examples. Adequate defenses against such mishaps must be shaped by the designer's knowledge of the particular application. Somewhat less conspicuous types of computational troubles can result from the processor's use of finite arithmetic: Some calculation may produce a result that simply cannot be expressed in the capacity (number of bits) available for it. In the next section we mention mechanisms that enable the programmer to intercept cases of underflow and overflow and preempt the system's response in favor of a more customized action. However, as part of a defensive programming attitude, it may be possible to reduce the propensity for such occurrences by more careful arrangement of computations. For instance, the lengthy but straightforward assignment

$$y = \frac{a*b*c*(d+h)}{e*f*(j-i)}$$

may tempt the implementer to follow the ''natural'' flow by developing the numerator, then developing the denominator, and finally performing a single division to obtain the desired result. Successive multiplications produce fairly vulnerable conditions, especially if the product keeps growing with each operation. A more cautious approach would intersperse divisions and multiplications as shown

$$y = \frac{a}{e}*\frac{b}{f}*\frac{c}{(j-i)}*(d+h)$$

so that intermediate results would be less likely to wander out of range. Overflow or underflow are not the only problems stemming from finite arithmetic. Computed results may be well within the expressible range with respect to magnitude, but not with respect to precision. Thus multiplication of two numbers, each with a long fraction, may yield a result in which several places are lost because there is no room for them. Here again, reordering of some computations, when possible, may avert the loss of significant figures.

Other situations may require more elaborate defense measures. For instance, a simple comparison for equality,

```
IF X = Y THEN ...
```

may be less innocent than it looks. It may be that one of the items being compared is a computed value, while the other was read as input or explicitly assigned. Specifically, let us suppose that X and Y both are declared (in PL/I) as FLOAT(6); X is read in as 37.24 and Y is the result of some computation. The implication is that the value of Y is to be compared to a (conceptual) value of 0.372400*10**2. The test will fail for a Y of 37.2402, for instance. For our purposes, it may be that 37.2402 (or even 37.2412) should be treated the same as 37.24; yet, unless we anticipate such a situation, this simple test may frequently fail when it should succeed. Suitable preparation for this type of problem may involve rounding the computed Y to the desired number of places (or truncating it if that is more appropriate) so that the two items being compared express the same precision. Alternatively, the test itself could be restated so that the requirement for strict equality is replaced by something more tolerant ("acceptably close"). Thus, the previous skeletal IF statement now might read

```
IF ABS(X-Y) < 0.01 THEN ...
```

8.1.3.2 Cries and alarms

Sensitivity to potential trouble spots, no matter how acute, cannot always prevent the development of difficulties as execution of a module progresses. For this reason it may be very effective to equip a module with specific code sequences that may have little or nothing to do with the actual algorithm being implemented. Instead, the specific purpose of these code sequences is to provide the module with more sensitive antennae for detecting and reacting to a variety of events threatening its correct operation.

In any but the simplest applications, it is impossible to check for everything. After various guidelines and general rules have been considered, it is ultimately a matter of the implementer's judgment to establish the most effective compromise between thoroughness and practicality for a particular application. Nevertheless, it still is helpful to point out some common sources of difficulty, along with appropriate safeguards.

1. *Improper data types.* The most frequent mishap along these lines occurs when a module expecting numeric data receives nonnumeric information instead. If left to automatic system mechanisms, such occurrences usually force execution to stop, in many instances unnecessarily. For example, a record-oriented data processing application may be dealing with each record independently, in which case it is appropriate to handle records with improper data by sidetracking them to an exception file and continuing normal processing. The ON CONVERSION and GET STRING statements in PL/I are convenient ways to detect inconsistencies in data types. The latter capability (essentially that of "rereading" data previously interpreted as character strings) also is available in FORTRAN 77.

2. *Inexpressible data values.* A surprisingly large number of computational conditions could lead to a generated result beyond the computer's expressible range. The ON OVERFLOW, ON UNDERFLOW, and ON FIXEDOVERFLOW statements in PL/I can be incorporated to replace automatic system responses with more appropriately tailored ones supplied by the designer.

3. *Data out of range.* Numerical data may be acceptable because their values can be represented internally, even though these values make no sense in the context of the

particular application. For example, a value of 312.85 is easily and accurately expressed in a computer, but it is completely unreasonable if it is supposed to represent the number of hours worked by an individual in a given week. Such inconsistencies, of course, depend on the particular application, and protective measures have to be tailored appropriately. The importance of such protection is underscored by the fact that one of the most conspicuous new features in the PASCAL language is the ability to define an acceptable range with each type of variable. Another aspect of data range protection is preventing improper addressing. For example, if a module computes or uses a reference to an array element, there is a possibility that the reference could fall beyond the array's bounds. In response, some systems terminate the run, which may be bad enough. More disastrously, there are systems which simply accept the reference as long as the resulting location is accessible. The ON SUBSCRIPTRANGE in PL/I provides the designer with the opportunity to intercede with a response that may be more appropriate to the application.

4. *Invalid data.* A more specialized difficulty may occur when a data item is in the right form and within the acceptable range but is not a "legal" value because it is erroneously entered or does not belong to a list of acceptable values. Many organizations run into this problem with illegal membership or employee identification numbers. If the consequences of an illegal value are judged to be sufficiently severe, effective defensive measures can be built into the data themselves, supported by additional processing steps. A common approach is to construct the data value as a "self-checking" number such that the basic value (for example, n digits long) is supplemented by an $(n + 1)$th digit computed from the others. Validation, upon input, then consists of duplicating the computation and comparing the resulting digit with the corresponding one submitted as part of the input. Various methods have been defined for computing such values. For example, a series of digits written onto a magnetic tape or disk often are accompanied by an additional number obtained by computing the sum of the other numbers. (This is called a *checksum.*) Then, when those data are to be read in for subsequent use, the checksum is recomputed in the same way and compared to the one generated previously. Because the mapping from user data to checksum is usually not one-to-one, use of this technique cannot guarantee that the data are correct. However, it will detect a significant fraction of incorrect data.

8.2 PERFECTION OF THE INDIVIDUAL MODULE

The best way to produce a completely correct module is to design it that way and to prove it is correct through formal analysis. Development under such circumstances would consist primarily of an iterative process in which a coded module is analyzed and, if found to be incorrect, adjusted until its correctness is proven. The enormous payoff implicit in such a capability, as well as the intellectual challenges involved, have motivated considerable activity among computer scientists to formulate and investigate theories and methodologies that support such analyses. These capabilities already exist, although their applicability is limited to very simple implementations. Just how far they can be extended and still remain practical—substantially less complex than the module whose correctness is being analyzed—is still a matter of some speculation. Even the most carefully designed and coded module must be evaluated by actually conducting tests that put it through its paces. This is where the major difficulty lies: Except for the impossible extreme of conducting all possible tests, there is no testing strategy to assure us that a given module has been "properly" exercised. (Even if exhaustive testing could be performed, no one would reasonably be expected to look through all the results.)

In the absence of such guarantees, we strive to identify a collection of techniques and guidelines that enhance the effectiveness of a limited testing effort. Before discussing them, it is important to emphasize a single precautionary note that may be more significant than any group of rules: Testing must be performed systematically, with a predefined plan in mind. Here again we draw on engineering practices established over centuries. The preparation of a test series is an intrinsic part of any product development process, and it generally takes place along with or prior to the construction of the product itself. Thus when a product is ready to be tested, the testing procedures are ready for it. It may be impossible to define appropriate secondary tests, that is, specific investigations prompted by results obtained from initial evaluations. However, the effectiveness resulting from a thoughtfully defined test strategy often makes these subsequent tests self-evident.

8.2.1 Syntax Checking and Correction

Before a module can be tested during execution, the syntax of its source version must be examined and certified. This is the easiest and most straightforward part of the implementation process. When a source program is written, it can be checked carefully for discrepancies that violate the programming language's grammatical rules. This is best done in two stages: A careful examination by the implementer, followed by an automated examination on the part of the language processor (compiler or assembler). The latter, of course, is more thorough and its analysis (by definition) is complete. However, a great deal of development time can be saved by checking the source code before submitting it for compilation or assembly. (In an interactive environment, such "desk checking" takes place almost subconsciously as the programmer examines each line of code before transmitting it. Much the same thing happens at the keypunch when batch processing is used.) Manual inspection usually finds the more blatant omissions and keying errors that often produce voluminous (and marginally useful) diagnostic messages when given to a language processor. Once a module has been purged of these errors, the diagnostic services of the compiler or assembler can be used to identify and remove the remaining syntax errors. This normally proceeds fairly rapidly. In a surprising number of instances, the resulting product, a syntactically correct module, is mistakenly assumed to be correct in all other respects as well. This is a very serious misapprehension as it produces the temptation to reduce (or even bypass) further tests. Such are the ingredients of disaster. *A "clean" source module is merely the first step.*

8.2.2 Evaluation of a Module's Behavior During Processing

In this section we shall look at a number of guidelines that have been found to be helpful in performing systematic testing. As such they are useful in shaping a strategy that anticipates a testing phase. Thus the assumption is that the first testable version of a module already reflects the existence of these aids.

8.2.2.1 *The instrumented module*
When we wish to test some product under development, it is helpful to provide that product with sensors attuned to pick up and report environmental information of interest. For example, when a newly designed turbine is being tested as an eventual component for a jet engine, it is equipped with a variety of devices to report the effects of the heated gases coming from the combustion chamber and rushing around the turbine blades. There are thermocouples to measure gas and metal temperatures, probes to show the pressure and direction of the gas, and strain gauges indicating the behavior of the blades under this continuous onrush. As trouble spots are found and corrected, some of these instruments will be removed or deactivated, while others remain to help monitor the turbine's behavior during regular use.

The need to do this is no less critical when it comes to the development of software modules. In this context, program statements become the "thermocouples," "pressure probes," and "strain gauges," but the idea remains the same: The most cleverly designed tests cannot be effective if the module being tested is not sensitized to them. We can identify some helpful instruments, several of which have been mentioned earlier but are well worth reemphasizing.

1. *Echoes.* A fundamental guideline for any processing situation is to make sure that "proper" information is available to begin with. Such verification starts simply by printing or displaying the input supplied to a module. This could be information actually read in, arguments supplied by another module, or values in some shared area; the idea is the same.

2. *Isolation of processing effects.* The essence of troubleshooting is to verify that certain things work, thereby eliminating each of them progressively until the observed difficulty is narrowed down to a small area of concern. For software modules, this process can be expedited by taking advantage of the uncluttered flow of events characteristic of structured programming: Since a well-structured module necessarily consists only of certain constructs, it is a relatively simple matter to instrument each construct at its boundaries. This gives us "before" and "after" information at a relatively specific level.

3. *Monitoring a cyclic process.* If the construct being instrumented is some kind of loop (for instance, a WHILE or REPEAT-UNTIL), it probably will not be sufficient just to know the state of the pertinent data before the entry and after the exit.

Additional help is provided by monitoring progress through the loop. The frequency with which such monitoring is done must be judged based on the number of cycles likely to be performed. Printing the index and pertinent data values for each of 1200 iterations, for example, might be too much of a good thing; every 50th iteration is likely to be sufficient in this case.

It is extremely difficult for a programmer to detect errors in his or her own coding by performing simple desk checking. After all, that person has produced the code in the first place, and it would not have taken the form it did unless the programmer thought it to be correct. Many implementation errors occur because of the programmer's misinterpretation of a specific construct in the implementation language. If this is the case, no amount of desk checking and hand simulation will uncover the error. (The hand simulation is based on the programmer's [erroneous] perception of the internal process, so it does not correspond to the actual events that occur.)

Continually reviewing the code and saying, ''This code is correct; why doesn't it work?'' becomes an exercise in futility. In these situations the programmer must compel the *system* to reveal what *it* thinks it is doing instead of assuming that *he or she* knows what it is doing. Thus instrumentation cannot be supplanted by external logical analysis of the code. The system knows what it is doing (by definition) and sometimes the programmer must make explicit inquiries about the system's activities instead of making assumptions about them.

8.2.2.2 Basic procedural tests

Distinct from the question of instrumentation is the question of defining the tests themselves. The most obvious starting point is to evaluate the module's behavior for its most common mode of processing. With rather rare exceptions, a module tends to have one path (or a small number of paths), which we expect to handle the bulk of the cases. Any other alternatives are perceived to be as exceptions. Tests designed to take the module through this ''ordinary'' processing provide a baseline—a body of results that tells us how the module behaves when all conditions are right.

The number of tests to be run for this purpose cannot be prescribed. There may be millions of cases possible, yet they may be so similar to each other (limited data ranges, restricted decision possibilities) that a dozen trials may constitute a sufficient demonstration of correctness. The opposite situation occurs all too often, but exhaustive testing is out of the question. One reasonable approach is to identify the range of possibilities and run a series of tests with values randomly distributed throughout that range.

For instance, a software product for payroll processing must accommodate an almost unlimited number of possibilities, all considered ordinary. However, there are well-defined limits on items such as the number of hours worked, the number of overtime hours, hourly pay rate, overtime increment, maximum paycheck size, maximum number of reported sick hours, and so on. Consequently, a desired number of tests can be constructed in which arbitrary combinations of the pertinent values (all within range) are submitted and processed. As errors are found and removed, increasingly longer sequences of test cases will be processed without mishap. When such sequences reach some minimum acceptable number (again a matter of judgment), we are ready to infer that ordinary processing capability has been demonstrated.

To alleviate the tedium and reduce the effort required to develop and submit such test cases, many installations use a software product for automatic generation of test cases. (Recall that some of the projects specified at the end of Chapter 3 address this specific issue.) Clearly, the major ingredients in such a mechanism include a pseudorandom number generator and a set of criteria that define the limits within which the generator must operate for that application.

Satisfactory completion of such tests represents a very encouraging step in the development process, but it does not constitute a complete evaluation. Additional necessities are discussed in the following sections.

8.2.2.3 *Testing at extreme conditions*
Once we are convinced that the module will run properly for most cases, we can begin investigating some of the less frequent but still prominent pathways and alternatives. Some of these may represent ridiculous but still legal conditions, in which case the module must be prepared to deal with them properly.

Areas in this category that are particularly vulnerable to mishaps are those at the extremes of the allowable data ranges. Experience, gathered the hard way, has demonstrated that errors in these regions occur often enough to warrant the use of tests that examine module behavior at these data limits. Some examples will clarify the point.

1. *Table management (look up, insertion, deletion).* Extreme conditions include an unsuccessful search, searching or deleting from an empty table, insertion into a full table, and rearranging a table with one entry (or none).

2. *Input operations.* Extremes include reading a file with one entry, reading an empty file, or reading the last entry in a file.

3. *Data extremes.* In this connection it is helpful to test specific cases in which variables take on their lowest and highest legitimate values. For instance, a payroll test series would include an "employee" who worked zero hours, maximum overtime hours, maximum overtime hours with zero straight hours, maximum number of dependents, zero dependents, and so on.

4. *Cyclic operations.* When the number of cycles through a loop is designed to vary from run to run, it is useful to include a test that causes exactly one cycle, as well as a situation forcing the loop to be bypassed (zero cycles). Similarly, if the loop has a prescribed limiting value, that limit should be tested.

8.2.2.4 *Tests with bad data*
An important part of any testing strategy involves explicit attempts to upset the processing. This is done by subjecting a module to conditions that stress it beyond its design limits. Clearly, the module (by definition) will not operate "normally" under such conditions. It is necessary to define precisely what the module will do when it cannot pursue its regular activities. Conse-

quently, every software evaluation must include runs in which the module is compelled to operate under outlandish, even unthinkable, conditions. The following are some examples.

1. *Data values*. In previous discussions we stressed the need to provide test conditions within and at the boundaries of acceptable ranges. In this phase, those limits are violated to see how the module reacts. For instance, there may be an integer variable that always takes on positive values. In the context of the application, it makes absolutely no sense for that variable ever to be zero or negative. This is an open invitation to a test with a negative value (and probably one of zero as well). A value of 81.5 is outlandish if it is supposed to represent a body temperature in degrees Celsius. However, it is worth a test to determine how the module reacts there. Similar tests will suggest themselves for each application once the designer is convinced that "impossibly bad" data values are not impossible at all.

2. *Decision mechanisms*. A common difficulty with selection processes is one in which the designer has left a loophole. If a situation logically calls for, say, three choices, the implementer sometimes is too quick to assume that the decision structure always will be presented with only one of those three choices. If possible, there should be a test in which the decision mechanism is forced to handle a situation that is "none of the above."

3. *Cyclic processes*. A possible hazard in loops, similar to one discussed earlier, occurs when starting and limiting values are computed dynamically. We already have mentioned the idea of forcing an extreme of zero cycles. This may need to be taken a step further by contriving the generation of a starting value that exceeds the ending value. Such a circumstance is likely to be caught by the operating environment anyway; however, the system's response may be more catastrophic than is necessary for that situation. Similarly, a loop dealing with element-by-element processing of an array invites a test in which the array bounds are intentionally violated.

4. *Miscellaneous data errors*. Included here are the more extreme errors that often result from oversights in the data preparation process. For example, the presence of letters or punctuation symbols in an expectedly numeric field is something worth investigating. Another, more radical situation is one in which a crucial data item is missing altogether.

Obviously, it is impossible to dictate standard responses to such erroneous or "impossible" operating conditions. The way a piece of software reacts or what it can salvage from such a situation will depend on the nature of the process. However, the important objective of this kind of testing is to make sure that the response is an intentional one—not one left to chance or the idiosyncrasies of a particular operating environment. For example, a particular situation may force an inevitable failure of the module, but there may be an opportunity to recover, rectify, and try again (or even bypass that part of the process). At the very worst, there is an opportunity to respond with specific information that helps pinpoint the reason for failure. This is particularly useful when we expand the idea of "failure" to include the type of situation that no system can be designed to detect: An error that is not catastrophic enough to disrupt the process but will produce the wrong results at the conclusion of the process.

8.2.3 Testing Aids

Nearly every operating environment provides some feature to help test software products. This assistance may range from rudimentary messages following a program's (normal or abnormal) termination to elaborate debugging packages that perform step-by-step traces. In some cases these features are embedded in a programming language (as exemplified by PL/I's ON CHECK feature); in others they reside in separate programs that can be superimposed on the product being tested.

When a system-supplied debugging aid is needed, it is helpful to approach its use with the following perspective: If we implement a module in a particular programming language (regardless of its level), we labor (willingly) under the delusion that the computing system operates only at that level. For example, if we are coding in PL/I, our perception of the system is that of a "PL/I machine." If the system is reasonably designed, anything going on outside a particular level is normally hidden from us. If the system design is effective (as well as reasonable), the hidden data and events are not required. We know all we need to know at our level of perception, and the illusion is preserved. In fact, any additional reference to information at any other level may cause confusion rather than clarification for many users.

The same is true with regard to a debugging package. If consistently designed, this package should supply evaluative and diagnostic information at the same level as the rest of the "machine" as we perceive it. If this isolation is broken, the illusion is shattered as well, and there is suddenly considerable additional—but unnecessary—complexity. For example, if we are coding in PASCAL, the information developed by a module test should be useful when viewed in conjunction with the source version of that module. If the debugging aid forces us to scrutinize information at a different level (for instance, the assembly language) the context of a PASCAL machine suddenly is lost: In addition to concerning ourselves with the properties of PASCAL, we now find ourselves having to worry about the assembler and, indirectly, the host machine's architecture. Similarly, a diagnostic service that supports PL/I programs breaks the boundaries of the (conceptual) PL/I machine if it refers to locations in terms of their hexadecimal displacements from some origin. This frame of reference belongs more properly with an "assembly-language machine"; PL/I locations are tied to sequential statement numbers or variable names. If a particular testing aid makes this transcendence of level unavoidable, or if the necessary debugging information cannot be obtained unless the implementer seeks such a level change (for instance, a FORTRAN programmer requesting a hexadecimal dump), it may be an opportune time to construct a simpler (less general) testing aid customized to the particular software product.

8.3 A SMALL EXAMPLE

To coalesce some of these testing guidelines around a concrete example, we shall consider a module intended as part of a business data-processing product. The business receives orders and fills them, updating its inventory. As part of the order processing activities, the software creates a shipping order and an invoice to the customer. In addition, it credits a particular salesperson with the order, thereby computing the commission and adding that amount to the salesperson's income. In computing the financial data relating to the sale, the company must prepare a shipping cost (which it pays) and add that amount to the cost of the sale. It is the computation of this freight cost with which our module is concerned.

In concept, freight costs are relatively simple quantities to compute. For our situation, however, there are complications because of the way the pricing works: First of all, there are several basic freight classes, where the class is determined by the weight of the goods being shipped. Each class has its own rate schedule. For a given point of origin (and, fortunately, we shall assume a single shipping point), the rates are determined according to the destination and class. Destinations are defined in terms of zones and the zones, in turn, depend on zip codes (specifically, the first three digits of the zip code). The entire set of zip codes maps into a smaller set of zones, with a different mapping for each shipping class. The rates change twice a year and the mappings change every other year. Current figures are summarized in Table 8.1.

The data structure used for this situation consists of a series of tables: First there is a collection of weight limits (WTLIM), delineating the different freight classes. For each of the six freight classes, there is a table that maps the zip code ranges to their respective rates. Internally, these tables are agglomerated into a single structural unit (FRTABL). The latter is allocated with some additional entries to handle anticipated expansion. Each entry in FRTABL consists of the first three digits of the zip code at each end of the acceptable range (ZIPMIN and ZIPMAX), and a corresponding shipping cost in dollars per pound (RATES). The boundaries in FRTABL for each freight class are defined in a vector ZNTBL, whose entries point to the upper limits of the respective freight classes. This is depicted schematically in Figure 8.1.

Based on this data organization, the processing module (implemented as a procedure named FREIGHT) receives the shipping weight and zip code, and it delivers the rate. The calling module then can compute the shipping costs as one of the cost components on an invoice. (There are no strong reasons for using a subroutine in preference to a function here; some slight advantages may emerge later, but the choice was arbitrary.)

FREIGHT's processing is straightforward: after finding the right weight class, it uses the appropriate ZNTBL data to bracket the pertinent section of FRTABL. A final search on zip code produces the desired rate.

Figure 8.2 gives an initial version of the coded module that looks up the desired rate. There are several inconsistencies in the coding despite the fact that it is syntactically correct. Before we can expect to define ways to track down these flaws and remedy them, we must deal with a basic shortcoming—the lack of instrumentation. As the module stands, its construction assumes that nothing will go wrong. Consequently, there is a good possibility that if something does go wrong, no one will know it.

TABLE 8.1 DATA CHARACTERISTICS FOR FREIGHT RATE DETERMINATION

Class	Weight Criterion		No. of Zipcode Groups
1	weight	less than 5000	40
2	weight	5000– 9999	36
3	weight	10000–13999	32
4	weight	14000–19999	24
5	weight	20000–24999	16
6	weight	25000 or more	10

Example Rate Table Segment (Weight Class 5):

Zipcode Range	Rate	Zipcode Range	Rate
00301–00375	0.375	59801–59989	0.250
00376–01089	0.340	60001–65689	0.245
01101–05989	0.325	65701–69989	0.255
06001–09989	0.320	70001–73789	0.260
10001–23689	0.320	73801–79989	0.275
23701–45089	0.310	80001–88889	0.340
45101–49987	0.300	88901–94989	0.385
50001–53789	0.285	95001–99989	0.400

Zipcode Range Characteristics (Illustrative only)

- No zipcodes below 00301
- No zipcode ending in 00
- No zipcode above nnn89

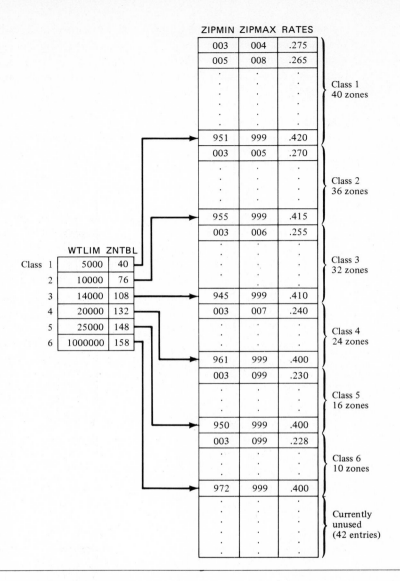

ZIPMIN	ZIPMAX	RATES	
003	004	.275	
005	008	.265	Class 1
.	.	.	40 zones
.	.	.	
.	.	.	
.	.	.	
951	999	.420	
003	005	.270	
.	.	.	Class 2
.	.	.	36 zones
.	.	.	
955	999	.415	
003	006	.255	
.	.	.	Class 3
.	.	.	32 zones
.	.	.	
945	999	.410	
003	007	.240	
.	.	.	Class 4
.	.	.	24 zones
961	999	.400	
003	099	.230	
.	.	.	Class 5
.	.	.	16 zones
950	999	.400	
003	099	.228	
.	.	.	Class 6
.	.	.	10 zones
972	999	.400	
.	.	.	Currently
.	.	.	unused
.	.	.	(42 entries)
.	.	.	

WTLIM ZNTBL

	WTLIM	ZNTBL
Class 1	5000	40
2	10000	76
3	14000	108
4	20000	132
5	25000	148
6	1000000	158

FIGURE 8.1 *Basic data structures for example in Section 8.3.*

Figure 8.3 shows another version of the module; we have equipped this version with some statements to provide visible indications of the module's progress.

- SUBSCRIPTRANGE is enabled to help monitor the table searches.

- There is a display of the basic tables (WTLIM, ZNTBL, and FRTABL) so that their accuracy can be verified against the corresponding source document. Once verified (and corrected, if necessary), this serves as a reference for comparison with the

```
FREIGHT: PROCEDURE(WGT,ZPCOD,FRATE);
        DECLARE
            WGT FIXED BINARY (31), ZPCOD CHARACTER(5),FRATE FLOAT BINARY,
            (WTLIM(6),ZNTBL(6)) FIXED BINARY (31),
            (RTWT,LOWEST,HIGHEST) FIXED BINARY (15),
            ZIPSTR CHARACTER (3),
            1 FRTABL (200),
                (2 ZIPMIN, 2 ZIPMAX) CHARACTER (3),
                2 RATES FLOAT BINARY;

/***********************************************************************/
/*                    INITIALIZE WTLIM, ZNTBL, FRTABL                  */
/*        WE SHALL SHOW A SMALL PART, JUST FOR ILLUSTRATION.           */
/***********************************************************************/

            ZIPMIN(133)='003';     ZIPMAX(133)='005';     RATES(133)=0.375;
            ZIPMIN(134)='006';     ZIPMAX(134)='010';     RATES(134)=0.340;
            ZIPMIN(135)='011';     ZIPMAX(135)='059';     RATES(135)=0.325;
            ZIPMIN(136)='060';     ZIPMAX(136)='099';     RATES(136)=0.320;
            ZIPMIN(137)='100';     ZIPMAX(137)='236';     RATES(137)=0.310;
            ZIPMIN(138)='237';     ZIPMAX(138)='450';     RATES(138)=0.300;
            ZIPMIN(139)='451';     ZIPMAX(139)='499';     RATES(139)=0.285;
            ZIPMIN(140)='500';     ZIPMAX(140)='537';     RATES(140)=0.260;
            ZIPMIN(141)='538';     ZIPMAX(141)='599';     RATES(141)=0.250;
            ZIPMIN(142)='600';     ZIPMAX(142)='656';     RATES(142)=0.245;
            ZIPMIN(143)='657';     ZIPMAX(143)='699';     RATES(143)=0.255;
            ZIPMIN(144)='700';     ZIPMAX(144)='737';     RATES(144)=0.260;
            ZIPMIN(145)='738';     ZIPMAX(145)='799';     RATES(145)=0.275;
            ZIPMIN(146)='800';     ZIPMAX(146)='888';     RATES(146)=0.340;
            ZIPMIN(147)='889';     ZIPMAX(147)='949';     RATES(147)=0.385;
            ZIPMIN(148)='950';     ZIPMAX(148)='999';     RATES(148)=0.400;

/***********************************************************************/
/*        FIND THE RIGHT FREIGHT CLASS BASED ON SHIPPING WEIGHT        */
/***********************************************************************/

            DO I = 1 TO 6;
            IF WGT < WTLIM(I) & WGT >= WTLIM(I-1) THEN RTWT = I;
            END;

/***********************************************************************/
/*        USE THE FREIGHT CLASS AND ZIPCODE TO FIND THE RATE;         */
/*        FIRST, DEFINE THE APPROPRIATE SECTION OF THE ZIPCODE/RATE    */
/*        TABLE, AND THEN SEARCH THAT PORTION FOR THE RATE.            */
/***********************************************************************/

            HIGHEST = ZNTBL(RTWT);
            LOWEST = ZNTBL(RTWT-1);

            ZIPSTR = SUBSTR(ZPCOD,1,3);
            DO I = LOWEST TO HIGHEST;
            IF ZIPSTR >= ZIPMIN(I) & ZIPSTR <= ZIPMAX(I)
            THEN FRATE = RATES(I);
            END;

            RETURN;
            END FREIGHT;
```

FIGURE 8.2 *PL/I code for freight-handling procedure.*

results generated later in the module. Since these tables represent a relatively voluminous amount of data, the PUT statements that print them may be deactivated once
an accurate set of tables has been printed. A very convenient way to do this is to
convert the instrumentation statements to comments. This removes them from the

```
                (SUBSCRIPTRANGE):
      FREIGHT:  PROCEDURE(WGT,ZPCOD,FRATE):
            DECLARE
                WGT FIXED BINARY (31), ZPCOD CHARACTER(5),FRATE FLOAT BINARY,
                XGT FIXED BINARY (31), XPCOD CHARACTER (5), XRATE FLOAT BINARY,
                WTLIM (6) FIXED BINARY (31) INITIAL (5000,10000,14000,20000,
                                                     25000,100000),
                ZNTBL (6) FIXED BINARY (15) INITIAL (40,76,108,132,148,158),
                (RTWT,LOWEST,HIGHEST) FIXED BINARY (15),
                ZIPSTR CHARACTER (3),
                1 FRTABL (200),
                    (2 ZIPMIN, 2 ZIPMAX) CHARACTER (3),
                    2 RATES FLOAT BINARY:

      /***********************************************************************/
      /*                 INITIALIZE WTLIM, ZNTBL, FRTABL                     */
      /*      WE SHALL SHOW A SMALL PART, JUST FOR ILLUSTRATION.              */
      /***********************************************************************/

                ZIPMIN(133)='003':    ZIPMAX(133)='005':    RATES(133)=0.375:
                ZIPMIN(134)='006':    ZIPMAX(134)='010':    RATES(134)=0.340:
                ZIPMIN(135)='011':    ZIPMAX(135)='059':    RATES(135)=0.325:
                ZIPMIN(136)='060':    ZIPMAX(136)='099':    RATES(136)=0.320:
                ZIPMIN(137)='100':    ZIPMAX(137)='236':    RATES(137)=0.310:
                ZIPMIN(138)='237':    ZIPMAX(138)='450':    RATES(138)=0.300:
                ZIPMIN(139)='451':    ZIPMAX(139)='499':    RATES(139)=0.285:
                ZIPMIN(140)='500':    ZIPMAX(140)='537':    RATES(140)=0.260:
                ZIPMIN(141)='538':    ZIPMAX(141)='599':    RATES(141)=0.250:
                ZIPMIN(142)='600':    ZIPMAX(142)='656':    RATES(142)=0.245:
                ZIPMIN(143)='657':    ZIPMAX(143)='699':    RATES(143)=0.255:
                ZIPMIN(144)='700':    ZIPMAX(144)='737':    RATES(144)=0.260:
                ZIPMIN(145)='738':    ZIPMAX(145)='799':    RATES(145)=0.275:
                ZIPMIN(146)='800':    ZIPMAX(146)='888':    RATES(146)=0.340:
                ZIPMIN(147)='889':    ZIPMAX(147)='949':    RATES(147)=0.385:
                ZIPMIN(148)='950':    ZIPMAX(148)='999':    RATES(148)=0.400:

                PUT PAGE:
                DO I=133 TO 148:
                PUT SKIP DATA(ZIPMIN(I),ZIPMAX(I),RATES(I)):
                END:
                PUT SKIP (2):
                DO I=1 TO 6: PUT SKIP DATA(WTLIM(I),ZNTBL(I)):   END:

      /***********************************************************************/
      /*       FIND THE RIGHT FREIGHT CLASS BASED ON SHIPPING WEIGHT         */
      /***********************************************************************/

                XGT=WGT:  PUT SKIP(2) DATA (XGT):
                ON SUBSCRIPTRANGE PUT SKIP LIST ('RTWT LOOP BAD AT I OF: ',I):
                RTWT=0:
            DO I = 1 TO 6:
            IF WGT < WTLIM(I) & WGT >= WTLIM(I-1) THEN RTWT = I:
            END:
                PUT DATA (RTWT):

      /***********************************************************************/
      /*      USE THE FREIGHT CLASS AND ZIPCODE TO FIND THE RATE:            */
      /*      FIRST, DEFINE THE APPROPRIATE SECTION OF THE ZIPCODE/RATE      */
      /*      TABLE, AND THEN SEARCH THAT PORTION FOR THE RATE.              */
      /***********************************************************************/
```

FIGURE 8.3 *Freight-handling procedures with interim
output statements.*

```
HIGHEST = ZNTBL(RTWT);
LOWEST = ZNTBL(RTWT-1);
     PUT SKIP DATA (LOWEST,HIGHEST);

ZIPSTR = SUBSTR(ZPCOD,1,3);
     XPCOD=ZPCOD;    PUT SKIP DATA(XPCOD,ZIPSTR);
     ON SUBSCRIPTRANGE PUT SKIP LIST('FRATE LOOP BAD AT I OF: ',I);
     FRATE=0;
DO I = LOWEST TO HIGHEST;
IF ZIPSTR >= ZIPMIN(I) & ZIPSTR <= ZIPMAX(I)
THEN FRATE = RATES(I);
END;
     XRATE=FRATE;    PUT DATA (XRATE);

RETURN;
END FREIGHT;
```

FIGURE 8.3 *(continued)*

flow of processing activities, but the text remains intact. Thus reactivation is trivial if it should become necessary. (The application of software engineering methodologies has not neutralized Dr. Murphy entirely, nor has it repeated his law: If testing statements are removed entirely from a processing module, there is a substantial increase in the likelihood that they will have to be installed again.)

● Just prior to the determination of freight class, there is an echo of the weight (WGT). The loop itself will be protected by initializing RTWT before entry. This offers an opportunity to compare RTWT before and after the loop. For convenience, RTWT is printed along with WGT.

● Proper selection of the rate table subset is monitored by the output statement, following the determination of LOWEST and HIGHEST.

● Finally, a display of FRATE (adjacent to ZPCOD for convenience) shows the results of the final loop. As with RTWT, FRATE is initialized for comparison.

With these additions, the module can be evaluated more effectively. A plausible beginning provides some tests at design conditions (we shall assume the tables are correct).

1. A midrange weight (22,500 lb) and zip code (80620).

2. A very low weight (408 lb) and zip code (38518).

3. A very high weight (82,118 lb) and zip code (45229).

4. A borderline weight (14,000 lb) and zip code (54321).

The results of the first test (Fig. 8.4) already are revealing: Progress through the RTWT loop is thwarted at the very start. With I at 1, the loop attempts to refer to WTLIM(0) and, of course, it cannot. Several simple remedies suggest themselves. We have chosen to bound the WTLIM table at its lower end; its declaration now reads

```
FRTABL.ZIPMIN(133)='003'                    FRTABL.ZIPMAX(133)='005'
FRTABL.RATES(133)= 3.750000E-01;
FRTABL.ZIPMIN(134)='006'                    FRTABL.ZIPMAX(134)='010'
FRTABL.RATES(134)= 3.399999E-01;
FRTABL.ZIPMIN(135)='011'                    FRTABL.ZIPMAX(135)='059'
FRTABL.RATES(135)= 3.249999E-01;
FRTABL.ZIPMIN(136)='060'                    FRTABL.ZIPMAX(136)='099'
FRTABL.RATES(136)= 3.199999E-01;
FRTABL.ZIPMIN(137)='100'                    FRTABL.ZIPMAX(137)='236'
FRTABL.RATES(137)= 3.099999E-01;
FRTABL.ZIPMIN(138)='237'                    FRTABL.ZIPMAX(138)='450'
FRTABL.RATES(138)= 2.999999E-01;
FRTABL.ZIPMIN(139)='451'                    FRTABL.ZIPMAX(139)='499'
FRTABL.RATES(139)= 2.849999E-01;
FRTABL.ZIPMIN(140)='500'                    FRTABL.ZIPMAX(140)='537'
FRTABL.RATES(140)= 2.599999E-01;
FRTABL.ZIPMIN(141)='538'                    FRTABL.ZIPMAX(141)='599'
FRTABL.RATES(141)= 2.500000E-01;
FRTABL.ZIPMIN(142)='600'                    FRTABL.ZIPMAX(142)='656'
FRTABL.RATES(142)= 2.449999E-01;
FRTABL.ZIPMIN(143)='657'                    FRTABL.ZIPMAX(143)='699'
FRTABL.RATES(143)= 2.549999E-01;
FRTABL.ZIPMIN(144)='700'                    FRTABL.ZIPMAX(144)='737'
FRTABL.RATES(144)= 2.599999E-01;
FRTABL.ZIPMIN(145)='738'                    FRTABL.ZIPMAX(145)='799'
FRTABL.RATES(145)= 2.749999E-01;
FRTABL.ZIPMIN(146)='800'                    FRTABL.ZIPMAX(146)='888'
FRTABL.RATES(146)= 3.399999E-01;
FRTABL.ZIPMIN(147)='889'                    FRTABL.ZIPMAX(147)='949'
FRTABL.RATES(147)= 3.849999E-01;
FRTABL.ZIPMIN(148)='950'                    FRTABL.ZIPMAX(148)='999'
FRTABL.RATES(148)= 3.999999E-01;


WTLIM(1)=           5000  ZNTBL(1)=         40;
WTLIM(2)=          10000  ZNTBL(2)=         76;
WTLIM(3)=          14000  ZNTBL(3)=        108;
WTLIM(4)=          20000  ZNTBL(4)=        132;
WTLIM(5)=          25000  ZNTBL(5)=        148;
WTLIM(6)=         100000  ZNTBL(6)=        158;

XGT=        22500;
RTWT LOOP BAD AT I OF;           1                   RTWT=          5;
LOWEST=       132        HIGHEST=       148;
XPCOD='60620'            ZIPSTR='606';       XRATE= 2.449999E-01;
FRTRT= 2.44999E-01;
```

FIGURE 8.4 *Output of procedure from Figure 8.3.*

```
... WTLIM(0:6) FIXED BINARY (31)
        INITIAL(0,5000,10000,14000,20000,25000,1000000),
```

Once we are alerted to this situation, it is apparent that ZNTBL, as declared, will cause the same problem: When RTWT is 1, the assignment of LOWEST will take ZNTBL out of range. The same repair will apply here:

```
...ZNTBL(0:6)FIXED BIN INIT(1,40,76,108,132,148,158),...
```

A repetition of the first test (Fig. 8.5) fares somewhat better. The freight class (RTWT) is assigned properly and the module runs to completion. Resisting the temptation to declare the module operational just because it gets all the way

```
XGT=              225001          RTWT=        51
RTWT LOOP BAD AT 1 OF:   1     RTWT=     51
LOWEST=        132      HIGHEST=     1481
XPCOD='60620'          ZIPSTR='606'         XRATE= 2.449999E-011
```

FIGURE 8.5 *Results of initial test of freight-handling procedure after bounding* WTLIM *table.*

through, we examine LOWEST and HIGHEST, the bounds of the selected subset of the rate table. For a RTWT of 5, we see (by comparing to the display of ZNTBL) that a LOWEST of 132 and HIGHEST of 148 do indeed correspond to entries for ZNTBL(4) and ZNTBL(5). However, that gives us a (supposed) mapping into 41 zip code zones and the specifications (Table 8.1) say that weight class 5 should map to 40. This discrepancy quickly can be traced back to an oversight in assigning LOWEST. Instead of merely using ZNTBL(RTWT-1), we need to increment that value by one because the ZNTBL entries indicate the end of each table segment and not the beginning of the next one. Accordingly, the assignment to LOWEST should read

```
LOWEST = ZNTBL(RTWT-1) + 1;
```

Moreover, the lower bound needs to be changed so that the revised assignment will be correct when RTWT is 1. As it stood before, that would have been the only time LOWEST would be correct. So, ZNTBL(0) is initialized to 0 instead of 1. Note that the erroneous assignment of LOWEST has no effect on the result of this test. Since the zip code used in the test (60620) is in the middle of the range, the appropriate portion of FRTABL is searched and the correct RATES value is assigned. A test using a very high zip code (such as 97708) would be needed to confirm the discrepancy.

This time a repetition of the first test (Fig. 8.6) produces the desired results: RTWT, LOWEST, HIGHEST, and FRATE are assigned properly. Subsequent tests (Fig. 8.7) show that the RTWT determination operates over the range of weight classes and at their borders.

The same approach can attend to the selection of FRATE based on weight class and zip code. Tests with very low (such as 00408), very high (such as 99821), and borderline (such as 73801) zip codes (Fig. 8.8) serve in this regard.

The most important realization now is that the testing is not at an end. We must assess the module's resistance to mayhem. (Obviously, this example has been left more vulnerable so that its flaws are conspicuous.) To simplify matters, we shall

```
XGT=            225001        RTWT=        51
LOWEST=         133     HIGHEST=    1481
XPCOD='60620'    ZIPSTR='606'1      XRATE= 2.449999E-011
```

FIGURE 8.6 *Results of freight-handling process after proper initialization of* ZNTBL.

```
XGT=              408;        RTWT=        1;
LOWEST=        1        HIGHEST=    40;
XPCOD='36518'   ZIPSTR='365';      XRATE= 2.13867E-01;
```

```
XGT=             62117;      RTWT=        6;
LOWEST=      149       HIGHEST=   159;
XPCOD='45229'   ZIPSTR='452';      XRATE= 2.871093E-01;
```

```
XGT=            14000;       RTWT=        4;
LOWEST=      109       HIGHEST=   132;
XPCOD='54321'   ZIPSTR='543';      XRATE= 2.578125E-01;
```

FIGURE 8.7 *Demonstration of freight-handling procedure over its designed range of weights.*

assume that a nonnumeric shipping weight would be caught before it reaches this module. However, this still leaves the possibility (admittedly remote) of a negative weight. As the coding stands, such an occurrence will force an assignment of 0 to RTWT, so the module is protected on that front. Zip code is another matter: Recall (Table 8.1) that not every 5-digit string is a legitimate zip code. Consequently, we must ascertain FREIGHT's behavior when confronted with an unacceptable zip code. (Because zip code is treated as a character string, a nonnumeric value (for example, 12I44) is no worse than an illegal numeric one (such as 12197).

Examination of the revised module (Fig. 8.9) in conjunction with the (hypo-

```
XGT=            22407;       RTWT=        5;
LOWEST=      133       HIGHEST=   148;
XPCOD='00408'   ZIPSTR='004';      XRATE= 3.750000E-01;
```

```
XGT=            22407;       RTWT=        5;
LOWEST=      133       HIGHEST=   148;
XPCOD=4
XPCOD='99821'   ZIPSTR='998';      XRATE= 3.999999E-01;
```

```
XGT=            22407;       RTWT=        5;
LOWEST=      133       HIGHEST=   148;
XGT='73801'     ZIPSTR='738';      XRATE= 2.749999E-01;
```

FIGURE 8.8 *Demonstration of freight-handling procedure over its designed range of zip codes.*

```
/*************************************************************************/
/*      USE THE FREIGHT CLASS AND ZIPCODE TO FIND THE RATE:              */
/*      FIRST, DEFINE THE APPROPRIATE SECTION OF THE ZIPCODE/RATE        */
/*      TABLE, AND THEN SEARCH THAT PORTION FOR THE RATE.                */
/*************************************************************************/
            HIGHEST = ZNTBL(RTWT);
            LOWEST = ZNTBL(RTWT-1);
                PUT SKIP DATA (LOWEST,HIGHEST);

            ZIPSTR = SUBSTR(ZPCOD,1,3);
                XPCOD=ZPCOD;   PUT SKIP DATA(XPCOD,ZIPSTR);
                ON SUBSCRIPTRANGE PUT SKIP LIST
                ('FRATE LOOP BAD AT I OF: ',I);
                FRATE=0;
            DO I = LOWEST TO HIGHEST;
            IF ZIPSTR >= ZIPMIN(I) & ZIPSTR <= ZIPMAX(I)
            THEN FRATE = RATES(I);
            END;
                XRATE=FRATE;    PUT DATA (XRATE);

            RETURN;
            END FREIGHT;
```

FIGURE 8.9 *Rate assignment procedure with limited detection of improper zip codes.*

thetical) zip code rules in Table 8.1 indicates that there is some limited built-in protection against improper zip codes. Note that the data structure for the zip code and rate table (Fig. 8.1) is contrived so that each zip code range is explicitly bounded. In contrast, ZNTBL is set up to use each entry as an upper limit for one weight class and (indirectly) as a lower limit for the next one. As a result, certain gaps in the succession of numerically possible zip codes (created by the definition of a proper zip code) will produce unsuccessful table searches. This behavior is confirmed with tests using a zip code of 00006 (Fig. 8.10). However, other discrepancies still cannot be detected: For example, a zip code of 45299, although illegal (in this illustration), is processed routinely because FREIGHT uses only the first three characters for table look up. Similarly (but more subtly), a zip code of 32A76 should be detected, but it is not: 32A76 (in the EBCDIC collating sequence) is "greater than" 237 and "less than" 450, so that a search of FRTABL with this string is successful (Fig. 8.11). In order to correct this situation, FREIGHT must be equipped with an explicit screen for improper zip codes. This modification is shown in Figure 8.12, and its effects on several illegal zip codes are shown in Figure 8.13.

8.4 SUMMARY

We have emphasized two important aspects of the design of modules.

A module must be designed with the expectation that it will be tested. Moreover, these tests will have to be performed on each module *by itself,* before it is combined with other modules in a software product.

```
XGT=            22407;        RTWT=         5;
LOWEST=         133      HIGHEST=      148;
XPCOD='00006'   ZIPSTR='000';       XRATE= 0.000000E+00;
```

FIGURE 8.10 *Output illustrating successful detection of improper zip codes.*

The tests that will be applied to a module should be designed systematically, as is the module itself. Although it is impossible to anticipate every necessary test, a predefined test sequence is extremely helpful in identifying weak spots and pointing to other useful tests.

The first of these practices calls for the inclusion of additional code whose purpose is to provide a detailed picture of the events that occur as the module goes through its activities. Some of this information may not be wanted when the module is used in actual production, in which case it can be deactivated. (One easy way to do this is to convert the code to comments). In a sense, we are instrumenting the module in much the same way that we equip a computer with special circuits whose only job is to measure and report on the machine's behavior.

The second practice mentioned above takes advantage of this module instrumentation to develop as complete a picture as possible of the module's performance under various operating conditions. It is usually impossible to test a module under every conceivable operating condition; we must seek to cover the widest range of conditions with what we consider to be a reasonable number of tests. It is helpful to categorize such tests as follows.

1. *Typical operating conditions.* The module's behavior must be established under normal conditions, that is, with input values within the ranges for which the module is designed.

2. *Boundary operating conditions.* Operating characteristics must also be evaluated at conditions that represent the extremes of the design range.

```
XGT=            22407;        RTWT=         5;
LOWEST=         133      HIGHEST=      148;
XPCOD='45299'   ZIPSTR='452';       XRATE= 2.849999E-01;
```

```
XGT=            22407;        RTWT=         5;
LOWEST=         133      HIGHEST=      148;
XPCOD='32A76'   ZIPSTR='32A';       XRATE= 2.999999E-01;
```

FIGURE 8.11 *Output illustrating failure to detect improper zip codes.*

```
/********************************************************************/
/*      USE THE FREIGHT CLASS AND ZIPCODE TO FIND THE RATE:         */
/*      FIRST, DEFINE THE APPROPRIATE SECTION OF THE ZIPCODE/RATE    */
/*      TABLE, AND THEN SEARCH THAT PORTION FOR THE RATE.           */
/********************************************************************/

        HIGHEST = ZNTBL(RTWT);
        LOWEST = ZNTBL(RTWT-1);
            PUT SKIP DATA (LOWEST,HIGHEST);

        ZIPSTR = SUBSTR(ZPCOD,1,3);
            XPCOD=ZPCOD;   PUT SKIP DATA(XPCOD,ZIPSTR);

        /********************************************************************/
        /*                      ZIPCODE TEST                                */
        /********************************************************************/
            IF      SUBSTR(ZPCOD,4,2) = '00'
            |       SUBSTR(ZPCOD,4,2) > '89'
            |       SUBSTR(ZPCOD,4,1) < '0'
            |       ZIPSTR < '003'
            THEN DO;
                    PUT SKIP LIST ('IMPROPER ZIPCODE');
                        FRATE = 0;   RETURN;
                    END;

            ON SUBSCRIPTRANGE PUT SKIP LIST
            ('FRATE LOOP BAD AT I OF: ',I);
            FRATE=0;
        DO I = LOWEST TO HIGHEST;
        IF ZIPSTR >= ZIPMIN(I) & ZIPSTR <= ZIPMAX(I)
        THEN FRATE = RATES(I);
        END;
            XRATE=FRATE;    PUT DATA (XRATE);

        RETURN;
        END FREIGHT;
```

FIGURE 8.12 *Revised rate assignment procedure with additional zip-code testing.*

3. *Illegal operating conditions.* Although we know ahead of time that the module will fail at these conditions, it is important to determine exactly how such failures occur and what happens afterward. This often points up oversights that can be missed even in the most careful design studies.

There are no specific recipes for ''proper testing'' of processing modules. However, awareness during the design stage of the need to test systematically—along with careful application of the guidelines given here—can help in avoiding expensive maintenance later on.

PROBLEMS

1. Given below are sketches for a variety of processes. Details are omitted so that actual structures, language, and even algorithms are unspecified. However, there is sufficient description to establish the nature of the processes. For each

```
XGT=            22407;          RTWT=           5;
LOWEST=          133          HIGHEST=      148;
XPCOD='00006'    ZIPSTR='000';
IMPROPER ZIPCODE



XGT=            22407;          RTWT=           5;
LOWEST=          133          HIGHEST=      148;
XPCOD='00006'    ZIPSTR='000';
IMPROPER ZIPCODE



XGT=            22407;          RTWT=           5;
LOWEST=          133          HIGHEST=      148;
XPCOD='45299'    ZIPSTR='452';
IMPROPER ZIPCODE



XGT=            22407;          RTWT=           5;
LOWEST=          133          HIGHEST=      148;
XPCOD='32A76'    ZIPSTR='32A';
IMPROPER ZIPCODE
```

FIGURE 8.13 *Output illustrating effect of additional zip-code testing.*

one, define a set of test conditions (pertinent data values) that would be particularly helpful in revealing the operational characteristics of the process, or pointing up its deficiencies, or both. (This emphasizes the notion that such tests can be defined well in advance of the actual implementation.)

a. This process computes the number of elapsed days between two dates, each expressed as *mm/dd/yy*.

Input: $mm1/dd1/yy1$, $mm2/dd2/yy2$.

Output: number of elapsed days

b. This process converts an integer, expressed in some number base $b1$, to the equivalent value expressed in some number base $b2$.

Input: the integer to be converted, $b1$, and $b2$

Output: the converted value

c. This process compares two tables T1 and T2 of (presumably) equal length to determine whether they contain identical values arranged in identical order.

Input: references to T1 and T2 and their respective lengths

Output: 1 if the tables are identical, 0 if they are not

d. This process compares two tables T1 and T2 of (presumably) equal length to determine whether they contain identical sets of entries.

Input: references to T1 and T2 and their respective lengths

Output: 1 if the tables are identical, 0 if they are not

e. This process searches a string S1 for occurrences of a (presumably) smaller string S2. The presence of S2's characters in any permutation counts as an occurrence, as long as there are no embedded extraneous characters. For instance, EGLIB counts as an occurrence of BILGE, but BIL7GE does not. Occurrences may overlap. For instance, if we were to search the string AAAA for occurrences of the string AA, the resulting count would be three.

Input: references to S1 and S2, along with their respective lengths

Output: number of occurrences of arbitrarily permuted S2 in S1

f. This process is basically the same as (*e*). However, it provides additional output.

Input: references to S1 and S2, along with their respective lengths

Output: number of occurrences in which the sequence is *identical* to that in S2, along with the starting position of each such occurrence; the number of occurrences of other permutations of S2, along with the starting position of each such occurrence

g. This process examines an arbitrarily long string S1 that may or may not contain parentheses. If there are parentheses, the process determines whether they are properly matched, nested, or both. All characters except left and right parentheses are ignored.

Input: reference to string S1, and its length

Output: 0 if they are no parentheses; 1 if there are parentheses and they are properly paired, matched and nested; −1 if there are parentheses but there is some form of mismatch

2. Examine the procedure PGAME presented in Section 7.3.

a. Write a driver to develop PGAME. Include instrumentation in PGAME so that its behavior becomes apparent.

b. Define a series of tests that can be submitted via the driver devised for (*a*) to establish the operating characteristics of PGAME. Indicate the purpose of each test.

c. Run the tests described in (*b*). Did they tell you everything you expected to find out?

---

3. Figure 5.6 shows the code for a module (GET_FORM) designed to read and translate an input card for the chemical formula processing software.

   a. Define a set of input cards for testing GET_FORM. Indicate how each of your tests contributes to an overall picture of the behavior of GET_FORM.

   b. Run GET_FORM with the data defined in (a).

   c. Did you find it necessary to introduce additional code into GET_FORM itself in order to increase the effectiveness of your tests? If so, describe the additional activities thus introduced.

   d. Repeat (a), (b), and (c) for the revised version of GET_FORM (Fig. 5.17).

4. Repeat Problem 3 for the module SCAN_FORM (Fig. 5.7).

5. Repeat Problem 3 for the module GET_SYM (Fig. 5.8).

6. Repeat Problem 3 for the module NUMBER (Fig. 5.9).

7. Repeat Problem 3 for the module EXEC_SYM (Fig. 5.19).

8. Repeat Problem 3 for the module INSERT (Fig. 5.20).

9. Repeat Problem 3 for the module CREATE (Fig. 5.23).

10. Repeat Problem 3 for the module CONNECT (Fig. 5.25).

11. Repeat Problem 3 for the module FILL (Fig. 5.26).

12. Devise a systematic group of tests for the polynomial evaluator addressed in Problem 2 of Chapter 7. Indicate the purpose of each test.

13. In Problem 5 of Chapter 7, you were asked to consider the possible difficulties that might be encountered by an updating process for frequency counters.

    a. Describe a series of tests that would be effective in determining whether your modifications (Chap. 7, Prob. 5(c)) provide the intended improvements.

    b. Run the tests described in (a).

14. Repeat Problem 13 for Problem 6, Chapter 7.

15. Repeat Problem 13 for Problem 8, Chapter 7.

16. Repeat Problem 13 for Problem 9, Chapter 7.

17. Repeat Problem 13 for the module PRINT_MOL (Fig. A.1 in the appendix).

Afterword

We have tried to present an integrated, systematic methodology for the production of software that is relatively insensitive to the nature or complexity of the process being implemented. We have emphasized the conceptual similarity between software and other engineered products, establishing a basis for the application of demonstrably effective engineering methods to the design, implementation, and testing of computer programs and their components.

Systematic exploitation of the principles and techniques discussed in the foregoing chapters heightens greatly the prospects of preparing software with highly desirable properties.

1. The procedural logic is *clear and straightforward*. Unnecessary complexity is avoided by decomposing an arbitrary process into an integrated collection of activities, each one sufficiently modest so that it can be analyzed and understood in its entirety. Careful establishment of precise boundaries between such components helps produce an overall process with a *readable* course of action.

2. Division of an arbitrarily long and complicated process into manageable components also means that we know precisely what each part does and how it fits with the others. Consequently, it is possible (and often easy) to certify that each part does what it is supposed to do. Ultimately, this paves the way to eventual assurance that the entire product does what *it* is supposed to do. The result is that the software is *verifiable*.

3. A fundamental property of a computer application is that it is likely to change. In fact, this tendency often serves as a qualitative indicator of the success of an application: Usage of an effective application evolves from initial delight and won-

derment to acceptance, and from there to a more ambitious perception that views the process as requiring improvement. Consequently, software that is easily *modifiable* places both its users and producers in a distinctly advantageous position. The approaches and attitudes presented throughout the text treat this property as an explicit objective.

4. Scarce resources often are wasted by producing software that is unnecessarily specific. With systematic design and implementation, it is fairly likely that these products, with little or no additional effort, can be made *reusable,* that is, applicable in a wide range of contexts without change.

5. One of the major claims made for this methodology is that the software produced in accordance with its precepts is much less likely to be burdened by errors than that prepared in an ad hoc manner. Valid as that claim has been shown to be, it is unrealistic to count on error-free software all the time. We can expect an occasional need to repair a flaw that eventually comes to light. The ease of identifying and correcting such flaws represents another major benefit of this methodology. Accordingly, such soft-ware is said to be highly *maintainable.*

The importance of these properties no longer is a matter of opinion. Detailed cost and effort studies conducted for a wide range of applications in a diverse collection of environments have established the significance of these attributes by documenting both the benefits of their presence and the consequences (operational and temporal, as well as financial) suffered by ignoring them. As a result, adaptation of these methods in industrial, commercial, military, and academic environments is rapidly becoming the rule rather than the exception.

In focusing our attention on the design, implementation, and testing of well-constructed software, we have deemphasized consideration of other, important phases of the overall software development cycle. These include the basic definition of the process itself, the precise definition of its requirements, and the activities concerned with reviewing the resulting design and verifying that it meets the requirements defined earlier. While these areas are outside the scope of this introductory text, the central material has been developed and presented with the anticipation that you will be concerned with these other phases in the future. Consequently, subsequent integration of those phases into your realm of expertise will be an extension of the precepts, techniques, and attitudes acquired here.

To summarize the major ideas that we have studied, it is helpful to review the essential aspect of each of the three phases addressed throughout the text.

DESIGN

The following are important factors in the design process.

1. *Modularity.* Recognition that arbitrarily large, complicated process can be handled effectively by representing them as syntheses of smaller, individually manageable

modules. The action stemming from this recognition (*decomposition*) must be an explicit part of the design process, with no immediate concern about how those modules will actually be coded. That concern is not part of the design activity.

2. *Functional isolation*. Each module must relate directly to an activity that is meaningful in the context of the application. Boundaries between such activities must be clear, well-defined, and sensible with regard to the scope of the activity they delineate. When such functional isolation is provided, it should be very easy to describe exactly what a particular module does and what it needs to do it.

Two tools are useful in supporting the design activity.

1. *Structure diagrams*. These graphical summaries of the relationships between software components provide a convenient overview of a software product's design. In addition to helping in verifying the validity of the design, a structure diagram is an excellent point of departure for the development of more detailed information about the software's construction.

2. *Pseudocode*. This narrative description of the flow of events in a software component is an effective complement to the structure diagram. Besides helping assure the correctness of a particular software item, the pseudocode description serves as a helpful guide in transforming processing requirements to program code.

IMPLEMENTATION

These factors are important in systematic implementation.

1. *Use of well-structured components*. One of the essential precepts in systematic programming is the insistence that all code be represented in terms of a small number of precisely defined *constructs* associated with good structure. While failure to use these constructs does not necessarily guarantee "poor" structure, it does increase the likelihood that the resulting code will be more obscure and (therefore) difficult to test, expand, or modify. These constructs may take different forms in different programming languages (depending on the available features), but the type of processing represented by each standard construct transcends the question of programming language.

2. *Documentation*. Clarity and legibility are very important objectives in systematic software production; thus informative, thorough documentation assumes a major role in the implementation process. Accordingly, it is treated as an integral part of implementation, so that coding and documentation (by means of comments throughout the code) become parts of the same activity. Many installations set carefully defined standards for such documentation, refusing to accept any code that violates them.

The progress of the implementation process is enhanced considerably by the use of the following tools and techniques.

1. *Indentation.* The clarity and legibility of programs are helped to a surprising extent by exploiting free-form capabilities of programming languages to highlight structural components. Use of indentation to segregate declarations, decision blocks, and other structural elements makes it easier to understand the relationships among these components.

2. *White Space.* Blank spaces and lines, when used with indentation, help improve the legibility of a module's listing. Particular structures can be emphasized without changing the nature or contents of a code sequence.

3. *Instrumentation.* A processing module (for example, a program, function, or subroutine) can include a variety of features in anticipation that the module is going to be tested. The exact form of these features, expressed as additional coding statements, will depend on the facilities available in the programming language being used, but the objective persists: to sensitize the module so that its (intended) operation is supplemented by information that reveals what it does and how it does it.

TESTING

An important aspect of systematic software production is the recognition that testing is an intrinsic part of the overall product cycle, not to be considered as an emergency measure. Factors that make the planned testing phase particularly fruitful include the following.

1. *Isolated testing.* The idea of decomposing a process into functionally isolated modules extends logically and consistently to include the testing of these modules as independent entities. The ultimate objective is to be able to assemble an effective, reliable software product by combining a number of components that have already been developed, tested, and certified to work properly.

2. *Systematic testing plans.* The idea of instrumenting a processing module as part of the implementation process is complemented by the inclusion of test definitions as part of that same activity. When a module is ready to be tested, it can be done according to a plan designed to reveal the maximum amount of useful information about the module's operating characteristics in the most economical manner. Although it is impossible to define a ''best'' set of general tests, some guidelines can be established. Besides using a basic set of tests that assess a module's behavior over the range of its operating conditions, it is particularly profitable to test the module at the limits of its intended operating conditions and also under conditions that exceed those limits. This procedure helps identify possible areas for further testing.

Two tools can be effectively exploited to realize the benefits of systematic, isolated testing.

1. *Drivers*. A processing module whose eventual role will be that of a component in some larger structure can be tested very effectively by simulating (to the minimum extent necessary) the *immediate* environment in which it will ultimately operate. The vehicle that provides this (illusory) environment, the *driver,* is rudimentary and can be discarded once the module's development is complete.

2. *Stubs*. Development and testing in isolation also can be applied to software components that use (invoke and act on the results generated by) other components. Until these other components are available, they can be represented by greatly simplified surrogates providing the required results without going through the processes that produce them. This type of surrogate, called a *stub,* enables the component being tested to operate with a complete (though unrealistic) flow of events. As the overall development activity progresses, a stub can be discarded and replaced with its more substantive counterpart. The substitution will have no effect on the other components.

The specific techniques supporting these methodologies are not immutable. We are at the beginning of what promises to be an extended, upward progression marked by increasing application of structure and discipline to what was thought to be purely an art. It is, thus, likely that the details of these approaches will continue to change. However, the essence of the attitude—that is, the progressive replacement of chaos by structure—has now been established.

Appendix: Printing the Structural-Formula

This appendix describes the subsystem of the chemical-formula evaluation project that prints the structural-formula. It completes the implementation presented in Chapter 5.

A.1 GENERAL APPROACH

How might we go about writing the two-dimensional structural-formula of a molecule on a chalkboard? We might envision a rectangular grid. For each position in the grid, there is another position above, below, to its left, and to its right. When starting to write the structural-formula, we select an arbitrary position and place an arbitrary atom of the molecule there. (The word *arbitrary* may be too strong, but at least there are many potentially productive choices.) Once an atom has been placed on the board, the atoms that are bonded to it must be identified and placed in adjacent positions with an appropriate notation that indicates the multiplicity of the bond. In determining the surrounding position in which a specific atom will be placed, positions can be scanned or interrogated to determine if they are currently available. (Obviously, we must be able to recognize when a position is not on the board.)

All these concepts (and more) must be incorporated into the software. The rectangular grid will be represented by a two-dimensional array MAP. The concepts of up, down, to the right, and to the left will be represented by numeric encodements. The concept of a position will be encoded into a numeric 2-tuple, which

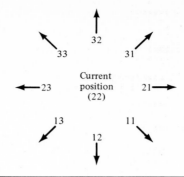

FIGURE A.1 *Direction encodements.*

specifies indices in MAP. The processes of determining bonded atoms, checking positions to determine if they are currently available (or off the board), and placing an atom (and bonding notation) at a specific position in MAP will be embedded in procedures.

Although they are similar, the computer-oriented algorithms presented here will differ slightly from those used by a person. A person has the option of erasing certain portions of a display and starting again. The approach of the computer algorithms will be more directed so that there will be no backtracking. Also, since the line printer cannot be backspaced (while a person can write in any direction), a complete *map* (the array MAP) of everything that will be printed is created before anything is sent to the printer.

The process of building this map is recursive in nature. Each time an atom is placed in MAP, it is "marked" to show it has been processed. When an atom is placed in MAP, one of the unprocessed atoms bonded to it is selected and placed in MAP in an appropriate position. (This constitutes the recursion.) Once this newly selected atom is completely processed (all the unprocessed atoms bonded to it have been placed in MAP), another unprocessed atom bonded to the original atom is selected. The recursion ends when there are no remaining unprocessed atoms.

A.2 THE ENCODEMENTS

Two major encodement schemes must be understood: the encodements for the four directions and the encodements placed in the MAP array that indicate what is to be printed in the corresponding printer position.

The direction encodements can be thought of as two-digit numbers expressed in base 4. The low-order digit indicates which way to move in the X-direction (1, right; 2, stay; 3, left), and the high-order digit indicates which way to move in the Y-direction (1, down; 2, stay; 3, up). Thus the base 10 encodements for the four directions are:

```
/**********************************************************************/
/*                                                                  */
/*                          PRINT_MOL                               */
/*                                                                  */
/*      THIS PROCEDURE PRINTS THE GRAPHICAL                         */
/*      REPRESENTATION OF THE MOLECULE.                            */
/*                                                                  */
/*          INPUT PARAMETERS:                                       */
/*              MOL - THE MOLECULE                                 */
/*                                                                  */
/**********************************************************************/

        PRINT_MOL:PROC(MOL);

            DCL 1 MOL,              /*  INTERNAL REPRESENTATION  */
                  2 REP,
                      3 CONNECTION(*,*) FIXED BIN(15),
                      3 ATOM_CORR(*) FIXED BIN(15),
                      3 P$NEXT FIXED BIN(15),
                  2 CONTEXT,
                      3 #BONDS FIXED BIN(15),
                      3 ATOM_PEND(*) FIXED BIN(15);


            DCL 1 POS,
                  2 X FIXED BIN(15) INIT(3),
                  2 Y FIXED BIN(15) INIT(16);

/**********************************************************************/
/*                                                                  */
/*      MAP IS AN INTERMEDIATE NUMERIC ARRAY USED                  */
/*      TO HOLD INFORMATION ABOUT WHERE ATOMS AND                  */
/*      LINKS SHOULD BE PRINTED ON THE OUTPUT PAGE.                */
/*                                                                  */
/*      ATOMS ARE ENCODED AS POSITIVE ENTRIES;                     */
/*      THEIR CODES CORRESPOND TO THE ATOM                         */
/*      NUMBERS.                                                    */
/*      LINKS ARE ENCODED AS NEGATIVE ENTRIES;                     */
/*      IF THE BOND IS HORIZONTAL, THE ENTRY IS                    */
/*      -#BONDS;  IF THE BOND IS VERTICAL, THE                     */
/*      ENTRY IS -8-#BONDS.                                         */
/*      ZERO ENTRIES INDICATE THAT NOTHING IS TO                   */
/*      BE PRINTED.                                                 */
/*                                                                  */
/**********************************************************************/


            DCL MAP(X_EXT,Y_EXT) FIXED BIN(15),

                PROCESSED(#MOL) BIT(1),

/**********************************************************************/
/*      THE FOUR DIRECTIONS, 9, 11, 6, AND 14, ARE                */
/*      PICKED FOR EASE OF DECODING.  THEY CAN BE                  */
/*      CONSIDERED AS 2-DIGIT NUMBERS IN BASE 4                    */
/*      ARITHMETIC.  THE LOW-ORDER DIGIT INDICATES                */
/*      THE X DIRECTION;  THE HIGH-ORDER DIGIT                     */
/*      INDICATES THE Y DIRECTION.                                 */
/*      THE SEPARATE DIGITS CORRESPOND TO:                         */
/*          1 - RIGHT (DOWN)                                       */
/*          2 - STAY                                               */
/*          3 - LEFT (UP)                                          */
/*                                                                  */
/*      THE COMBINED NUMERIC VALUES CORRESPOND TO:                */
/*          RIGHT: 9 = 2*4 + 1                                     */
/*          LEFT: 11 = 2*4 + 3                                     */
/*          UP:   14 = 3*4 + 2                                     */
/*          DOWN:  6 = 1*4 + 2                                     */
/*                                                                  */
/**********************************************************************/
```

FIGURE A.2 *PL/I code for* PRINT_MOL.

THE ENCODEMENTS

```
                    DIRECTION(2,4) FIXED BIN(15) INIT(
                        9,11,6,14,
                        14,6,11,9),


                    (
                    $INSIDE INIT(1),
                    $OUTSIDE INIT(2),
                    D$UP INIT(14),
                    D$DOWN INIT(6),
                    D$RIGHT INIT(9),
                    D$LEFT INIT(11),
                    X_EXT INIT(59),
                    Y_EXT INIT(28)
                        ) FIXED BIN(15),


                    F$ERROR BIT(1) INIT('0'B);


                MAP = 0;
                PROCESSED = FALSE;
                CALL BLD_MAP(ONE,POS);
                IF ¬F$ERROR THEN CALL PRINT_MAP;


            END PRINT_MOL;
```

FIGURE A.2 *(continued)*

Right: $9 = 2 * 4 + 1$

Left: $11 = 2 * 4 + 3$

Up: $14 = 3 * 4 + 2$

Down: $6 = 1 * 4 + 2$

This type of numeric encodement was chosen because a general X-Y-direction can be represented by *one* scalar value, and yet the direction information can be extracted easily. Notice that although it is not employed here, this encodement scheme also can encode diagonal directions (Fig. A.1). More high-order digits can also be added to specify how far to move in the given direction.

The encodements placed in the MAP array indicate what is to be printed. Positive entries specify atoms, zero entries specify blanks, and negative entries specify bonds. Entries between -7 and -1 specify horizontal bonds (and indicate multiplicity), and entries between -15 and -9 specify vertical bonds.

A.3 THE CODE

The data context and coordinating function of PRINT_MOL is shown in Figure A.2. All the remaining procedures must be embedded within PRINT_MOL in order to reside in the correct data context.

BLD_MAP (Fig. A.3) contains the major portion of the code that coordinated the placement of entries in MAP. In this procedure, the concepts of an *inside*

APPENDIX: PRINTING THE STRUCTURAL-FORMULA

```
/**************************************************************************/
/*                                                                      */
/*                          BLD_MAP                                     */
/*                                                                      */
/*     THIS PROCEDURE RECURSIVELY BUILDS THE MAP                        */
/*     MATRIX GIVEN THE CONNECTION MATRIX.                              */
/*                                                                      */
/*         INPUT PARAMETERS:                                            */
/*             (EXPLICIT)                                               */
/*             P$A1 - POINTER TO BASE ATOM                              */
/*             A1_POS - POSITION OF BASE ATOM                           */
/*             (GLOBAL)                                                 */
/*             MOL - THE MOLECULE                                       */
/*         OUTPUT PARAMETERS:                                           */
/*             (GLOBAL)                                                 */
/*             PROCESSED - INDICATES PROCESSED ATOMS                    */
/*         INPUT-OUTPUT PARAMETERS:                                     */
/*             (GLOBAL)                                                 */
/*             F$ERROR - INDICATES AN ERROR                             */
/*                                                                      */
/**************************************************************************/



        BLD_MAP: PROC(P$A1,A1_POS) RECURSIVE;


            DCL 1 A1_POS,
                  2 X FIXED BIN(15),
                  2 Y FIXED BIN(15);


            DCL 1 A2_POS,
                  2 X FIXED BIN(15),
                  2 Y FIXED BIN(15);


            DCL(
                P$A1,       /*  POINTER TO ATOM1  */
                P$A2,       /*  POINTER TO ATOM2  */
                T$A2,       /*  TYPE OF ATOM2  */
                DIR,        /*  DIRECTION  */
                I,          /*  DO LOOP PARAMETER  */
                #BONDS      /*  NUMBER OF BONDS  */
                     ) FIXED BIN(15);


            CALL INSERT_MAP(A1_POS,ATOM_CORR(P$A1));
            PROCESSED(P$A1) = TRUE;
            IF F$ERROR THEN RETURN;


            P$A2 = FIND_NEXT(P$A1);
            DO WHILE(P$A2 < P$NEXT);
                #BONDS = CONNECTION(P$A1,P$A2);
                IF ATOM_CORR(P$A2) ¬= A$CONN THEN DO;


                            /*  DETERMINE INSIDE OR OUTSIDE  */
                    IF #BONDS = ATOM_TAB(ATOM_CORR(P$A2)).BONDS
                        THEN T$A2 = $OUTSIDE;
                    ELSE T$A2 = $INSIDE;
```

FIGURE A.3 *PL/I code for* BLD_MAP.

```
                          /*  DETERMINE DIRECTION  */
          DIR = $NULL;
          DO I = 1 TO 4 WHILE(DIR = $NULL);
               DIR = CHK_DIR(A1_POS,DIRECTION(T$A2,I)
                    ,A2_POS);
          END;
          IF DIR = $NULL THEN DO;
               CALL ERROR(E$NO_DIR);
               F$ERROR = TRUE;
          END;
          ELSE DO;    /* LINK AND RECURSE  */
               CALL SET_LINK(A1_POS,DIR,#BONDS);
               CALL BLD_MAP(P$A2,A2_POS);
          END;
     END;
     ELSE        /*  MUST BE CONNECTOR ATOM  */
          CALL SPEC_HAND(P$A1,A1_POS,P$A2);


     IF F$ERROR THEN RETURN;


          P$A2 = FIND_NEXT(P$A1);
     END;


  END BLD_MAP;
```

FIGURE A.3 *(continued)*

atom and an *outside* atom are used to determine in which position an atom will be placed. An outside atom is one that is bonded to only one other atom. (Thus it is not in the spine and can be printed perpendicular to the spine.) An inside atom is bonded to at least two other atoms.

A different direction priority is associated with inside and outside atoms. The software tries to select positions in the following order for inside atoms: right, left, down, and up. The order for outside atoms is up, down, left, right. (See array DIRECTION in Fig. A.2. Notice that this array-driven approach can be modified easily.)

The following procedures are used to support BLD_MAP.

INSERT_MAP (Fig. A.4) inserts and entry into a specific position in MAP.

FIND_NEXT (Fig. A.5) finds the next unprocessed atom bonded to a given atom.

CHK_DIR (Fig. A.6) determines whether the position in a specific direction is currently unused (available) and returns the encodement of that position.

SET_LINK (Fig. A.7) inserts bonding information into MAP.

CALC_POS (Fig. A.8) calculates a new position given an old position and a direction.

SPEC_HAND (Fig. A.9) is an ad hoc algorithm for handling the *W* group.

PRINT_MAP (Fig. A.10) coordinates printing the contents of the MAP array. There are two supporting procedures.

PROC_LINE1 (Fig. A.11) prints atoms, horizontal bonds, and vertical bonds (with their multiplicity).

PROC_LINE2 (Fig. A.12) prints the multiplicity of horizontal bonds.

```
/ ********************************************************************/
/ *                                                                */
/ *                        INSERT_MAP                              */
/ *                                                                */
/ *     THIS PROCEDURE INSERTS A SPECIFIC VALUE                    */
/ *     INTO THE MAP MATRIX AT A SPECIFIC SPOT.                    */
/ *                                                                */
/ *         INPUT PARAMETERS:                                      */
/ *             POS - THE POSITION                                 */
/ *             VALUE - THE VALUE TO BE INSERTED                   */
/ *         OUTPUT PARAMETERS:                                     */
/ *             (GLOBAL)                                           */
/ *             MAP - THE MAP MATRIX                               */
/ *             F$ERROR - INDICATES AN ERROR                       */
/ *                                                                */
/ ********************************************************************/

              INSERT_MAP: PROC(POS,VALUE);


                  DCL 1 POS,
                        2 X FIXED BIN(15),
                        2 Y FIXED BIN(15);


                  DCL VALUE FIXED BIN(15);


                  IF X<1 | X>X_EXT | Y<1 | Y>Y_EXT THEN DO;
                      CALL ERROR(E$MAP_OVER);
                      F$ERROR = TRUE;
                      RETURN;
                  END;
                  ELSE MAP(X,Y) = VALUE;


              END INSERT_MAP;
```

FIGURE A.4 *PL/I code for* INSERT_MAP.

Numerous examples of the output produced by PRINT_MOL can be found in Chapter 3. Most of the structural-formulas presented there were produced by this version of PRINT_MOL.

```
/ ********************************************************************/
/ *                                                                */
/ *                        FIND_NEXT                               */
/ *                                                                */
/ *     THIS PROCEDURE FINDS THE NEXT                              */
/ *     UNPROCESSED ATOM.                                          */
/ *                                                                */
/ *         INPUT PARAMETERS:                                      */
/ *             (EXPLICIT)                                         */
/ *             P$A1 - ROW OF CONNECTION MATRIX                    */
/ *             (GLOBAL)                                           */
/ *             PROCESSED - INDICATES PROCESSED ATOMS              */
/ *             MOL - THE MOLECULE                                 */
/ *         OUTPUT PARAMETER:                                      */
/ *             NEXT - NEXT UNPROCESSED ATOM                       */
/ *                                                                */
/ ********************************************************************/
```

FIGURE A.5 *PL/I code for* FIND_NEXT.

```
        FIND_NEXT: PROC (P$A) RETURNS (FIXED BIN (15));

        DCL (
              P$A,        /*  CURRENT ATOM  */
              NEXT        /*  NEXT SPOT  */
                     ) FIXED BIN (15);

        DO NEXT = 1 TC P$NEXT-1 WHILE (PROCESSED (NEXT)  |
                         CONNECTION (P$A, NEXT) =0);
        END;
        RETURN (NEXT);

    END FIND_NEXT;
```

FIGURE A.5 *(continued)*

```
/ *******************************************************************/
/ *                                                                 */
/ *                        CHK_DIR                                  */
/ *                                                                 */
/ *    THIS PROCEDURE DETERMINES THE POSITION OF                    */
/ *    AN ATOM TO BE INSERTED GIVEN THE POSITION                    */
/ *    OF AN ALREADY INSERTED ATOM AND A DIRECTION IN               */
/ *    WHICH TO MCVE.  IT ALSO CHECKS TO SEE THAT THE               */
/ *    NEW POSITION IS WITHIN THE BOUNDS OF THE                     */
/ *    MAP MATRIX AND THAT THERE IS NO ATOM IN THE                  */
/ *    NEWLY CALCULATED POSITION.                                   */
/ *                                                                 */
/ *        INPUT PARAMETERS:                                        */
/ *            (EXPLICIT)                                           */
/ *            POS - THE OLD POSITION                               */
/ *            DIR - THE DIRECTION TO MOVE                          */
/ *            (GLOBAL)                                             */
/ *            MAP - THE MAP MATRIX                                 */
/ *        OUTPUT PARAMETERS:                                       */
/ *            NEW_POS - THE NEW POSITION                           */
/ *                                                                 */
/ *******************************************************************/


        CHK_DIR: PROC (POS, CIR, NEW_POS) RETURNS (FIXED BIN (15));


        DCL 1 PGS,
              2 X_POS FIXED BIN (15),
              2 Y_POS FIXED BIN (15);


        DCL 1 NEW_POS,
              2 X FIXED BIN (15),
              2 Y FIXED BIN (15);


        DCL DIR FIXED BIN (15);
```

FIGURE A.6 *PL/I code for CHK_DIR.*

```
                CALL CALC_POS(POS,DIR,NEW_POS);
                IF X<1 | X>X_EXT | Y<1 | Y>Y_EXT THEN RETURN($NULL);


                IF MAP(X,Y) = 0 THEN RETURN(DIR);
                ELSE RETURN($NULL);


        END CHK_DIR;
```

FIGURE A.6 *(continued)*

```
        /*******************************************************/
        /*                                                     */
        /*                    SET_LINK                         */
        /*                                                     */
        /*    THIS PROCEDURE SETS THE LINK VALUE IN            */
        /*    THE MAP MATRIX.                                  */
        /*        INPUT PARAMETERS:                            */
        /*            POS - THE ORIGINAL POSITION              */
        /*            DIR - THE DIRECTION OF MOVEMENT          */
        /*            #BONDS - THE NUMBER OF BONDS TO BE INSERTED */
        /*                                                     */
        /*******************************************************/


            SET_LINK: PROC(POS,DIR,#BONDS);


                DCL 1 POS,
                      2 X_POS FIXED BIN(15),
                      2 Y_POS FIXED BIN(15);


                DCL 1 L_POS,
                      2 X FIXED BIN(15),
                      2 Y FIXED BIN(15);


                DCL (
                      DIR,       /*   DIRECTION  */
                      #BONDS,    /* NUMBER OF BONDS  */
                      XI,        /*   X INCREMENT  */
                      YI         /*   Y INCREMENT  */
                          ) FIXED BIN(15);


                XI = 2 - MOD(DIR,4);
                YI = 2 - TRUNC(DIR/4);
                X = X_POS + XI;
                Y = Y_POS + YI;


                IF XI ¬= 0 THEN CALL INSERT_MAP(L_POS,-#BONDS);
                ELSE CALL INSERT_MAP(L_POS,-(8+#BONDS));


            END SET_LINK;
```

FIGURE A.7 *PL/I code for* SET_LINK.

THE CODE

```
/*******************************************************************/
/*                                                                 */
/*                         CALC_POS                                */
/*                                                                 */
/*      THIS PROCEDURE CALCULATES A NEW POSITION                   */
/*      GIVEN AN OLD POSITION AND A DIRECTION IN                   */
/*      WHICH TO MOVE.                                             */
/*                                                                 */
/*         INPUT PARAMETERS:                                       */
/*              OLD_POS - THE OLD POSITION                         */
/*              DIR - THE DIRECTION TO MOVE                        */
/*         OUTPUT PARAMETERS:                                      */
/*              NEW_POS - THE NEW POSITION                         */
/*                                                                 */
/*******************************************************************/

         CALC_POS: PROC(OLD_POS,DIR,NEW_POS);

             DCL 1 OLD_POS,
                   2 X_POS FIXED BIN(15),
                   2 Y_POS FIXED BIN(15);

             DCL 1 NEW_POS,
                   2 X FIXED BIN(15),
                   2 Y FIXED BIN(15);

             DCL (
                   DIR          /*  DIRECTION  */
                        ) FIXED BIN(15);

             X = X_POS + 2*(2-MOD(DIR,4));
             Y = Y_POS + 2*(2-TRUNC(DIR/4));

         END CALC_POS;
```

FIGURE A.8 *PL/I code for* CALC_POS.

```
/*******************************************************************/
/*                                                                 */
/*                         SPEC_HAND                               */
/*                                                                 */
/*      THIS PROCEDURE PERFORMS SOME SPECIAL                       */
/*      HANDLING FOR TAKING CARE OF THE 'W'                        */
/*      CONSTRUCT.   IT IS AN AD HOC IMPLEMENTATION                */
/*      BASED ON KNOWING THE CONTEXT IN WHICH THE                  */
/*      'W' CONSTRUCT CAN OCCUR AND SPECIFICALLY                   */
/*      KNOWING THE SEQUENCE IN WHICH THE                          */
/*      ATOMS OF THE 'W' CONSTRUCT ARE INSERTED                    */
/*      INTO THE CONNECTION MATRIX.   MINOR CHANGES                */
/*      ELSEWHERE IN THE SYSTEM WOULD PRODUCE MAJOR                */
/*      CHANGES HERE.                                              */
/*                                                                 */
/*         INPUT PARAMETERS:                                       */
/*              (EXPLICIT)                                         */
/*              P$A1 - POINTER TO BASE (OXYGEN) ATOM               */
/*              A1_POS - POSITION OF BASE ATOM                     */
/*              P$A2 - POINTER TO CONNECTOR ATOM                   */
/*         OUTPUT PARAMETERS:                                      */
/*              (GLOBAL)                                           */
/*              PROCESSED - INDICATES PROCESSED ATOMS              */
/*              F$ERROR - INDICATES AN ERROR                       */
/*                                                                 */
/*******************************************************************/
```

FIGURE A.9 *PL/I code for* SPEC_HAND.

```
SPEC_HAND: PROC(P$A1,A1_POS,P$A2);


        DCL 1 A1_POS,
             2 X FIXED BIN(15),
             2 Y FIXED BIN(15);


        DCL 1 A2_POS,
             2 X FIXED BIN(15),
             2 Y FIXED BIN(15);


        DCL 1 A3_POS,
             2 X FIXED BIN(15),
             2 Y FIXED BIN(15);


        DCL (
             P$A1,      /*  POINTER TO ATOM1   */
             P$A2,      /*  POINTER TO ATOM2   */
             P$A3,      /*  POINTER TO ATOM3   */
             DIR        /* DIRECTION  */
                  ) FIXED BIN(15);

        DIR = CHK_DIR(A1_POS,D$UP,A2_POS);
        IF DIR = $NULL THEN DO;
             CALL ERROR(E$CONN);
             F$ERROR = TRUE;
             RETURN;
        END;
        CALL SET_LINK(A1_POS,DIR,ONE);
        CALL INSERT_MAP(A2_POS,A$CONN);
        PROCESSED(P$A2) = TRUE;
        P$A3 = FIND_NEXT(P$A2);
        IF P$A1 = 1 THEN DIR = D$RIGHT;    /*  W AT BEGINNING  */
        ELSE DIR = D$LEFT;       /* W AT END */
        DIR = CHK_DIR(A2_POS,DIR,A3_POS);
        IF DIR = $NULL THEN DO;
             CALL ERROR(E$CONN);
             F$ERROR = TRUE;
             RETURN;
        END;
        CALL SET_LINK(A2_POS,DIR,ONE);
        CALL INSERT_MAP(A3_POS,ATOM_CORR(P$A3));
        PROCESSED(P$A3) = TRUE;
        CALL SET_LINK(A3_POS,D$DOWN,ONE);


    END SPEC_HAND;
```

FIGURE A.9 *(continued)*

```
/***********************************************************************/
/*                                                                     */
/*                          PRINT_MAP                                  */
/*                                                                     */
/*    THIS PROCEDURE DOES THE ACTUAL PRINTING OF                       */
/*    THE GRAPHICAL REPRESENTATION ON THE PRINTED                      */
/*    PAGE.  IT REFERENCES THE VARIABLE 'MAP' TO                       */
/*    DETERMINE WHAT TO PRINT.                                         */
/*                                                                     */
/*        INPUT PARAMETERS:                                            */
/*            (GLOBAL)                                                 */
/*            MAP - THE MAP OF THE PRINTED PAGE                        */
/*                                                                     */
/***********************************************************************/
```

FIGURE A.10 *PL/I code for* PRINT_MAP.

```
PRINT_MAP: PROC;

    DCL (
         ROW,         /*  ROW OF MAP MATRIX  */
         COL          /*  COLUMN OF MAP MATRIX  */
              ) FIXED BIN(15),

         F$EMPTY BIT(1);

    PUT PAGE EDIT('GRAPHICAL REPRESENTATION OF MOLECULE') (A);
    PUT SKIP(3);
    DO ROW = 1 TO Y_EXT;
         F$EMPTY = TRUE;
         DO COL = 1 TO X_EXT WHILE(F$EMPTY);
              F$EMPTY = MAP(COL,ROW) = 0;
         END;

         IF ¬F$EMPTY THEN DO;
              CALL PROC_LINE1(ROW);
              CALL PROC_LINE2(ROW);
         END;
    END;

    END PRINT_MAP;
```

FIGURE A.10   *(continued)*

```
/*******************************************************************/
/*                                                                 */
/*                       PROC_LINE1                                */
/*                                                                 */
/*   THIS PROCEDURE PROCESSES A ROW OF THE MAP                     */
/*   MATRIX FOR THE FIRST TIME.  IT PRINTS ATOMS                   */
/*   AND BONDS AND NUMBERS FOR MULTIPLE VERTICAL                   */
/*   BONDS.                                                        */
/*                                                                 */
/*       INPUT PARAMETERS:                                         */
/*           (EXPLICIT)                                            */
/*           ROW - THE ROW OF THE MAP MATRIX                       */
/*           (GLOBAL)                                              */
/*           MAP - THE MAP MATRIX                                  */
/*                                                                 */
/*******************************************************************/

         PROC_LINE1: PROC(ROW);

              DCL (
                   ROW,      /*  ROW OF MAP MATRIX  */
                   COL,      /*  COLUMN OF MAP MATRIX  */
                   ENT,      /*  ENTRY OF MAP MATRIX  */
                   #BONDS,   /*  EXTRACTED CODE FROM ENTRY  */
                   X_Y_DIR   /*  X OR Y DIRECTION  */
                        ) FIXED BIN(15);
```

FIGURE A.11   *PL/I code for PROC_LINE1.*

```
                    /*   PROCESS LINE FOR FIRST TIME   */
            PUT SKIP;
            DO COL = 1 TO X_EXT;
                ENT = MAP(COL,ROW);
                IF ENT = 0 THEN
                    PUT EDIT('  ')(A);
                ELSE IF ENT > 0 THEN
                    PUT EDIT(ATOM_TAB(ENT).SYMBOL,' ')(A);
                ELSE IF ENT < 0 THEN DO;
                    ENT = -ENT;
                    #BONDS = MOD(ENT,8);
                    X_Y_DIR = ENT/8;
                    IF X_Y_DIR = 0 THEN PUT EDIT('- ')(A);
                    ELSE DO;
                        PUT EDIT('|')(A);
                        IF #BONDS > 1 THEN
                            PUT EDIT(#BONDS)(F(1));
                        ELSE PUT EDIT(' ')(A);
                    END;
                END;
            END;

        END PROC_LINE1;
```

FIGURE A.11 *(continued)*

```
/**********************************************************************/
/*                                                                    */
/*                         PROC_LINE2                                 */
/*                                                                    */
/*     THIS PROCEDURE PROCESSES A ROW OF THE                          */
/*     MAP MATRIX FOR THE SECOND TIME TO                              */
/*     DETERMINE IF THERE IS A MULTIPLE BOND                          */
/*     ON A HORIZONTAL BOND.                                          */
/*                                                                    */
/*         INPUT PARAMETERS:                                          */
/*            (EXPLICIT)                                              */
/*            ROW - THE ROW OF THE MAP MATRIX                         */
/*            (GLOBAL)                                                */
/*            MAP - THE MAP MATRIX                                    */
/*                                                                    */
/**********************************************************************/

        PROC_LINE2: PROC(ROW);

            DCL (
                ROW,      /*  ROW OF MAP MATRIX  */
                COL,      /*  COLUMN OF MAP MATRIX  */
                ENT,      /*  ENTRY OF MAP MATRIX  */
                #BONDS,   /*  EXTRACTED CODE FROM ENTRY  */
                X_Y_DIR   /*  X OR Y DIRECTION  */
                   ) FIXED BIN(15);
```

FIGURE A.12 *PL/I code for* PROC_LINE2.

```
                    /* PROCESS LINE FOR SECOND TIME  */
          PUT SKIP;
          DO COL = 1 TO X_EXT;
                ENT = MAP(COL,ROW);
                IF ENT >= 0 THEN PUT EDIT('  ')(A);
                ELSE DO;
                      #BONDS = MOD(-ENT,8);
                      X_Y_DIR = (-ENT)/8;
                      IF X_Y_DIR = 0 & #BONDS > 1 THEN
                            PUT EDIT(#BONDS,' ')(F(1),A);
                      ELSE PUT EDIT('  ')(A);
                END;
          END;

          END PROC_LINE2;
```

FIGURE A.12 *(continued)*

Index

Index

Algorithms:
    for the case study 63–68, 71
    for a data file generator, 97
    description of, 37, 43
    for display of chemical formulas, 297–310
    for evaluation of expressions, 118
    for infix-to-postfix conversion, 104
    for a polynomial integrator, 82–87
    for processing of chemical formulas, 128ff
    for a pseudorandom number generator, 89
    for sorting, 232
    for symbolic differentiation, 124
    for text formatting, 133
    verification of, 8, 40
    versus programs, 33

(PL/I *Continued*)

    IF-THEN-ELSE construct in, 141

    implementation of the case study in, 169–211

    organization of programs in, 215

    REPEAT-UNTIL construct in, 142

    WHILE construct in, 140

Polish notation. *See* postfix expressions

Polynomials, integration of, 82–87, 229

Postfix expressions:

    conversion from infix expressions, 101

    evaluation of, 118

Problems in software production, 3, 261

Program modules:

    connections among, 27, 163, 201, 244

    error detection in, 245

    functional independence in, 164, 241

    guidelines for design of, 240–246, 292–293

    instrumentation for, 269

    size of, 242–244

    tests for, 270–273

Programming:

    as an artistic activity, 4, 9

    for clarity, 10, 37, 214

    defensive, 263

    for ease of implementation, 163

    for ease of modification 12, 176, 291

    for error detection, 245

    for generality, 292

    modular approach to, 11, 19, 27, 31, 164, 201, 213 ff, 239 ff, 291

    safe practices for, 264–266

    a structured approach to, 7, 19, 29, 139–151

    structured components in, 32–34

    traditional approaches to, 4

Programs:

    blueprints for, 29, 32, 37, 78, 220, 253

    building blocks for, 34–37, 239, 249

    connections among components of 27, 163, 201, 244

    declarations in, 139–142

    design versus implementation of, 20, 292–293

    documentation for, 37, 43, 150, 223

    functional independence in, 164, 199, 239

characteristics of, 29
examples of, 31, 33, 72, 73, 78, 220, 253
notation for, 30
Structured programming:
avoidance of defaults in, 140
control of scope in, 142
documentation as part of, 223
error detection as part of, 245, 262
error prevention as part of, 264–266
and the GOTO statement, 137
guidelines for declarations in, 139–142
implementation of constructs in, 138–144
major components in, 7, 32–37
modularization as a technique in, 11, 29, 164, 201, 213, 239
and module organization, 213–219, 253
and pseudocode, 32–38
and structure diagrams, 29–31
stubs as implementation tools in, 167, 295
Subprograms:
comparison of internal and external, 217–219
error detection in, 245
size of, 242–244
subroutines versus functions, 220
transmission of data among, 27, 144, 163, 201, 217–219
Subroutines. *See* Subprograms
Symbolic differentiation, 124

Testing of programs:
aids for, 273
with bad data, 271
effect on module size, 243
example, 274–283
exploitation of functional independence for, 263
importance of, 150, 204
instrumentation for, 269
in PL/I, 246–247
techniques for, 269–273, 294
Text formatting, 131

Tools:
   for documentation, 223–224
   for error detection, 245, 273
   for implementation of software, 167–168
   for instrumentation of software, 269
   for program testing, 273, 295
   for structured design, 27–38
   for structured programming, 140–144
Top-down design:
   for the case study problem, 69–70
   characteristics of, 25
   decomposition in, 26, 163
   pseudocode in, 32–34, 293
   stepwise refinement in, 25
   structure diagrams in, 29
Trees, as data structures, 121

Variables:
   declaration of, in structured programs, 139–141
   dictionaries for, 224
   names for, 147
   scope of, in structured programs, 142, 144, 146, 201
Verification:
   of programs, 150, 245
   in structured design, 8, 40

WHILE construct:
   basic characteristics of, 35
   flowchart for, 140
   implementation of, 140